The MCSE™ SQL 2000 Administration Cram Sheet

This Cram Sheet contains the distilled, key facts about Exam 70-228, Installing, Configuring, and Administering SQL Server 2000. Review this information last thing before you enter the test room, paying special attention to those areas where you feel you need the most review. You can transfer any of these facts onto a blank sheet of paper before beginning the exam.

OVERVIEW

1. Data collections: attributes, records, tables, databases, and instances

2. Relational databases create relationships between records in tables using Primary and Foreign keys.

CLIENT/SERVER

3. Two-tier architecture provides a client-side interface that communicates with the DBMS located on a server.

4. Three-tier architecture places a middle tier between the client and server that handles business logic and transaction services.

5. The n-tier architecture places more than a single middle-tier layer between the client and server. Also called multitier architectures.

6. Collaborative Enterprise architecture considerations include clustered servers, replicated databases, load balancing, distributed transaction processing, and mobile disconnected users.

SQL SERVER 2000 DATABASES

7. System databases used by SQL Server: **master**, **modal**, **tempdb**, and **msdb**.

8. User databases contain user data. Samples by default: **Northwind** and **pubs**.

9. Database file types: Primary data file (.mdf), secondary data files (.ndf), and transaction log files (.ldf).

10. Versions of SQL Server 2000: Enterprise, Evaluation, Standard, Personal, Developer, Windows CE, and Desktop Engine.

PLANNING INSTALLATION

11. An instance maintains multiple databases. Multiple instances can be installed on a single server.

12. Only one default instance can exist. SQL Server 6.5 and 7.0 instances are always the default instance.

13. One or more named instances can exist. SQL Server 2000 supports named instances.

14. Multiple versions of SQL Server can run on a single machine using SQL Server 2000 named instances.

15. Components available during installation of SQL Server 2000: Server Components, Management Tools, Development Tools, MDAC SDKs, Client Connectivity Components, SQL Server 2000 Books Online, Code Samples, English Query, and Analysis Services.

16. Network libraries provide network connectivity for database access: Multiprotocol, Named Pipes, NWLink IPX/SPX, TCP/IP Sockets, AppleTalk, and Banyan VINES.

58. Three types of replication are available: Snapshot, Merge, and Transactional.

59. Replication involves three elements: Publishers, Distributors, and Subscribers.

60. Linked servers allow for the use of distributed transactions across multiple remote heterogeneous OLE DB data sources.

SECURITY

61. Authentication involves the establishment of a connection to the database. Two authentication modes are provided: Windows and SQL Server (Mixed-Mode provides both). Access can be granted, not granted (revoked), or denied to Windows users, Windows groups, and SQL users. If denial is assigned or inherited, no other grant of access will allow access.

62. Connection using the guest, dbo, sa, or any other SQL login requires SQL Server authentication. Required for access without a Windows domain user account.

63. Windows logins can be managed using **sp_grantlogin** and **sp_denylogin**.

64. SQL logins can be managed using **sp_addlogin**.

65. Logins grant can be removed using **sp_revokelogin**.

66. Authorization involves the ability to access, update, and delete databases and database objects. Authorization can be granted, not granted (revoked), or denied to logins or roles. If denial is assigned or inherited, no other grant of permission will allow access.

67. Permissions include rights granting or preventing access to functions and database objects. Permissions can be assigned to roles and logins assigned to those roles.

68. There are three types of permissions: Object (**DELETE**, **EXECUTE**, **INSERT**, **SELECT**, and **UPDATE**), Statement (**BACKUP**, **RESTORE**, and **CREATE**), and Implied (inherited through role membership or object ownership).

69. Roles are groupings of permissions that can be assigned to logins. Roles are created at two levels: Server (**bulkadmin**, **dbcreator**, **diskadmin**, **processadmin**, **securityadmin**, **serveradmin**, **setupadmin**, and **sysadmin**) and Database (**db_accessadmin**, **db_backupoperator**, **db_datareader**, **db_datawriter**, **db_denydatareader**, **db_denydatawriter**, **db_ddladmin**, **db_owner**, and **db_securityadmin**, User-defined).

70. User-defined roles can be created using **sp_addrole** and dropped using **sp_droprole**. Members can be added to and removed from database roles using **sp_addrolemember** and **sp_droprolemember**. Members can be added to and removed from server roles using **sp_addsrvrolemember** and **sp_dropsrvrolemember**.

71. C2 security is a detailed, complex set of security provisions required for some governmental systems.

AUTOMATION

72. Automation involves three components: Jobs, Alerts, and Operators. Jobs can be organized into categories. Alerts can notify operators by three methods: email, pager (email), and net send. The fail-safe operator is notified if all pager notification attempts have failed.

73. The SQL Server Agent is required for multiserver administration. Members of the **sysadmin** role can make changes on the master server, but not on the target servers. Multiserver administration involves the creation of a master server, enlistment of target servers, and defection of target servers.

74. Automation depends on three services: SQLServerAgent, SQLAgentMail, and SQL Mail. Both mail services require access to MAPI-compliant mail services.

75. The Database Maintenance Planning Wizard can be used to schedule recurring automated tasks including Log Shipping.

CORIOLIS™
Certification Insider Press

38. When shrinking databases, data files reduce in size immediately, but log files will not reduce in size until the next truncation of the log.

39. The **ALTER DATABASE** command-line function can be used for altering a database, including expanding and shrinking the database.

40. Database objects such as tables, view, and stored procedures can be edited after creation.

41. Indexes improve data access time in large tables. A clustered index reorganizes tabular data. A non-clustered index creates an organized reference based on specified criteria, avoiding the need to search the entire table for a specified datum. Indexes can be rebuilt or recreated.

DISASTER RECOVERY

42. Three primary types of data backup: Full, Differential, and Transaction Log.

43. File and filegroup backups are also available if not using the Simple recovery model.

44. Three standard recovery models (the default model is Full): Simple, Full, and Bulk-logged. The recovery model can be changed during SQL Server 2000 operation without restarting the instance.

45. To perform the most up-to-date recovery:
    • Restore the most recent Full backup.
    • Restore the most recent Differential backup since the last Full backup.
    • Restore all Transaction Log backups since the most recent Differential (or Full) backup.

46. A cold standby server can be created using backup and restoration of a primary database to the standby server. A warm standby server utilizes DTS Log Shipping to synchronize transaction logs on the standby server automatically.

ENFORCING INTEGRITY

47. Table relationships allow cascading updates to maintain data integrity between tables by avoiding the creation of orphaned records.

48. The UNIQUE constraint prevents the creation of duplicate data in the appropriate field.

49. The Check constraint allows input data to be checked before a record is created or updated

50. Deadlocking occurs when two processes are mutually holding necessary locks. SQL Server 2000 automatically resolves deadlocks.

MONITORING

51. SQL Server 2000 and Windows 2000 monitoring tools: SQL Profiler, System Monitor, Error logs, Enterprise Manager, Transact-SQL (T-SQL), DBCC statements, and sqldiag.

52. SQL Profiler traces can be saved for later reuse. Each monitored instance requires a separate trace.

53. T-SQL Query analyzer monitoring commands include: **sp_lock**, **sp_monitor**, **sp_spaceused**, and **sp_who**.

54. DBCC statements fall into four categories:
    • Maintenance: **DBCC DBREINDEX**, **DBCC DBREPAIR**, **DBCC INDEXDEFRAG**, **DBCC SHRINKDATABASE**, **DBCC SHRINKFILE**, **DBCC UPDATEUSAGE**.
    • Status: **DBCC INPUTBUFFER**, **DBCC OPENTRAN**, **DBCC OUTPUTBUFFER**, **DBCC PROCCACHE**, **DBCC SHOWCONTIG**, **DBCC SHOW_STATISTICS**, **DBCC SQLPERF**, **DBCC TRACESTATUS**, **DBCC USEROPTIONS**.
    • Validation: **DBCC CHECKALLOC**, **DBCC CHECKCATALOG**, **DBCC CHECKCONSTRAINTS**, **DBCC CHECKDB**, **DBCC CHECKFILEGROUP**, **DBCC CHECKIDENT**, **DBCC CHECKTABLE**, **DBCC NEWALLOC**.
    • Miscellaneous: **DBCC dllname (FREE)**, **DBCC HELP**, **DBCC PINTABLE**, **DBCC ROWLOCK**, **DBCC TRACEOFF**, **DBCC TRACEON**, **DBCC UNPINTABLE**.

EXTRACTING AND TRANSFORMING DATA

55. Transact-SQL (T-SQL) bulk update statements: **INSERT**, **BULK INSERT**, and **SELECT INTO**.

56. The bcp command-line bulk update utility can be called by batch files.

57. Data Transformation Services (DTS) packages can be scheduled for later or recurring operation.

7. Collations define collections of alphabetic character sets and the rules for them including sort order. SQL Server 2000 provides both Unicode and non-Unicode character variable types.

REQUIREMENTS

18. SQL Server 2000 does not have a hardware compatibility list (HCL) of its own.
    - Hardware minimums: 166MHz CPU, 64MB RAM (128MB for Enterprise Edition), 250MB HDD, VGA monitor, MS-compatible mouse, and CD-ROM.
    - Software minimums: IE 5.0 and: Enterprise (NT 4.0 Server-SP5, or Windows 2000 Server), Developer (same as Enterprise, plus NT 4.0 Workstation and Windows 2000 Professional), Standard (same as Enterprise), Personal (same as Enterprise and Developer, plus Windows ME and Windows 98).

19. Each instance requires two services for operation: SQL Server and SQL Server Agent. Each service can have a different service account.

20. SQL Server 2000 provides two types of login authentication: Windows Authentication and Mixed-Mode Authentication.

INSTALLATION

21. The three installation types: Typical, Minimal, and Custom. Additional components can be added or removed after installation.

22. Remote Installation allows SQL Server 2000 to be installed from a central location. Remote Uninstallation is not supported.

23. Unattended Installation use an unattended installation setup initialization (.iss) file to perform preconfigured installations without user input during installation. Sample .iss and batch files are provided during installation.

24. Registry Rebuild is used to recover from a corrupted registry without requiring a full reinstallation of SQL Server 2000. You must have a record of all of the choices used in the original installation configuration.

25. Failover clustering allows multiple servers to share database processing between several servers (called *nodes*). An SQL Server instance on a clustered server is called a *virtual server*. In the event of the loss of a node, process ownership is automatically changed to another node. If the clustering software fails to detect a node's heartbeat signal, the node is treated as a failed server.

UPGRADES

26. SQL Server 6.5 database upgrades use the Upgrade Wizard. You must upgrade earlier versions to SQL Server 6.5 before an upgrade to SQL Server 2000 becomes possible.

27. SQL Server 7.0 database can be upgraded in place or using the Copy Database Wizard.

28. Earlier versions of SQL Server 2000 can be upgraded in place or using the Copy Database Wizard.

CREATING DATABASES

29. The Enterprise Manager is a graphical user interface (GUI) utility for database management.

30. The SQL Query Analyzer is a command-line interface for database management that includes templates for many standard actions.

31. Data files can be grouped into filegroups to allow for detailed allocation and placement of files and tables.

32. Databases can be created using the **CREATE DATABASE** command and deleted using the **DROP DATABASE** command.

MANAGING DATABASES

33. Database access can be restricted to a single user, members of the **db_owner**, **dbcreator**, and **sysadmin** roles, or unrestricted.

34. Databases can be set read-only to prevent updates.

35. Detaching a database removes a database from the SQL Server instance but does not delete the data and transaction log files.

36. A detached database can be attached to another instance of SQL Server 2000 to move a database between servers. A database can be attached to only one instance at a time.

37. Databases expand by default if not configured with restrictions. If not restricted, databases can expand to fill all available space on a drive.

MCSE™
SQL 2000
Administration

Kalani Kirk Hausman

MCSE™ SQL 2000 Administration Exam Cram

Limits of Liability and Disclaimer of Warranty

The author and publisher of this book have used their best efforts in preparing the book and the programs contained in it. These efforts include the development, research, and testing of the theories and programs to determine their effectiveness. The author and publisher make no warranty of any kind, expressed or implied, with regard to these programs or the documentation contained in this book.

The author and publisher shall not be liable in the event of incidental or consequential damages in connection with, or arising out of, the furnishing, performance, or use of the programs, associated instructions, and/or claims of productivity gains.

Trademarks

Trademarked names appear throughout this book. Rather than list the names and entities that own the trademarks or insert a trademark symbol with each mention of the trademarked name, the publisher states that it is using the names for editorial purposes only and to the benefit of the trademark owner, with no intention of infringing upon that trademark.

The Coriolis Group, LLC
14455 N. Hayden Road
Suite 220
Scottsdale, Arizona 85260

(480)483-0192
FAX (480)483-0193
www.coriolis.com

Library of Congress Cataloging-in-Publication Data
Hausman, Kalani Kirk
    MCSE SQL 2000 administration / by Kalani Kirk Hausman.
        p.   cm. -- (Exam cram)
    Includes index.
    ISBN 1-58880-033-4
    1. Electronic data processing personnel--Certification.   2. Microsoft
software--Examinations--Study guides.   3. SQL (Computer program
language)   4. Database management--Examinations--Study
guides.   I. Title.   II. Series.
QA76.3.H375   2001
005.75'65--dc21   2001028386
                                                      CIP

Publisher
Steve Sayre

Acquisitions Editor
Lee Anderson

Project Editor
Sybil Ihrig,
Helios Productions

Technical Reviewer
Sumit Pal

Production
Coordinator
Sybil Ihrig,
Helios Productions

Cover Designer
Jesse Dunn

Layout Designer
April Nielsen

Printed in the United States of America
10 9 8 7 6 5 4 3 2 1

The Coriolis Group, LLC • 14455 North Hayden Road, Suite 220 • Scottsdale, Arizona 85260

A Note from Coriolis

Our goal has always been to provide you with the best study tools on the planet to help you achieve your certification in record time. Time is so valuable these days that none of us can afford to waste a second of it, especially when it comes to exam preparation.

Over the past few years, we've created an extensive line of *Exam Cram* and *Exam Prep* study guides, practice exams, and interactive training. To help you study even better, we have now created an e-learning and certification destination called **ExamCram.com**. (You can access the site at **www.examcram.com**.) Now, with every study product you purchase from us, you'll be connected to a large community of people like yourself who are actively studying for their certifications, developing their careers, seeking advice, and sharing their insights and stories.

We believe that the future is all about collaborative learning. Our **ExamCram.com** destination is our approach to creating a highly interactive, easily accessible collaborative environment, where you can take practice exams and discuss your experiences with others, sign up for features like "Questions of the Day," plan your certifications using our interactive planners, create your own personal study pages, and keep up with all of the latest study tips and techniques.

We hope that whatever study products you purchase from us—*Exam Cram* or *Exam Prep* study guides, *Personal Trainers, Personal Test Centers*, or one of our interactive Web courses—will make your studying fun and productive. Our commitment is to build the kind of learning tools that will allow you to study the way you want to, whenever you want to.

Visit ExamCram.com now to enhance your study program.

Help us continue to provide the very best certification study materials possible. Write us or email us at **learn@examcram.com** and let us know how our study products have helped you study. Tell us about new features that you'd like us to add. Send us a story about how we've helped you. We're listening!

Good luck with your certification exam and your career. Thank you for allowing us to help you achieve your goals.

ExamCram.com Connects You to the Ultimate Study Center!

To Susan Cook for her assistance, patience, and constant support.

About the Author

Kalani Kirk Hausman has been an IT professional for more than 20 years in the roles of consultant, trainer, programmer, database administrator, IT manager, and network administrator. He is currently working as a Computer Systems Manager within the Texas A&M University system, where he is active in many university-wide ERP planning committees and multidepartmental database development efforts. He is also employed as the North American Online Manager for Fujitsu/ICL's online training division, KnowledgePool, Inc.

Mr. Hausman's studies include computer science, electronics technology, electrical engineering, mechanical engineering, and philosophy as well as consulting in the IT field. His hobbies include designs in high-speed transportation, submersible propulsion, cosmology, interactive telepresence, technology in education, and virtual reality for use by those with disabling conditions. Any spare time is spent attempting to determine whether a human can learn multiprocessing after a sufficient period of sleep deprivation.

His current independent projects include development of a shared interactive telepresence system designed to allow remote experience of widely varying environments by students regardless of geographic location or disabling condition. He is also working on implementing a zoological wireless telepresence system that is capable of allowing remote observation of animals in both natural and human-created environments.

Acknowledgments

Thanks go to Michael Shannon for contacting me initially about this book. I would also like to extend thanks to Lee Anderson, my acquisitions editor at Coriolis, for making this book possible, and to my production manager, Sybil Ihrig of Helios Productions, for her indispensable assistance. Appreciation is also due to Colleen Brosnan for her excellent copyediting and to my technical reviewer, Sumit Pal, for his technical comments and suggestions. Finally, thanks to Fred Montgomery, Systems Analyst at Texas A&M University, for his unflagging enthusiasm and assistance.

Contents at a Glance

Table of Contents

Chapter 5
Advanced Installation and Upgrade 97

Introduction

Welcome to *MCSE SQL 2000 Administration Exam Cram*. Whether this is your first or your fifteenth *Exam Cram* book, you'll find information here and in Chapter 1 that will help ensure your success as you pursue knowledge, experience, and certification. The purpose of this book is to help you get ready to take—and pass—Microsoft Certification Exam 70-228: Installing, Configuring, and Administering Microsoft SQL Server 2000 Enterprise Edition. This Introduction explains Microsoft's certification programs in general and how the *Exam Cram* series can help you prepare for Microsoft's SQL Server 2000 Certification Exams.

Exam Cram books help you understand and appreciate the subjects and materials you need to pass Microsoft certification exams. *Exam Cram* books are aimed strictly at test preparation and review. They do not teach you everything you need to know about a topic. Instead, I present and dissect the questions and problems I've found that you're likely to encounter on the Microsoft Certification Exams.

Nevertheless, to completely prepare yourself for any Microsoft test, you should begin by taking the Self-Assessment that immediately follows this Introduction. This tool will help you evaluate your knowledge base against the requirements for an MCSE under both ideal and real circumstances.

Based on what you learn from this exercise, you may decide to begin your studies with some classroom training or some background reading. On the other hand, you may decide to read one of the many study guides available from Microsoft or third-party vendors on certain topics, including The Coriolis Group's *Exam Prep* series. I recommend that you supplement your study program with visits to **ExamCram.com** to receive additional practice questions, get advice, and track the MCSE program.

I also strongly recommend that you install, configure, and play with the software that you'll be tested on, because nothing beats hands-on experience and familiarity when it comes to understanding the questions you're likely to encounter on a certification test. Book learning is essential, but hands-on experience is the best teacher.

Microsoft Certified Professional (MCP) Program

The Microsoft Certified Professional (MCP) program currently includes the following separate tracks, each of which boasts its own special acronym (as a certification candidate, you need to have a high tolerance for alphabet soup of all kinds):

➤ *MCP (Microsoft Certified Professional)*—This is the least prestigious of all the certification tracks from Microsoft. Passing one of the major Microsoft exams qualifies an individual for the MCP credential. Individuals can demonstrate proficiency with additional Microsoft products by passing additional certification exams.

➤ *MCP+SB (Microsoft Certified Professional + Site Building)*—This certification program is designed for individuals who are planning, building, managing, and maintaining Web sites. Individuals with the MCP+SB credential must have demonstrated the ability to develop Web sites that include multimedia and searchable content and Web sites that connect to and communicate with a back-end database. It requires one MCP exam, plus two of these three exams: 70-055: Designing and Implementing Web Sites with Microsoft FrontPage 98; 70-057: Designing and Implementing Commerce Solutions with Microsoft Site Server 3.0, Commerce Edition; and 70-152: Designing and Implementing Web Solutions with Microsoft Visual InterDev 6.0. Microsoft will retire Exam 70-055 on June 30, 2001, and the MCP+SB certification on June 30, 2002.

➤ *MCSE (Microsoft Certified Systems Engineer)*—Anyone who has a current MCSE is warranted to possess a high level of networking expertise with Microsoft operating systems and products. This credential is designed to prepare individuals to plan, implement, maintain, and support information systems, networks, and internetworks built around Microsoft Windows 2000 and its BackOffice Server 2000 family of products.

To obtain an MCSE, an individual must pass four core Operating System exams, one optional core exam, and two elective exams. The Operating System exams require that individuals prove their competence with desktop and server operating systems and networking/internetworking components.

For a Windows NT 4 MCSE, the Accelerated exam, 70-240: Microsoft Windows 2000 Accelerated Exam for MCPs Certified on Microsoft Windows NT 4.0, is an option. This free exam covers all of the material tested in the Core Four exams. The hitch in this plan is that you can take the test only once. If you fail, you must take all four core exams to recertify. The Core Four exams are 70-210: Installing, Configuring, and Administering Microsoft Windows

2000 Professional, 70-215: Installing, Configuring, and Administering Microsoft Windows 2000 Server, 70-216: Implementing and Administering a Microsoft Windows 2000 Network Infrastructure, and 70-217: Implementing and Administering a Microsoft Windows 2000 Directory Services Infrastructure.

To fulfill the fifth core exam requirement, you can choose from four Design exams: 70-219: Designing a Microsoft Windows 2000 Directory Services Infrastructure, 70-220: Designing Security for a Microsoft Windows 2000 Network, 70-221: Designing a Microsoft Windows 2000 Network Infrastructure, or 70-226: Designing Highly Available Web Solutions with Microsoft Windows 2000 Server Technologies. You are also required to take two elective exams. An elective exam can be from any number of subject or product areas, primarily BackOffice Server 2000 components. The two Design exams that you don't select as your fifth core exam also qualify as electives. If you are on your way to becoming an MCSE and have already taken some exams, visit **www.microsoft.com/trainingandservices/** for information on how to complete your MCSE certification.

If you are an MCSE and want to remain certified after December 31, 2001, you must upgrade your certification on or before that date. For more detailed information, visit **www.microsoft.com/trainingandservices/**.

New MCSE candidates must pass seven tests to meet the MCSE requirements. It's not uncommon for the entire process to take over a year, and many individuals find that they must take a test more than once to pass. The primary goal of the *Exam Prep* and *Exam Cram* test preparation books is to make it possible, given proper study and preparation, to pass all Microsoft certification tests on the first try. Table 1 shows the required and elective exams for the Windows 2000 MCSE certification.

➤ *MCSD (Microsoft Certified Solution Developer)*—The MCSD credential reflects the skills required to create multi-tier, distributed, and Component Object Model (COM)-based solutions using new technologies, in addition to desktop and Internet applications. To obtain an MCSD, an individual must demonstrate the ability to analyze and interpret user requirements; select and integrate products, platforms, tools, and technologies; design and implement code; customize applications; and perform necessary software tests and quality assurance operations.

To become an MCSD, you must pass a total of four exams: three core exams and one elective exam. Each candidate must choose one of these three desktop Application exams: 70-016: Designing and Implementing Desktop Applications with Microsoft Visual C++ 6.0, 70-156: Designing and Implementing

Table 1   MCSE Windows 2000 Requirements.

Core

If you have not passed these 3 Windows NT 4 exams	
Exam 70-067	Implementing and Supporting Microsoft Windows NT Server 4.0
Exam 70-068	Implementing and Supporting Microsoft Windows NT Server 4.0 in the Enterprise
Exam 70-073	Microsoft Windows NT Workstation 4.0
then you must take these 4 exams	
Exam 70-210	Installing, Configuring, and Administering Microsoft Windows 2000 Professional
Exam 70-215	Installing, Configuring, and Administering Microsoft Windows 2000 Server
Exam 70-216	Implementing and Administering a Microsoft Windows 2000 Network Infrastructure
Exam 70-217	Implementing and Administering a Microsoft Windows 2000 Directory Services Infrastructure
If you have already passed exams 70-067, 70-068, and 70-073, you may take this exam	
Exam 70-240	Microsoft Windows 2000 Accelerated Exam for MCPs Certified on Microsoft Windows NT 4.0

5th Core Option

Choose 1 from this group	
Exam 70-219	Designing a Microsoft Windows 2000 Directory Services Infrastructure
Exam 70-220	Designing Security for a Microsoft Windows 2000 Network
Exam 70-221	Designing a Microsoft Windows 2000 Network Infrastructure
Exam 70-226	Designing Highly Available Web Solutions with Microsoft Windows 2000 Server Technologies

Elective*

Choose 2 from this group	
Exam 70-019	Designing and Implementing Data Warehouse with Microsoft SQL Server 7.0
Exam 70-056	Implementing and Supporting Web Sites Using Microsoft Site Server 3.0
Exam 70-080	Implementing and Supporting Microsoft Internet Explorer 5.0 by Using the Internet Explorer Administration Kit
Exam 70-085	Implementing and Supporting Microsoft SNA Server 4.0
Exam 70-086	Implementing and Supporting Microsoft Systems Management Server 2.0
Exam 70-222	Migrating from Microsoft Windows NT 4.0 to Microsoft Windows 2000
Exam 70-223	Installing, Configuring, and Administering Microsoft Clustering Services by Using Microsoft Windows 2000 Advanced Server
Exam 70-224	Installing, Configuring, and Administering Microsoft Exchange 2000 Server
Exam 70-225	Designing and Deploying a Messaging Infrastructure with Microsoft Exchange 2000 Server
Exam 70-227	Installing, Configuring, and Administering Microsoft Internet Security and Acceleration (ISA) Server 2000 Enterprise Edition
Exam 70-228	Installing, Configuring, and Administering Microsoft SQL Server 2000 Enterprise Edition
Exam 70-229	Designing and Implementing Databases with Microsoft SQL Server 2000 Enterprise Edition
Exam 70-244	Supporting and Maintaining a Microsoft Windows NT Server 4.0 Network

This is not a complete listing—you can still be tested on some earlier versions of these products. However, we have included mainly the most recent versions so that you may test on these versions and thus be certified longer. We have not included any tests that are scheduled to be retired.

* 5th Core Option exams may also be used as electives, but can only be counted once toward a certification. You cannot receive credit for an exam as both a core and an elective in the same track.

Desktop Applications with Microsoft Visual FoxPro 6.0, or 70-176: Designing and Implementing Desktop Applications with Microsoft Visual Basic 6.0. In addition, one of these three distributed Application exams are required: 70-015: Designing and Implementing Distributed Applications with Microsoft Visual C++ 6.0, 70-155: Designing and Implementing Distributed Applications with Microsoft Visual FoxPro 6.0, or 70-175: Designing and Implementing Distributed Applications with Microsoft Visual Basic 6.0. The third core exam is 70-100: Analyzing Requirements and Defining Solution Architectures. Elective exams cover specific Microsoft applications and languages, including Visual Basic, C++, the Microsoft Foundation Classes, Access, SQL Server, Excel, and more.

➤ *MCDBA (Microsoft Certified Database Administrator)*—The MCDBA credential reflects the skills required to implement and administer Microsoft SQL Server databases. To obtain an MCDBA, an individual must demonstrate the ability to derive physical database designs, develop logical data models, create physical databases, create data services by using Transact-SQL, manage and maintain databases, configure and manage security, monitor and optimize databases, and install and configure Microsoft SQL Server.

To become an MCDBA, you must pass a total of three core exams and one elective exam. The required core exams are 70-028: Administering Microsoft SQL Server 7.0 or 70-228: Installing, Configuring, and Administering Microsoft SQL Server 2000 Enterprise Edition; 70-029: Designing and Implementing Databases with Microsoft SQL Server 7.0 or 70-229: Designing and Implementing Databases with Microsoft SQL Server 2000 Enterprise Edition; and 70-215: Installing, Configuring, and Administering Microsoft Windows 2000 Server.

The elective exams that you can choose from cover specific uses of SQL Server and include 70-015: Designing and Implementing Distributed Applications with Microsoft Visual C++ 6.0, 70-019: Designing and Implementing Data Warehouses with Microsoft SQL Server 7.0, 70-155: Designing and Implementing Distributed Applications with Microsoft Visual FoxPro 6.0, 70-175: Designing and Implementing Distributed Applications with Microsoft Visual Basic 6.0, and one exam relating to Windows 2000: 70-216: Implementing and Administering a Microsoft Windows 2000 Network Infrastructure.

If you have taken the three core Windows NT 4 exams on your path to becoming an MCSE, you qualify for the Accelerated exam (it replaces the Network Infrastructure exam requirement). The Accelerated exam covers the objectives of all four of the Windows 2000 core exams. In addition to taking the Accelerated exam, you must take only the two SQL exams (70-228 and 70-229): Administering and Database Design.

Note that the exam covered by this book is a core requirement for the MCDBA certification. Table 2 shows the requirements for the MCDBA certification.

➤ *MCT (Microsoft Certified Trainer)*—Microsoft Certified Trainers are deemed able to deliver elements of the official Microsoft curriculum, based on technical knowledge and instructional ability. Thus, it is necessary for an individual seeking MCT credentials (which are granted on a course-by-course basis) to pass the related certification exam for a course, complete the official Microsoft training in the subject area, and demonstrate an ability to teach.

This teaching skill criterion may be satisfied by proof of training certification (from Novell, Banyan, Lotus, the Santa Cruz Operation, or Cisco) or by taking a Microsoft-sanctioned workshop on instruction. Microsoft makes it clear that MCTs are important cogs in the Microsoft training channels. Instructors must be MCTs before Microsoft allows them to teach in any of its official training channels, including Microsoft's affiliated Certified Technical Education Centers (CTECs) and its online training partner network. As of January 1, 2001, MCT candidates must also possess a current MCSE, MCSSD, or MCDBA certification.

Microsoft has announced that the MCP+I and MCSE+I credentials will not be continued when the MCSE exams for Windows 2000 are in full swing because the skill set for the Internet portion of the program has been included in the new MCSE program. For details on these tracks, go to **www.microsoft.com/trainingandservices/**.

Technology continues to change, and new products replace older ones. When a Microsoft product becomes obsolete, MCPs typically have to recertify on current versions. (If individuals do not recertify, their certifications become invalid.) For this reason, Microsoft grants MCSEs 12 months past the scheduled retirement date for Windows NT 4 exams to recertify on Windows 2000 topics. (Note that this means taking at least two exams, if not more.)

For the most current information on Microsoft's certification programs, go to **www.microsoft.com/trainingandservices/**. Because Microsoft's Web site changes often, this URL may not work, so try the Search tool on Microsoft's site using either MCP or the quoted phrase Microsoft Certified Professional as a search string.

Table 2   MCDBA Requirements

Core

If you have not passed these 3 Windows NT 4 exams	
Exam 70-067	Implementing and Supporting Microsoft Windows NT Server 4.0
Exam 70-068	Implementing and Supporting Microsoft Windows NT Server 4.0 in the Enterprise
Exam 70-073	Microsoft Windows NT Workstation 4.0
you must take this exam	
Exam 70-215	Installing, Configuring and Administering Microsoft Windows 2000 Server
plus these 2 exams	
Exam 70-228	Installing, Configuring, and Administering Microsoft SQL Server 2000 Enterprise Edition
Exam 70-229	Designing and Implementing Databases with Microsoft SQL Server 2000 Enterprise Edition

Elective

Choose 1 of the following exams	
Exam 70-015	Designing and Implementing Distributed Applications with Microsoft Visual C++ 6.0
Exam 70-019	Designing and Implementing Data Warehouses with Microsoft SQL Server 7.0
Exam 70-155	Designing and Implementing Distributed Applications with Microsoft Visual FoxPro 6.0
Exam 70-175	Designing and Implementing Distributed Applications with Microsoft Visual Basic 6.0
Exam 70-216	Implementing and Administering a Microsoft Windows 2000 Network Infrastructure

OR

If you have already passed exams 70-067, 70-068, and 70-073, you may take this exam	
Exam 70-240	Microsoft Windows 2000 Accelerated Exam for MCPs Certified on Microsoft Windows NT 4.0
plus these 2 exams	
Exam 70-228	Installing, Configuring, and Administering Microsoft SQL Server 2000 Enterprise Edition
Exam 70-229	Designing and Implementing Databases with Microsoft SQL Server 2000 Enterprise Edition

This is not a complete listing—you can still be tested on some earlier versions of these products. However, we have tried to include the most recent versions so that you may test on these versions and thus be certified longer.

Taking a Certification Exam

After you've prepared for your exam, you need to register for the exam with a testing center. Each computer-based MCP exam costs $100; if you don't pass, retests are an additional $100 each. In the United States and Canada, tests are administered by Prometric and by Virtual University Enterprises (VUE). Here's how you can contact them:

➤ *Prometric*—You can sign up for a test through the company's Web site at **www.2test.com**. Within the United States and Canada, you can register by phone at (800) 755-EXAM. If you live outside this region, check the company's Web site for the appropriate phone number.

➤ *Virtual University Enterprises*—You can sign up for a test or get the phone numbers for local testing centers through the Web page at **www.vue.com/ms/**.

To sign up for a test, you may pay with a valid credit card or by check (only in the United States). Contact the company for mailing instructions if paying by check. Your payment must be verified before you can actually register for a test.

To schedule an exam, either call the company or visit its Web page at least one day in advance. To cancel or reschedule an exam, you must call before 7 P.M. Pacific Standard Time the day before the scheduled test time (if you don't contact the company, you may be charged even if you don't take the test). When you want to schedule a test, have the following information ready:

➤ Your name, organization, and mailing address.

➤ Your Microsoft Test ID. (In the United States, your Test ID is your Social Security number; citizens of other nations should call ahead to find out what type of identification number is required to register for a test.)

➤ The name and number of the exam you wish to take.

➤ A method of payment. (As I've already mentioned, a credit card is the most convenient method, but alternate means can be arranged in advance, if necessary.)

After you have signed up for a test, you'll be informed when and where the test is scheduled. Try to arrive at least 15 minutes early. You must supply two forms of identification—one of which must be a photo ID—to be admitted into the testing room.

All exams are completely closed-book. You may not take anything with you into the testing area, but you will be furnished with a blank sheet of paper and a pen or, in some cases, an erasable plastic sheet and an erasable pen. I suggest that you immediately write down on that sheet of paper all of the information you've memorized for the test. In *Exam Cram* books, this information appears on a tear-out sheet inside the front cover of each book. You will have some time to compose yourself, record this information, and take a sample orientation exam before you begin the real thing. I suggest you take the orientation test before taking your first exam. However, you probably won't need to do this more than once because the exams are fairly identical in layout, behavior, and controls.

When you complete a Microsoft Certification Exam, the software lets you know whether you've passed or failed. If you need to retake an exam, you'll have to schedule a new test with Prometric or VUE and pay another $100.

The first time you fail a test, you can retake the test the next day. However, if you fail a second time, you must wait 14 days before retaking that test. The 14-day waiting period remains in effect for all retakes after the second failure.

Tracking MCP Status

As soon as you pass any Microsoft exam (except Networking Essentials), you'll attain Microsoft Certified Professional (MCP) status. Microsoft also generates transcripts that indicate which exams you have passed. You can view a copy of your transcript at any time by going to the MCP secured site and selecting Transcript Tool. This tool allows you to print a copy of your current transcript and confirm your certification status.

After you pass the necessary set of exams, you are certified. Official certification normally takes anywhere from six to eight weeks, so don't expect to get your credentials overnight. When the package for a qualified certification arrives, it includes a Welcome Kit that contains a number of elements (see Microsoft's Web site for other benefits of specific certifications):

➤ A certificate suitable for framing, along with a wallet card and lapel pin.

➤ A license to use the MCP logo, thereby allowing you to use the logo in advertisements, promotions, and documents, and on letterhead, business cards, and so on. Along with the license, you'll receive an MCP logo sheet, which includes camera-ready artwork. (Note: Before using any of the artwork, individuals must sign and return a licensing agreement that indicates they'll abide by its terms and conditions.)

➤ A subscription to *Microsoft Certified Professional Magazine*, which provides ongoing data about testing and certification activities, requirements, and changes to the program.

Many people believe that the benefits of MCP certification go well beyond the perks that Microsoft provides to newly anointed members of this elite group. An increasing number of job listings request or require applicants to have an MCP, MCSE, and so on, and many individuals who complete the program qualify for increases in pay and/or responsibility. As an official recognition of hard work and broad knowledge, an MCP credential is a badge of honor in many IT organizations.

Preparing for a Certification Exam

To prepare for any SQL Server 2000-related test (including Installing, Configuring, and Administering Microsoft SQL Server 2000 Enterprise Edition), you must obtain and study materials designed to provide comprehensive information about the product and its capabilities. The following list of materials will help you prepare:

➤ The SQL Server 2000 product CD includes comprehensive online documentation and related materials. This should be a primary resource when you are preparing for the test.

➤ The exam preparation materials, practice tests, and self-assessment exams on the Microsoft Training and Services page at **www.microsoft.com/ trainingandservices/default.asp?PageID=mcp**. The Testing Innovations link offers samples of the new question types found on the Windows 2000 MCSE exams. Find the materials, download them, and use them.

➤ The exam preparation advice, practice tests, questions of the day, and discussion groups on the **ExamCram.com** e-learning and certification destination Web site (**www.examcram.com**).

In addition, you'll probably find the following materials useful in your quest for SQL Server 2000 expertise:

➤ *Microsoft training kits*—Microsoft Press offers a training kit that specifically targets Certification Exam 70-228. For more information, visit: **http:// mspress.microsoft.com/findabook/list/series_ak.htm**. This training kit contains information that you will find useful in preparing for the test.

➤ *Microsoft TechNet CD*—This monthly CD-based publication delivers numerous electronic titles that include coverage of SQL Server 2000 and related topics on the Technical Information (TechNet) CD. Its offerings include product facts, technical notes, tools and utilities, and information on how to access the Seminars Online training materials for SQL Server 2000. A subscription to TechNet costs $299 per year, but it is well worth the price. Visit **www.microsoft.com/technet/**, and check out the information under the TechNet Subscription menu entry for more details.

➤ *Study guides*—Several publishers (such as The Coriolis Group) offer SQL Server 2000 titles. The Coriolis Group series includes the following:

➤ *The Exam Cram series*—These books give you information about the material you need to know to pass the tests.

➤ *The Exam Prep series*—These books provide a greater level of detail than the *Exam Cram* books and are designed to teach you everything you need to know from an exam perspective. Each book comes with a CD that contains interactive practice exams in a variety of testing formats.

➤ *The SQL Server 2000 Black Book*— An excellent reference to keep close at hand during installation of SQL Server 2000. This is a necessary book in any DBA's library, as it has many solutions to commonly experienced issues.

➤ *Multimedia*—These Coriolis Group materials are designed to assist your study—whether you learn best by reading or doing:

➤ *The Exam Cram Personal Trainer*—Offers a unique, personalized self-paced training course based on the exam.

➤ *The Exam Cram Personal Test Center*—Features multiple test options that simulate the actual exam, including Fixed-Length, Random, Review, and Test All. Explanations of correct and incorrect answers reinforce concepts learned.

➤ *Classroom training*—CTECs, online partners, and third-party training companies (such as Wave Technologies, Learning Tree, Data-Tech, and others) all offer classroom training on SQL Server 2000. The aim of these companies is to help you prepare to pass and score well on Exam 70-228. Although the cost of such training is approximately $350 per day, most individuals find it to be quite worthwhile.

➤ *Other publications*—There's no shortage of materials available about SQL Server 2000. Refer to the resource sections at the end of each chapter in this book for additional sources of information.

About this Book

Each topical *Exam Cram* chapter follows a regular structure, along with graphical cues about important or useful information. Here's the structure of a typical chapter:

➤ *Opening hotlists*—Each chapter begins with a list of the terms, tools, and techniques that you must learn and understand before you can be fully conversant with that chapter's subject matter. Following the hotlists are one or two introductory paragraphs that explain what will be discussed in the chapter.

➤ *Topical coverage*—After the opening hotlists, each chapter covers a series of topics related to the chapter's subject title. Throughout this section, topics or concepts likely to appear on a test are highlighted using a special Exam Alert layout, like this:

This is what an Exam Alert looks like. Normally, an Exam Alert stresses concepts, terms, software, or activities that relate to one or more certification test questions.

Pay close attention to material flagged as an Exam Alert because this indicates that the information is really important. Most of the information that appears on The Cram Sheet appears as Exam Alerts within the text. You'll also find that the meat of each chapter is worth knowing, too, when preparing for the test. Because material in this book is very condensed, I recommend that you use this book along with other resources to achieve the maximum benefit.

In addition to the Exam Alerts, tips are provided that will help you build a better foundation for SQL Server 2000 Administration knowledge. Although the information may not be on the exam, it is related and will help you become a better test-taker.

 This is how tips are formatted. Keep your eyes open for these, and quickly you'll become a SQL Server 2000 guru.

➤ *Practice questions*—Although I talk about test questions and topics throughout the book, a section at the end of each chapter presents a series of mock test questions and explanations of both correct and incorrect answers.

➤ *Details and resources*—Every chapter ends with a section titled Need to Know More? This section provides direct pointers to Microsoft and third-party resources offering more details on the chapter's subject. In addition, this section rates the quality and thoroughness of the topic's coverage by each resource. Select the resources you find most useful in this collection, but don't feel compelled to use all of them. I recommend only resources that I use on a regular basis, so none are a waste of your time or money (however, purchasing them all at once probably represents an expense that many network administrators and would-be MCPs and MCDBAs may find hard to justify).

The bulk of the book follows this chapter structure slavishly, but there are a few other elements that I'd like to point out. Chapter 14 includes a sample test that provides a good review of the material presented throughout the book to ensure you're ready for the exam. Chapter 15 is an answer key to the sample test that appears in Chapter 14. In addition, you'll find a handy glossary and an index.

Finally, the tear-out Cram Sheet attached to the inside front cover of this *Exam Cram* book represents a condensed and compiled collection of facts and tips that are useful to memorize before taking the test. Because you can write this information onto a piece of paper before taking the exam, you can master this information by brute force—you need to remember it only long enough to write it down when you walk into the test room. I suggest that you review it just before you walk in to take the test.

How to Use this Book

I've structured the topics in this book to build on each other. Therefore, some topics in later chapters make more sense after you've read earlier chapters. That's why I suggest you read this book from front to back for your initial test preparation. If you need to brush up on a topic or you have to bone up for a second try, use the index or table of contents to go straight to the topics and questions that you need to study. Beyond helping you prepare for the test, this book serves a tightly focused reference to some of the most important aspects of SQL Server 2000.

Given all the book's elements and its specialized focus, I've tried to create a tool that will help you prepare for—and pass—Microsoft Exam 70-228. Please share your feedback on the book with us, especially if you have ideas about how I can improve it for future test-takers. I'll consider everything you say carefully, and I'll respond to all suggestions.

Send your questions or comments to me at **learn@examcram.com**. Please remember to include the title of the book in your message so I won't have to guess which book you're writing about. Also, be sure to check out the Web pages at **www.examcram.com**, where you'll find information updates, commentary, and certification information.

Thanks, and enjoy the book!

Self-Assessment

The purpose of this Self-Assessment is to help you evaluate your readiness to tackle Microsoft Certified Systems Engineer (MCSE) certification. It should also help you understand what you need to know to master the topic of this book—namely, Exam 70-228, Installing, Configuring, and Administering Microsoft SQL Server 2000 Enterprise Edition. Before you take this Self-Assessment, you should think about the concerns you have about pursuing an MCSE for Windows 2000 and what an "ideal" MCSE candidate is.

MCSEs in the Real World

The next section describes the "ideal" MCSE candidate, although very few real candidates meet all of the requirements. In fact, some of those requirements may seem impossible to fulfill, especially with the ongoing changes made to the program to support Windows 2000. Although the requirements for obtaining an MCSE may seem formidable, they are by no means unattainable. However, it does take time, involves some expense, and requires real effort to get through the process.

Increasing numbers of people are attaining Microsoft certifications, and you can also reach that goal. If you're willing to tackle the process seriously and work toward obtaining the necessary experience and knowledge, you can take—and pass—all of the certification tests involved in obtaining an MCSE. In fact, Coriolis has designed *Exam Preps*, the companion *Exam Crams*, *Exam Cram Personal Trainers*, and *Exam Cram Personal Test Centers* to assist you in studying for these exams. Coriolis has also greatly expanded its Web site, **www.examcram.com**, to provide a host of resources to help you prepare for the complexities of Windows 2000.

In addition to MCSE, other Microsoft certifications include the following:

➤ Microsoft Certified Solution Developer (MCSD), which is aimed at software developers and requires one specific exam, two more exams on client and distributed topics, plus a fourth elective exam drawn from a different, but limited, pool of options.

➤ Microsoft certifications that require one test, such as Microsoft Certified Professional (MCP), or several tests, such as Microsoft Certified Professional + Site Building (MCP+SB) and Microsoft Certified Database Administrator (MCDBA).

Who Is an Ideal Windows 2000 MCSE Candidate?

Just to give you some idea of the qualifications an ideal MCSE candidate should have, here are some relevant statistics about background and experience. Don't worry if you don't meet these qualifications, or don't come that close—this is a far from ideal world, and if you fall short, it just means that you simply have more work to do in those areas.

➤ Academic or professional training in network theory, concepts, and operations. This includes everything from networking media and transmission techniques through network operating systems, services, and applications.

➤ Three-plus years of professional networking experience, including experience with Ethernet, token ring, modems, and other networking media. This must include installation, configuration, upgrade, and troubleshooting experience.

Note: The Windows 2000 MCSE program is much more rigorous than the previous NT MCSE program; therefore, you'll really need some hands-on experience. Some of the exams require you to solve real-world case studies and network design issues, so the more hands-on experience you have, the better.

➤ Two-plus years in a networked environment that includes hands-on experience with Windows 2000 Server, Windows 2000 Professional, Windows NT Server, Windows NT Workstation, and Windows 95 or Windows 98. A solid understanding of each system's architecture, installation, configuration, maintenance, and troubleshooting is also essential.

➤ Knowledge of the various methods for installing Windows 2000, including manual and unattended installations.

➤ A thorough understanding of key networking protocols, addressing, and name resolution, including TCP/IP, IPX/SPX, and NetBEUI.

➤ A thorough understanding of NetBIOS naming, browsing, and file and print services.

➤ Familiarity with key Windows 2000 TCP/IP-based services, including hypertext transfer protocol (HTTP), dynamic host configuration protocol

(DHCP), windows internet naming server (WINS), domain name service (DNS), plus familiarity with one or more of the following: Internet Information Server (IIS), Index Server, and Proxy Server.

➤ An understanding of how to implement security for key network data in a Windows 2000 environment.

➤ Working knowledge of NetWare 3.x and 4.x, including IPX/SPX frame formats; NetWare file, print, and directory services; and both Novell and Microsoft client software. Working knowledge of Microsoft's Client Service for NetWare (CSNW), Gateway Service for NetWare (GSNW), NetWare Migration Tool (NWCONV), and NetWare Client For Windows (NT, 95, and 98) is essential.

➤ A good working understanding of Active Directory. The more you work with Windows 2000, the more you'll realize that this new operating system is quite different from Windows NT. New technologies such as Active Directory have really changed the way that Windows is configured and used. I recommend that you find out as much as you can about Active Directory and acquire as much experience using this technology as possible. The time you take learning about Active Directory will be time very well spent!

Fundamentally, this boils down to a bachelor's degree in computer science, plus three years' experience working in a position involving network design, installation, configuration, and maintenance. The Coriolis Group believes that well under half of all certification candidates meet these requirements, and that most meet less than half of these requirements—at least, when they begin the certification process. However, many candidates have survived this ordeal and become certified. You can also survive it—especially if you heed what our Self-Assessment can tell you about what you already know and what you need to learn.

Put Yourself to the Test

The following series of questions and observations is designed to help you determine what you must do to pursue Microsoft certification and what kinds of resources you may consult on your quest. Be absolutely honest in your answers, or you'll end up wasting money on exams that you're not yet ready to take. There are no right or wrong answers—only steps along the path to certification. Only you can decide where you really belong in the broad spectrum of aspiring candidates.

At the very minimum, you should have the following:

➤ Some background in computer science, even a limited one

➤ Hands-on experience with Microsoft products and technologies

Educational Background

Following are some questions to help you determine if you need further education and training before attempting to take an exam:

1. Have you ever taken any computer-related classes? [Yes or No]

   If Yes, proceed to Question 2; if No, proceed to Question 4.

2. Have you taken any classes on computer operating systems? [Yes or No]

   If Yes, you will probably be able to handle Microsoft's architecture and system component discussions. If you're rusty, brush up on basic operating system concepts, especially virtual memory, multitasking regimes, user mode versus kernel mode operation, and general computer security topics.

   If No, consider some basic reading in this area. I strongly recommend a good general operating systems book, such as *Operating System Concepts, 5th Edition*, by Abraham Silberschatz and Peter Baer Galvin (John Wiley & Sons, 1998, ISBN 0-471-36414-2). If this title doesn't appeal to you, check out reviews for other, similar titles at your favorite online bookstore.

3. Have you taken any networking concepts or technologies classes? [Yes or No]

   If Yes, you will probably be able to handle Microsoft's networking terminology, concepts, and technologies (brace yourself for frequent departures from normal usage). If you're rusty, brush up on basic networking concepts and terminology, especially networking media, transmission types, the OSI Reference Model, and networking technologies such as Ethernet, Token Ring, FDDI, and WAN links.

   If No, you may want to read one or two books in this topic area. The two best books that I know of are *Computer Networks, 3rd Edition*, by Andrew S. Tanenbaum (Prentice Hall, 1996, ISBN 0-13-083617-6) and *Computer Networks and Internets, 2nd Edition*, by Douglas E. Comer and Ralph E. Droms (Prentice Hall, 1998, ISBN 0-130-83617-6).

   Skip to the next section, "Hands-on Experience."

4. Have you done any reading on operating systems or networks? [Yes or No]

   If Yes, review the requirements stated in the first paragraphs after Questions 2 and 3. If you meet those requirements, move on to the next section. If No, consult the recommended reading for both topics. A strong background will help you prepare for the Microsoft exams better than anything else.

Hands-On Experience

The most important key to success on all of the Microsoft tests is hands-on experience, especially with Windows 2000 Server and Professional, plus the many add-on services and BackOffice components around which so many of the Microsoft certification exams revolve. After taking this Self-Assessment, you should learn at least this—there's no substitute for time spent installing, configuring, and using the various Microsoft products on which you'll be tested repeatedly and in depth.

5. Have you installed, configured, and worked with the following:

   ➤ Windows 2000 Server? [Yes or No]

   If Yes, make sure that you understand the basic concepts as covered in Exam 70-215. You should also study the TCP/IP interfaces, utilities, and services for Exam 70-216, plus implementing security features for Exam 70-220.

 You can download objectives, practice exams, and other data about Microsoft exams from the Training and Certification page at **www.microsoft.com/trainingandservices/default.asp?PageID=mcp**. Use the "Exams" link to obtain specific exam information.

   If you haven't worked with Windows 2000 Server, you must obtain one or two machines and a copy of Windows 2000 Server. Then, learn the operating system and whatever other software components on which you'll also be tested.

   In fact, I recommend that you obtain two computers—each with a network interface—and set up a two-node network on which to practice. With decent Windows 2000-capable computers selling for about $500 to $600 apiece these days, this shouldn't be too much of a financial hardship. You may have to scrounge to come up with the necessary software, but if you scour the Microsoft Web site you can usually find low-cost options to obtain evaluation copies of most of the software that you'll need.

   ➤ Windows 2000 Professional? [Yes or No]

   If Yes, make sure you understand the concepts covered in Exam 70-210.

   If No, you should obtain a copy of Windows 2000 Professional and learn how to install, configure, and maintain it. You can use *MCSE Windows 2000 Professional Exam Cram* to guide your activities and studies or work straight from Microsoft's test objectives if you prefer.

For any and all of these Microsoft exams, the Resource Kits for the topics involved are a good study resource. You can purchase softcover Resource Kits from Microsoft Press (search for them at **http:// mspress.microsoft.com/**), but they also appear on the TechNet CDs (**www.microsoft.com/technet**). Along with *Exam Crams* and *Exam Preps*, I believe that Resource Kits are among the best tools you can use to prepare for Microsoft exams.

6. For any specific Microsoft product that is not itself an operating system (for example, SQL Server), have you installed, configured, used, and upgraded this software? [Yes or No]

> If Yes, skip to the next section. If No, you must get some experience. Read on for suggestions on how to do this.
>
> Experience is a must with any Microsoft product exam, be it something as simple as FrontPage 2000 or as challenging as SQL Server 2000. For trial copies of other software, search Microsoft's Web site using the name of the product as your search term. Also, search for bundles like "BackOffice" or "Small Business Server."

If you have the funds, or your employer will pay your way, consider taking a class at a Certified Training and Education Center (CTEC) or at an Authorized Academic Training Partner (AATP). In addition to classroom exposure to the topic of your choice, you get a copy of the software that is the focus of your course, along with a trial version of whatever operating system it needs and the training materials for that class.

> Before you even think about taking any Microsoft exam, make sure that you've spent enough time with the related software to understand how it may be installed and configured, how to maintain such an installation, and how to troubleshoot that software when things go wrong. This will help you in the exam, and in real life!

Testing Your Exam-Readiness

Whether you attend a formal class on a specific topic to get ready for an exam or use written materials to study on your own, some preparation for the Microsoft certification exams is essential. At $100 a try, pass or fail, you want to do everything you can to pass on your first try. That's where studying comes in.

I have included a practice exam in this book, so if you don't score that well on the test, you can study more and then take the test again. The Coriolis Group also has exams that you can take online through the **ExamCram.com** Web site at **www.examcram.com**. If you still don't hit a score of at least 70 percent after these tests, you'll want to investigate the other practice test resources mentioned in this section.

For any given subject, consider taking a class if you've tackled self-study materials, taken the test, and failed. The opportunity to interact with an instructor and fellow students can make all the difference in the world, if you can afford that privilege. For information about Microsoft classes, visit the Training and Certification page at **www.microsoft.com/education/partners/ctec.asp** for Microsoft Certified Education Centers or **www.microsoft.com/aatp/default.htm** for Microsoft Authorized Training Providers.

If you can't afford to take a class, visit the Training and Certification page anyway, because it also includes pointers to free practice exams and to Microsoft Certified Professional Approved Study Guides and other self-study tools. If you can't afford to spend much at all, you should still invest in some low-cost practice exams from commercial vendors.

7. Have you taken a practice exam on your chosen test subject? [Yes or No]

> If Yes, and you scored 70 percent or better, you're probably ready to tackle the real thing. If your score isn't above that threshold, keep at it until you break that barrier.

> If No, obtain all of the free and low-budget practice tests you can find and start working. Keep at it until you can break the passing threshold comfortably.

When it comes to assessing your test readiness, there is no better way than to take a good-quality practice exam and pass with a score of 70 percent or better. When I'm preparing myself, I shoot for 80-plus percent, just to leave room for the "weirdness factor" that sometimes shows up on Microsoft exams.

Assessing Readiness for Exam 70-228

In addition to the general exam-readiness information in the previous section, there are several things you can do to prepare for the Installing, Configuring, and Administering Microsoft SQL Server 2000 Enterprise Edition exam. As you're getting ready for Exam 70-228, visit the Exam Cram Resource Center at **www.examcram.com/studyresource/**. Another valuable resource is the Exam Cram Insider newsletter. Sign up at **www.examcram.com** or send a blank email message to **subscribe-ec@mars.coriolis.com**. I also suggest that you join an active MCSE or MCDBA mailing list. One of the better ones is managed by Sunbelt Software. Sign up at **www.sunbelt-software.com** (look for the Subscribe button).

You can also cruise the Web looking for "braindumps" (recollections of test topics and experiences recorded by others) to help you anticipate topics that you're likely to encounter on the test. The MCSE mailing list is a good place to ask where the useful braindumps are.

> You can't be sure that a braindump's author can provide correct answers. Thus, use the questions to guide your studies, but don't rely on the answers in a braindump to lead you to the truth. Double-check everything you find in any braindump.

Microsoft also recommends checking the Microsoft Knowledge Base (available on its own CD-ROM as part of the TechNet collection or on the Microsoft Web site at **http://support.microsoft.com/support/**) for "meaningful technical support issues" that relate to your exam's topics. Although I'm not sure exactly what the quoted phrase means, I have also noticed some overlap between technical support questions on particular products and troubleshooting questions on the exams for those products.

Onward, through the Fog!

Once you've assessed your readiness, undertaken the right background studies, obtained the hands-on experience that will help you understand the products and technologies at work, and reviewed the many sources of information to help you prepare for a test, you'll be ready to take a round of practice tests. When your scores come back positive enough to get you through the exam, you're ready to go after the real thing. If you follow this assessment regime, you'll know what you need to study and when you're ready to make a test date at Prometric or VUE. Good luck!

Microsoft
Certification Exams

. . . .

Terms you'll need to understand:

✓ Case study

✓ Multiple-choice question formats

✓ Build-list-and-reorder question format

✓ Create-a-tree question format

✓ Drag-and-connect question format

✓ Select-and-place question format

✓ Fixed-length tests

✓ Simulations

✓ Adaptive tests

✓ Short-form tests

Techniques you'll need to master:

✓ Assessing your exam-readiness

✓ Answering Microsoft's varying question types

✓ Altering your test strategy depending on the exam format

✓ Practicing (to make perfect)

✓ Making the best use of the testing software

✓ Budgeting your time

✓ Guessing (as a last resort)

Exam-taking is not something that most people anticipate eagerly, no matter how well prepared they may be. In most cases, familiarity helps offset test anxiety. In plain English, this means you probably won't be as nervous when you take your fourth or fifth Microsoft certification exam as you'll be when you take your first one.

Whether it's your first exam or your tenth, understanding the details of taking the new exam (how much time to spend on questions, the environment you'll be in, and so on) and the new exam software will help you concentrate on the material rather than on the setting. Likewise, mastering a few basic exam-taking skills should help you recognize (and perhaps even outfox) some of the tricks and snares you're bound to find in some exam questions.

This chapter explains the exam environment and software and describes some proven exam-taking strategies that you can use to your advantage.

Assessing Exam-Readiness

I strongly recommend that you read through and take the Self-Assessment included with this book (it appears just before this chapter). This will help you compare your knowledge base to the requirements for obtaining an MCSE, and it will also help you identify parts of your background or experience that may need improvement, enhancement, or further learning. If you get the right set of basics under your belt, obtaining Microsoft certification will be that much easier.

Once you've gone through the Self-Assessment, you can remedy those topical areas in which your background or experience may be lacking. You can also tackle subject matter for individual tests at the same time, so you can continue making progress while you're catching up in some areas.

Once you've worked through an *Exam Cram*, have read the supplementary materials, and have taken the practice test, you'll have a pretty clear idea of when you should be ready to take the real exam. Although I strongly recommend that you keep practicing until your scores top the 75 percent mark, 80 percent is a better goal because it gives some margin for error when you are in an actual, stressful exam situation. Keep taking practice tests and studying the materials until you attain that score. You'll find more pointers on how to study and prepare in the Self-Assessment. But now, on to the exam itself.

What to Expect at the Testing Center

When you arrive at the testing center where you scheduled your exam, you must sign in with an exam coordinator and show two forms of identification, one of which must be a photo ID. After you've signed in and your time slot arrives, you'll be asked to deposit any books, bags, or other items you brought with you. Then, you'll be escorted into a closed room.

All exams are completely closed-book. Although you are not permitted to take anything with you into the testing area, you are furnished with a blank sheet of paper and a pen (in some cases, an erasable plastic sheet and an erasable pen). Before the exam, try to memorize as much of the important material as you can, so you can write that information on the blank sheet as soon as you are seated in front of the computer. You can refer to this piece of paper during the test, but you'll have to surrender the sheet when you leave the room.

You will have some time to compose yourself, write down information on the paper you're given, and take a sample orientation exam before you begin the real thing. I suggest you take the orientation test before taking your first exam (because the exams are generally identical in layout, behavior, and controls, you probably won't need to do this more than once).

Typically, the room has one to six computers, and each workstation is separated from the others by dividers. Most test rooms feature a wall with a large picture window. This permits the exam coordinator to monitor the room, prevent exam-takers from talking to one another, and observe anything out of the ordinary. The exam coordinator will have preloaded the appropriate Microsoft certification exam (for this book, Exam 70-228), and you'll be permitted to start as soon as you're seated in front of the computer.

All Microsoft certification exams allow a certain maximum amount of time in which to complete your work (this time is indicated on the exam by an on-screen counter/clock, so you can check the time remaining whenever you like). All Microsoft certification exams are computer-generated. In addition to multiple choice, you'll encounter select and place (drag and drop), create a tree (categorization and prioritization), drag and connect, and build list and reorder (list prioritization) on most exams. The questions are constructed to check your mastery of basic facts and figures about SQL Server 2000 and to require you to evaluate one or more sets of circumstances or requirements. Often, you'll be asked to give more than one answer to a question. You may also be asked to select the best or most effective solution to a problem from a range of choices, all of which are technically correct. Taking the exam is quite an adventure, and it involves real thinking. This book shows you what to expect and how to deal with the potential problems, puzzles, and predicaments.

In the next section, you'll learn more about the format of Microsoft test questions and how to answer them.

Exam Layout and Design

The format of Microsoft SQL Server 2000 exams can vary. For example, the Design exam (70-229) consists of a series of case studies, with six types of questions. For the Core Four exams (70-210, 70-215, 70-216, 70-217), as well as this exam (70-228), the same six types of questions can appear, but you are not likely to encounter complex multiquestion case studies.

For some Design exams, each case study (or "testlet") presents a detailed problem that you must read and analyze. Figure 1.1 shows an example of what a case study looks like. You must select the different tabs in the case study to view the entire case.

Following each case study is a set of questions related to the case study. These questions can be one of six types (which are discussed next). Careful attention to details provided in the case study is the key to success. Be prepared to toggle frequently between the case study and the questions as you work. Some of the case studies also include diagrams (called *exhibits*) that you'll need to examine closely to understand how to answer the questions.

After you complete a case study, you can review all of the questions and your answers. However, when you move on to the next case study, you cannot return to the previous case study and make any changes.

Following are the six types of question formats:

➤ Multiple choice, single answer

➤ Multiple choice, multiple answers

➤ Build list and reorder (list prioritization)

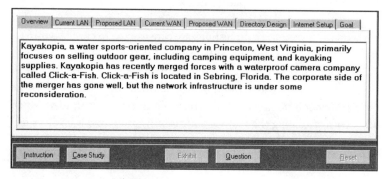

Figure 1.1   This is a typical case study.

➤ Create a tree

➤ Drag and connect

➤ Select and place (drag and drop)

For multiple choice, multiple answer questions, you must include all of the correct responses in your answer in order to receive any credit for the question.

*Note: Exam formats might vary by test center location. You may want to call the test center or visit **ExamCram.com** to see if you can find out which type of test you'll encounter.*

Multiple-Choice Question Format

Some exam questions require you to select a single answer, whereas others ask you to select multiple correct answers. The following multiple-choice question requires you to select a single correct answer. Following the question is a brief summary of each potential answer and why it is either right or wrong.

Question 1

> You have three domains connected to an empty root domain under one contiguous domain name: **tutu.com**. This organization is formed into a forest arrangement with a secondary domain called **frog.com**. How many Schema Masters exist for this arrangement?
>
> ○ a. 1
> ○ b. 2
> ○ c. 3
> ○ d. 4

Answer a is correct because only one Schema Master is necessary for a forest arrangement. The other answers (b, c, and d) are misleading because they try to make you believe that Schema Masters may be in each domain or that you should have one for each contiguous namespaced domain.

This sample question format corresponds closely to the Microsoft Certification Exam format (of course, questions are not followed by answer keys on the exam). To select an answer, you position the cursor over the radio button next to the answer and click the mouse button to select the answer.

Let's examine a question where one or more answers are possible. This type of question provides checkboxes rather than radio buttons for marking all appropriate selections.

Question 2

How can you seize FSMO roles? [Check all correct answers]

❑ a. The ntdsutil.exe utility

❑ b. The Replication Monitor

❑ c. The secedit.exe utility

❑ d. Active Directory Domains and FSMOs

Answers a and b are correct. You can seize FSMO roles from a server that is still running through the Replication Monitor, or in the case of a server failure, you can seize roles with the ntdsutil.exe utility. The secedit.exe utility is used to force group policies into play; therefore, answer c is incorrect. Active Directory Domains and Trusts are a combination of truth and fiction; therefore, answer d is incorrect.

For this particular question, two answers are required. Microsoft sometimes gives partial credit for partially correct answers. For Question 2, you have to check the boxes next to answers a and b to obtain credit for a correct answer. Notice that picking the right answers also means knowing why the other answers are wrong.

Build-List-and-Reorder Question Format

Questions in the build-list-and-reorder format present two lists of items: one on the left and one on the right. To answer the question, you must move items from the list on the right to the list on the left. The final list must then be reordered into a specific order.

These questions are usually in the form, "From the following list of choices, pick the choices that answer the question. Arrange the list in a certain order." To give you practice with this type of question, some questions of this type are included in this study guide. Here's an example of how they appear in this book; for a sample of how they appear on the test, see Figure 1.2.

Question 3

From the following list of famous people, pick those that have been elected President of the United States. Arrange the list in the order in which they served.

Thomas Jefferson

Ben Franklin

Abe Lincoln

George Washington

Andrew Jackson

Paul Revere

The correct answer is:

George Washington

Thomas Jefferson

Andrew Jackson

Abe Lincoln

On an actual exam, the entire list of famous people would initially appear in the list on the right. You would move the four correct answers to the list on the left and then reorder the list on the left. Notice that the answer to the question did not include all items from the initial list. However, this may not always be the case.

To move an item from the right list to the left list, first select the item by clicking on it and then clicking the Add button (left arrow). Once you move an item from one list to the other, you can move the item back by first selecting the item and then clicking the appropriate button (either the Add button or the Remove button). After items have been moved to the left list, you can reorder the list by selecting an item and clicking the up or down button.

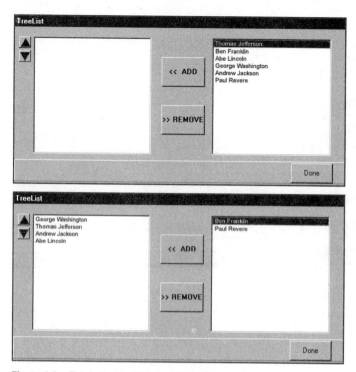

Figure 1.2 This is how build-list-and-reorder questions appear.

Create-a-Tree Question Format

Questions in the create-a-tree format also present two lists: one on the left and one on the right. The list on the right consists of individual items, and the list on the left consists of nodes in a tree. To answer the question, you must move items from the list on the right to the appropriate node in the tree.

These questions are basically a matching exercise. Items from the list on the right are placed under the appropriate category in the list on the left. Here's an example of how they appear in this book; for a sample of how they appear on the test, see Figure 1.3.

Question 4

The calendar year is divided into four seasons:

Winter

Spring

Summer

Fall

Identify the season when each of the following holidays occurs:

Christmas

Fourth of July

Labor Day

Flag Day

Memorial Day

Washington's Birthday

Thanksgiving

Easter

The correct answer is:

Winter

Christmas

Washington's Birthday

Spring

Flag Day

Memorial Day

Easter

Summer

Fourth of July

Labor Day

Fall

Thanksgiving

In this case, all of the items in the list were used. However, this may not always be the case.

To move an item from the right list to its appropriate location in the tree, you must first select the appropriate tree node by clicking on it. Then, you select the item to be moved and click the Add button. If one or more items have been added to a tree node, the node is displayed with a "+" icon to the left of the node name. You can click this icon to expand the node and view whatever was added. If any item has been added to the wrong tree node, you can remove it by selecting it and clicking the Remove button (see Figure 1.3).

Drag-and-Connect Question Format

Questions in the drag-and-connect format present a group of objects and a list of "connections." To answer the question, you must move the appropriate connections between the objects.

This type of question is best described using graphics. Here's an example.

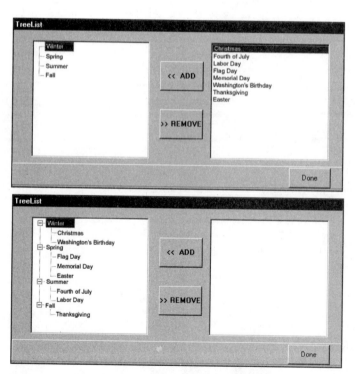

Figure 1.3   This is how create-a-tree questions appear.

Question 5

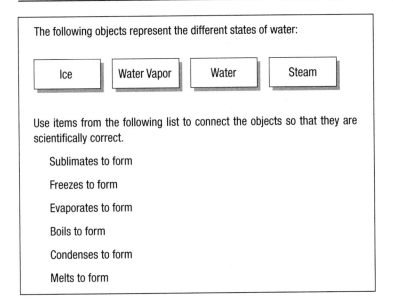

The following objects represent the different states of water:

| Ice | Water Vapor | Water | Steam |

Use items from the following list to connect the objects so that they are scientifically correct.

Sublimates to form

Freezes to form

Evaporates to form

Boils to form

Condenses to form

Melts to form

The correct answer is:

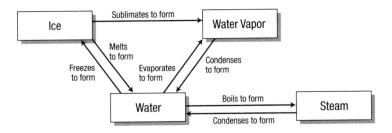

For this type of question, it's not necessary to use every object, but each connection can be used multiple times by dragging the answer to multiple locations. Dragging an answer away from its position removes it.

Select-and-Place Question Format

Questions in the select-and-place (drag-and-drop) format present a diagram with blank boxes and a list of labels that must be dragged to fill in the blank boxes. To answer the question, you must move the labels to their appropriate positions on the diagram.

This type of question is best described using graphics. Here's an example.

Question 6

Place the items in their proper order, by number, on the following flow-chart. Some items may be used more than once, and some items may not be used at all.

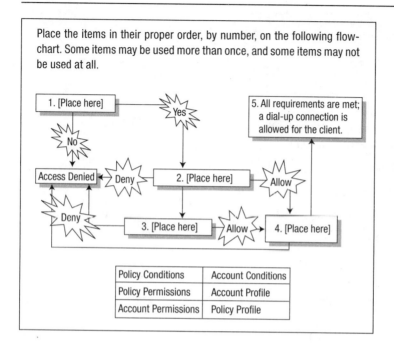

Policy Conditions	Account Conditions
Policy Permissions	Account Profile
Account Permissions	Policy Profile

The correct answer is:

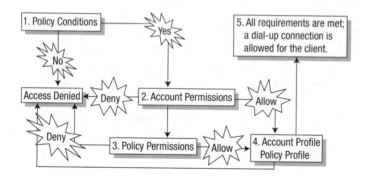

Microsoft's Testing Formats

Currently, Microsoft uses four different testing formats:

➤ Case study

➤ Fixed length

➤ Adaptive

➤ Short form

As mentioned earlier, the case study approach has been used with past versions of Microsoft's SQL Server Design exam. That exam consists of a set of case studies that you must first analyze to answer questions related to the case studies. Such exams include one or more case studies (tabbed topic areas), each of which is followed by 4 to 10 questions. The question types for both the SQL Server 2000 Design and Administration exams are multiple choice, build list and reorder, create a tree, drag and connect, and select and place. Depending on the test topic, some exams are totally case-based, whereas others are not.

Other Microsoft exams employ advanced testing capabilities that may not be immediately apparent. Although the questions that appear are primarily multiple choice, the logic in *fixed-length tests*, which use a fixed sequence of questions, is more complex than that in older Microsoft tests. Some questions employ a sophisticated user interface (which Microsoft calls a *simulation*) to test your knowledge of particular software and systems in a simulated "live" environment that behaves just like the original. The Testing Innovations link at **www.microsoft.com/ trainingandservices/default.asp?PageID=mcp** includes a downloadable practice simulation.

For some exams, Microsoft has turned to a well-known technique, called *adaptive testing*, to establish a test-taker's level of knowledge and product competence. Adaptive exams look the same as fixed-length exams, but they determine the level of difficulty at which an individual test-taker can correctly answer questions. Test-takers with differing levels of knowledge or ability see different sets of questions; individuals with high levels of knowledge or ability are presented with a smaller set of more difficult questions, whereas individuals with lower levels of knowledge are presented with a larger set of easier questions. Two individuals may answer the same percentage of questions correctly, but the test-taker with a higher knowledge or ability level scores higher because his or her questions are weighted more heavily.

Also, lower-level test-takers may answer more questions than more-knowledgeable colleagues. This explains why adaptive tests use ranges of values to define the number of questions and the amount of time needed to complete the tests.

Adaptive tests work by evaluating the test-taker's most recent answer. A correct answer leads to a more difficult question (also raising the test software's estimate of the test-taker's knowledge and ability level). An incorrect answer leads to a less difficult question (also lowering the test software's estimate of the test-taker's knowledge and ability level). This process continues until the test targets the test-taker's true ability level. The exam ends when the test-taker's level of accuracy meets a statistically acceptable value (in other words, when his or her performance demonstrates an acceptable level of knowledge and ability) or when the maximum number of items has been presented (in which case, the test-taker is almost certain to fail).

Microsoft also introduced a short-form test for its most popular tests. This test consists of 25 to 30 questions, with a time limit of exactly 60 minutes. This type of exam is similar to a fixed-length test because it allows readers to jump ahead or return to earlier questions and to cycle through the questions until the test is done. Microsoft does not use adaptive logic in this test; it claims that statistical analysis of the question pool is such that the 25 to 30 questions delivered during a short-form exam conclusively measure a test-taker's knowledge of the subject matter in much the same way as an adaptive test. The short-form test is like a "greatest hits exam" (that is, the most important questions are covered) version of an adaptive exam on the same topic.

Note: Some of the Microsoft exams may contain a combination of adaptive and fixed-length questions.

Because you won't know in which form the Microsoft exam might be, you should be prepared for an adaptive exam instead of a fixed-length or a short-form exam: The penalties for answering incorrectly are built into the test itself on an adaptive exam, whereas the layout remains the same for a fixed-length or short-form test, no matter how many questions you answer incorrectly.

 The biggest difference between adaptive tests and fixed-length or short-form tests is that you can revisit questions on fixed-length or short-form tests after you've read them. On an adaptive test, you must answer the question when it is presented and cannot go back to that question.

Strategies for Different Testing Formats

Before you choose a test-taking strategy, you must determine what type of test it is: case studies, fixed length, short form, or adaptive.

➤ Case study tests consist of a tabbed window that allows you to navigate easily through the sections of the case.

➤ Fixed-length tests consist of 50 to 70 questions with a checkbox. You can return to these questions if you want.

➤ Short-form tests have 25 to 30 questions with a checkbox. You can return to these questions if you want.

➤ Adaptive tests are identified in the introductory material of the test. They have no checkbox and can be visited (and answered) only once.

Some tests contain a variety of testing formats. For example, a test may start with a set of adaptive questions, followed by fixed-length questions.

You'll be able to tell for sure if you are taking an adaptive, fixed-length, or short-form test by the first question. Fixed-length or short-form tests include a checkbox that allows you to mark the question for later review. Adaptive test questions include no such checkbox and can be visited (and answered) only once.

Case Study Exam Strategy

Most test-takers find that the case study type of test used for some versions of the Design exam is the most difficult to master. When it comes to studying for a case study test, your best bet is to approach each case study as a standalone test. The biggest challenge you'll encounter is that you'll feel that you won't have enough time to get through all of the cases that are presented.

Each case provides a lot of material that you'll need to read and study before you can effectively answer the questions that follow. The trick to taking a case study exam is to first scan the case study to get the highlights. Make sure you read the overview section of the case so that you understand the context of the problem at hand. Then, quickly move on and scan the questions.

As you are scanning the questions, make mental notes to yourself so that you'll remember which sections of the case study you should focus on. Some case studies may provide a fair amount of extra information that you don't really need to answer the questions. The goal with this scanning approach is to avoid having to study and analyze material that is not completely relevant.

When studying a case, read the tabbed information carefully. It is important to answer each and every question. You will be able to toggle back and forth from case to questions, and from question to question within a case testlet. However, after you leave the case and move on, you may not be able to return to it. I suggest that you take notes while reading useful information to help you when you tackle the test questions. It's hard to go wrong with this strategy when taking any kind of Microsoft certification test.

Fixed-Length and Short-Form Exam Strategy

A well-known principle when taking fixed-length or short-form exams is first to read through the entire exam from start to finish. Answer only those questions that you feel absolutely sure you know. On subsequent passes, you can dive into more complex questions more deeply, knowing how many such questions you have left.

There's at least one potential benefit to reading the exam over completely before answering the trickier questions: Sometimes, information supplied in later questions sheds more light on earlier questions. At other times, information you read in later questions may jog your memory about facts, figures, or behavior that helps you answer earlier questions. Either way, you'll come out ahead if you answer only those questions on the first pass that you're absolutely confident about.

Fortunately, the Microsoft exam software for fixed-length and short-form tests makes the multiple-visit approach easy to implement. At the top-left corner of each question is a checkbox that permits you to mark that question for a later visit.

Note: Marking questions makes review easier, but you can return to any question by clicking the Forward or Back button repeatedly.

Here are some question-handling strategies that apply to fixed-length and short-form tests. Use them if you have the chance:

➤ When returning to a question after your initial read-through, read every word again; otherwise, your mind can fall quickly into a rut. Sometimes, revisiting a question after turning your attention elsewhere lets you see something you missed, but the strong tendency is to see what you've seen before. Try to avoid that tendency at all costs.

➤ If you return to a question more than twice, try to articulate to yourself what you don't understand about the question, why answers don't appear to make sense, or what appears to be missing. If you chew on the subject awhile, your subconscious may provide the missing details, or you may notice a "trick" that points to the right answer.

As you work your way through the exam, another counter that Microsoft provides comes in handy—the number of questions completed and questions outstanding. For fixed-length and short-form tests, it's wise to budget your time by making sure that you've completed one-quarter of the questions one-quarter of the way through the exam period, and three-quarters of the questions three-quarters of the way through.

If you're not finished when only five minutes remain, use that time to guess your way through any remaining questions. Remember, guessing is potentially more valuable than not answering. Blank answers are always wrong, but a guess may turn out to be right. If you don't have a clue about any of the remaining questions, pick answers at random or choose all a's, b's, and so on. Questions left unanswered are counted as answered incorrectly, so a guess is better than nothing at all.

 At the very end of your exam period, you're better off guessing than leaving questions unanswered.

Adaptive Exam Strategy

If there's one principle that applies to taking an adaptive test, it's "Get it right the first time." You cannot elect to skip a question and move on to the next one when taking an adaptive test, because the testing software uses your answer to the current question to select whatever question it plans to present next. You also cannot return to a question because the software gives you only one chance to answer the question. You can, however, take notes as you work through the test. Sometimes, information supplied in earlier questions may help you answer later questions.

Also, when you answer a question correctly, you are presented with a more difficult question next, to help the software gauge your level of skill and ability. When you answer a question incorrectly, you are presented with a less difficult question, and the software lowers its current estimate of your skill and ability. This continues until the program settles into a reasonably accurate estimate of what you know and can do.

The good news is that if you know the material, you'll probably finish most adaptive tests in 30 minutes or so. The bad news is that you must really know the material well to do your best on an adaptive test. That's because some questions are so convoluted, complex, or hard to follow that you're bound to miss one or two, at a minimum. Therefore, the more you know, the better you'll do on an adaptive test, even accounting for the occasionally weird or unfathomable questions that appear on these exams.

 Because you can't always tell in advance if a test is fixed length, short form, or adaptive, you should prepare for the exam as if it were adaptive. That way, you will be prepared to pass, no matter what kind of test you take. If the test turns out to be fixed length or short form, remember the tips from the preceding section, which will help you improve on what you could do on an adaptive test.

If you encounter a question on an adaptive test that you can't answer, you must guess an answer immediately. (However, you may suffer for your guess on the next question if you guess correctly, because the software will give you a more difficult question next!)

Question-Handling Strategies

For those questions that have only one right answer, usually two or three of the answers will be obviously incorrect, and two of the answers will be plausible. Unless the answer leaps out at you (if it does, reread the question to look for a trick; sometimes those are the ones you're most likely to get wrong), begin the process of answering by eliminating those answers that are most obviously wrong.

At least one answer out of the possible choices for a question can usually be eliminated immediately because it matches one of these conditions:

➤ The answer does not apply to the situation.

➤ The answer describes a nonexistent issue, an invalid option, or an imaginary state.

After you eliminate all answers that are obviously wrong, you can apply your retained knowledge to eliminate further answers. Look for items that sound correct but refer to actions, commands, or features that are not present or not available in the situation that the question describes.

If you're still faced with a blind guess among two or more potentially correct answers, reread the question. Try to picture how each of the possible remaining answers would alter the situation. Be especially sensitive to terminology; sometimes the choice of words ("remove" instead of "disable") can make the difference between a right answer and a wrong one.

You should guess at an answer only after you've exhausted your ability to eliminate answers and are still unclear about which of the remaining possibilities is correct. An unanswered question offers you no points, but guessing gives you at least some chance of getting a question right; just don't be too hasty when making a blind guess.

Note: If you're taking a fixed-length or a short-form test, you can wait until the last round of reviewing marked questions (just as you're about to run out of time or unanswered questions) before you start making guesses. You will have the same option within each case study testlet (but once you leave a testlet, you may not be allowed to return to it). If you're taking an adaptive test, you'll have to guess to move on to the next question if you can't figure out an answer some other way. Either way, guessing should be your technique of last resort!

Numerous questions assume that the default behavior of a particular utility is in effect. If you know the defaults and understand what they mean, this knowledge will help you cut through many Gordian knots.

Mastering the Inner Game

In the final analysis, knowledge breeds confidence, and confidence breeds success. If you study the materials in this book carefully and review all of the practice questions at the end of each chapter, you should become aware of those areas where additional learning and study are required.

After you've worked your way through the book, take the practice exam in the back of the book. Taking this test provides a reality check and helps you identify areas to study further. Make sure you follow up and review materials related to the questions you miss on the practice exam before scheduling a real exam. Don't schedule your exam appointment until after you've thoroughly studied the material and feel comfortable with the whole scope of the practice exam. You should score 80 percent or better on the practice exam before proceeding to the real thing (otherwise, obtain some additional practice tests so you can keep trying until you hit this magic number).

If you take a practice exam and don't get at least 80 to 85 percent of the questions correct, keep practicing. Microsoft provides links to practice exam providers and also offers self-assessment exams at **www.microsoft.com/trainingandservices/**. You should also check out **ExamCram.com** for downloadable practice questions.

Armed with the information in this book and with the determination to augment your knowledge, you should be able to pass the certification exam. However, you need to work at it, or you'll spend the exam fee more than once before you finally pass. If you prepare seriously, you should do well.

The next section covers other sources you can use to prepare for the Microsoft Certification Exams.

Additional Resources

A good source of information about Microsoft Certification Exams comes from Microsoft itself. Because its products and technologies—and the exams that go with them—change frequently, the best place to go for exam-related information is online.

If you haven't already visited the Microsoft Certified Professional site, do so right now. The MCP home page resides at **www.microsoft.com/trainingandservices** (see Figure 1.4).

Note: This page may be replaced by something new and different by the time you read this, because things change regularly on the Microsoft site. Should this happen, please read the sidebar titled "Coping with Change on the Web."

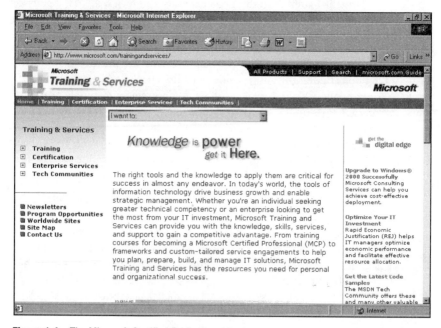

Figure 1.4　The Microsoft Certified Professional home page.

Coping with Change on the Web

Sooner or later, all of the information I've shared with you about the Microsoft Certified Professional pages and the other Web-based resources mentioned throughout the rest of this book will go stale or be replaced by newer information. In some cases, the URLs you find here may lead you to their replacements; in other cases, the URLs will go nowhere, leaving you with the dreaded "404 File not found" error message. When that happens, don't give up.

There's always a way to find what you want on the Web if you're willing to invest some time and energy. Most large or complex Web sites (such as the Microsoft site) offer a search engine. On all of Microsoft's Web pages, a Search button appears along the top edge of the page. As long as you can get to the Microsoft site (it should stay at **www.microsoft.com** for a long time), use this tool to help you find what you need.

The more focused you can make a search request, the more likely the results will include information you can use. For example, you can search for the string

```
"training and certification"
```

to produce a lot of data about the subject in general, but if you're looking for the preparation guide for Exam 70-228, "Installing, Configuring, and Administering Microsoft SQL Server 2000 Enterprise Edition," you'll be more likely to get there quickly if you use a search string similar to the following:

```
"Exam 70-228" AND "preparation guide"
```

Likewise, if you want to find the Training and Certification downloads, try a search string such as this:

```
"training and certification" AND "download page"
```

Finally, feel free to use general search tools—such as **www.search.com**, **www.altavista.com**, and **www.excite.com**—to look for related information. Although Microsoft offers great information about its certification exams online, there are plenty of third-party sources of information and assistance that need not follow Microsoft's party line. Therefore, if you can't find something immediately, intensify your search.

SQL Server 2000 Overview

Terms you'll need to understand:

✓ Database

✓ Record

✓ Table

✓ Instance

✓ Database Management System (DBMS)

✓ Relational database (RDB)

✓ Attribute

✓ Client/server

✓ System databases

✓ User databases

Techniques you'll need to master:

✓ Understanding basic database structure

✓ Recognizing system and user databases

✓ Recognizing database files by file type extension

✓ Identifying the versions of SQL Server 2000

Modern business practices involve the coordination and organization of tremendous amounts of data. Efficient access to stored data can mean the success or failure of a business, whether the business is a cutting-edge, Internet-based, online storefront or a bricks-and-mortar specialty store. Information technology has infiltrated the business world to such a degree that few businesses can function without the ability to provide updated information to their global clients easily and rapidly.

SQL Server 2000, Microsoft's latest product, supports the organization and presentation of the information required in today's business environment. The details provided in this chapter provide a brief review of database structure, implementation, and the basic databases within SQL Server 2000 installations, as well as an overview of the available versions of SQL Server 2000 and their uses. Additional references are listed at the end of this chapter.

Database Basics

Databases are organized collections of related information stored so that users can easily access the information and add, delete, update, and display subsets of it based on criteria specified by the user. Databases can vary in form and implementation. For example, the card catalog in a library is one form of a paper-based database. In this book, I focus on an electronic form of database implemented using Microsoft's SQL Server 2000 Database Management System.

Within a database, information is grouped in successively larger categories (see Table 2.1) that represent the manner in which the information is organized. Each instance of SQL Server 2000 contains several databases. Details on the types of databases contained within an instance of SQL Server 2000 are covered later in this chapter.

Table 2.1	Terminology for categories of data within SQL Server 2000 in ascending order by size.	
Category	**Contains**	**Example**
Attribute	A specific datum	Last name, ZIP code
Record	A collection of attributes related to a single item	Address (contains street, city, state, and ZIP code)
Table	A class of records objects	Members (contains name, membership type, and status)
Database	A collection of tables	Club membership (contains members and contact information)
Instance	A collection of databases	A complete installation of SQL Server 2000

Data stored within a database is more highly organized than in a simple file system. If properly designed, a database minimizes storage of duplicated data and provides a method for rapidly extracting specific items of information from the mass of stored data. Each database has two main portions: the files containing stored data, and the software that provides access to this data, which is referred to as a *Database Management System (DBMS)*. SQL Server 2000 is one type of DBMS. The DBMS is responsible for enforcing database structure and rules, maintaining relationships between data, and providing access for client applications, presented in a clear and useful manner.

Relational Databases

Organization of the data within a database may be accomplished in many ways. SQL Server 2000 utilizes a *Relational database (RDB)* structure. RDBs organize data into related tables, each representing a class of information deemed important. Each table has a series of columns and rows. Each column corresponds to an attribute of the object represented by the table, and each row characterizes an instance of the object class.

Relationships are established between tables through the use of keys or shared common attributes. If two tables each have a Primary Key, a relationship in its simplest form may be established between them by placing a related Foreign Key in one table that references the Primary Key in another.

An example of this would be in the case of two tables: **EMPLOYEES** and **INVOICES**. The Primary Key for the **EMPLOYEES** table is **EmpID**, while the Primary Key for the **INVOICES** table is **InvID**. Records in the **INVOICES** table are related to records in the **EMPLOYEES** table through the use of a Foreign Key **EmpID,** which relates to the Primary Key by the same name in the **EMPLOYEES** table. The Relationship provides a mechanism by which all **INVOICES** for a selected **EMPLOYEE** may be extracted and manipulated.

Table 2.2 provides an example of an object class (table) called **Employees**. In this example, the columns **EmpID**, **Name**, **Salary**, and **Hire Date** are examples of attributes of this table. All data in the row for employee **1001** represents one record in this table.

RDBs utilize separate tables for each type of data and then create a *relationship* between these tables. For example, a relational database structure may consist of an **Employees** table that contains information identifying each employee and an **Addresses** table that contains mailing address information such as **Street**, **City**, **State**, and **Zip code** fields. A client wanting to track all addresses that a particular employee has had during the term of his or her employment may find several entries in the **Addresses** table for each entry in the **Employees** table.

Table 2.2	Employees table format.		
EmpID	**Name**	**Salary**	**Hire Date**
1001	Robert Jenkins	35,152	4/13/1985
1002	Jenny Levine	37,016	8/14/1986
1003	Martin Adams	18,485	1/21/1996

 Normalization is the process by which information is organized and segmented in order to improve the efficiency of data storage and access. A database administrator (DBA) should be very comfortable with the methods used in this process to perform such administrative tasks well. This information is covered in much greater detail in Microsoft's Certification Exam 70-229: Designing and Implementing Databases with Microsoft SQL Server 2000 Enterprise Edition.

It is easy to see how the relational database structure is more efficient than a single-table solution. In a single-table format, if only one set of address attributes is present, only one set of information may be kept for each employee. However, if address history must be maintained, space must be allocated for all employees by adding attributes such as **OldStreet, OldCity, OldState**, and **OldZip**. This is inefficient because, although new hires start out with only a single address entry, eventually they may change addresses, creating the need to include additional address entries, which is difficult in a single-table format.

In a relational database, the same information can be maintained by adding a single entry in the **Employees** table identifying each employee and a single entry in the **Addresses** table for each address that a particular employee has had. Thus, a new hire has one entry in each table, but a long-term employee may have many address entries in the **Addresses** table that are related to the single entry in the **Employees** table.

Client/Server

Originally used in the 1980s to describe personal computers (PCs) in a networked environment, the term *client/server* describes a topology in which distributed *client* computers access shared resources located on centralized *server* machines. Earlier, monolithic mainframes provided all of the computing power, and access was provided through terminals, which were just networked monitors and keyboards with little or no storage or processing capability of their own.

Early PC networks utilized file-sharing architectures in which individual PCs downloaded files from centralized machines and performed all information processing locally. This type of architecture was not scaleable to allow for the number of simultaneous users found in modern networking environments.

Later, developments in graphical user interfaces (GUIs) and large-scale networked resources involving hundreds or thousands of simultaneous connections created the need to distribute user interfaces to PC clients, while providing centralized database server access that replaced the earlier file-sharing architecture.

 The term *thin client* is often used interchangeably with the term *client*. A thin client, however, is a user interface that has been optimized to provide the least data manipulation possible for the task and the least impact on system and network performance on the client side.

Network performance is improved by allowing the server to transmit only the required subset of data to the client PC, which in turn transmits back only the necessary updates without having to move entire files back and forth across the network. Remote Procedure Calls (RPCs) and Structured Query Language (SQL) statements are used to communicate between the client and server in this type of architecture.

Two-Tier Architecture

The most basic client/server architecture is the two-tier architecture in which the client-side user interface is accessed via the user's desktop environment, and the user interface communicates via the network with the DBMS located on a server. In this design, processing is divided between the client, which provides presentation and user interface processing, and the server, which provides access to triggers and stored procedures. Business logic functions may be present in either tier in this architecture.

Two-tier architectures are useful for large workgroups but begin to suffer in larger implementations. Network overhead is not fully optimized in this architecture, and performance issues may arise when there are more than several dozen users or when record-locking issues produce errors during multiple-user access.

Three-Tier Architecture

Large-scale distributed database scenarios involving a larger user base have evolved into the three-tier model (also called a *multitier* architecture). This model expands the two-tiered approach by adding an intermediary layer to handle business logic and transaction services between the user interface client layer and the DBMS.

In this model, performance can be significantly improved by allowing the client to pass an update to the middle tier, which queues the update until server access is available and then passes notification back to the client when the update is completed. Another advantage of the multitiered approach involves the use of modular programming, which enables rapid updating of business rules (such as a change in sales tax) without requiring an update in all clients. Changes to shared middle-tier components are obviously much easier to implement and roll out than are changes that involve thousands of clients.

The multitiered approach also makes migration between servers and platforms significantly easier because a middle-tier routing component may be redirected, including any changes to data access requirements, without requiring systemwide changes. Intelligent routing components can also improve server performance by directing requests or updates to different servers through middle-tier switching based on client-side input.

n-Tier Architectures

Multitiered architectures that involve multiple layers between the client and server layers are referred to as *n-tier* models. These are identical in terms of deployment and accessibility as the basic three-tier architecture, except they implement more than a single middle layer.

Collaborative Enterprise Architectures

Modern database management solutions often require the ability to distribute processing power between multiple clustered servers and replicated multiple database instances. Additional features for enterprise-level models include replication to mobile disconnected users and load-balancing capabilities to handle high traffic demands from global-scale Internet access.

Microsoft's SQL Server 2000 Enterprise Edition is designed with an emphasis on scalability and high-availability, making it ideally suited to huge database implementations demanding access by thousands of simultaneous users in a global marketplace.

SQL Server 2000 Databases

An instance of SQL Server 2000 includes several databases. These are broken down into two types: *system* and *user* databases. The SQL Server 2000 engine uses the system databases to perform various tasks. The user databases contain the various classes of data deemed important, as well as users, stored procedures, rules, and other information associated with the data.

System Databases

Each instance of SQL Server 2000 has four system databases: **master, modal, tempdb,** and **msdb.** These databases are used by the DBMS to maintain state information, provide a template for new databases, provide temporary storage, and manage scheduled tasks.

Table 2.3 provides details on the four system databases and the function of each.

User Databases

User databases include the collections of tables that contain the data within the database. An instance of SQL Server 2000 will have one or more user databases, potentially more depending on the business requirements of the specific DBMS solution.

Each user database contains objects such as tables, views, stored procedures, users, roles, rules, user-defined functions, and data types. Two sample databases are included when SQL Server 2000 is installed: **Northwind** and **pubs.** (These may be deleted if not needed.)

 It is helpful to be familiar with the structure of the sample databases and their tables, as many of the scenarios presented in the exam might be based on these or very similar databases.

Table 2.3	SQL Server 2000 system databases.
Database	**Function**
master	Represents the database schema. Maintains state information such as disk space usage, configuration information, and object information including the other databases. This is sometimes referred to as the *catalog* database because it provides information on all databases managed by the DBMS.
modal*	Forms the template for all new databases created within the instance.
tempdb	Provides temporary storage for data utilized by the SQL server during its operation. This database is a volatile database derived from the modal database. It loses all information each time the server is stopped and restarted.
msdb	Allows scheduling of tasks by the SQL Server Agent for later action. A scheduled backup event is one example of the use of this database.

*The modal database may not be present in some distributed database solutions if no new database will ever be created.

Database File Types

Each database is maintained in two or more physical files: a *primary data file*, one or more *log files*, and possibly one or more *secondary data files*. These files are identified by their file extensions (see Table 2.4) and should be located for optimum access based on the hardware configuration of the server.

The best practice is to separate data and log files onto separate disks to improve recoverability, especially if no hardware redundancy is present.

Versions of SQL Server 2000

Microsoft offers a number of different versions based on the SQL Server 2000 platform (see Table 2.5). The specific version utilized in a particular DBMS solution will be based on the number of users, expected scope, and other factors. This book focuses on the Enterprise version of SQL Server 2000 because the certification test is based on that platform.

Know these basic types well so you can quickly rule out obviously incorrect choices when answering scenario questions that specify a particular variant.

Table 2.4 Database file types.

Extension	File Type	Purpose
.mdf	Primary data file	Data
.ndf	Secondary data files*	Additional data
.ldf	Log files	Transaction logs

*There could be no secondary data files, or several.

Table 2.5 Versions of SQL Server 2000.	
Edition	**Use**
Enterprise	Fully featured production version of SQL Server 2000, designed to be scalable up to the largest enterprise-level requirements
Enterprise Evaluation	120-day evaluation version of the full Enterprise Edition
Standard	Designed for small workgroup environments
Personal	Standalone version for mobile users with a limit of five concurrent batch processes
Developer	Fully featured but only licensed for development; not for use as a production server
Windows CE	Designed for replication of data on Windows CE devices with a primary SQL Server 2000 database
Desktop Engine	A component that may be distributed with applications, having a limit of five concurrent batch processes and a 2GB database

Practice Questions

Question 1

Which of the following PC architectures are examples of client/server database models? [Check all correct answers]

- ❑ a. Two-tier
- ❑ b. n-tier
- ❑ c. Three-tier
- ❑ d. Mainframe
- ❑ e. Multitier

Answers a, b, c, and e are correct. Two-tier, three-tier, multitier, and n-tier architectures are all examples of client/server database architectures. Mainframe database architectures are not used for PCs. Therefore, answer d is incorrect.

Question 2

Which of the following is the database grouping of a class of record objects?

- ○ a. Database
- ○ b. Instance
- ○ c. Record
- ○ d. Attribute
- ○ e. Table

Answer e is correct. A table is a class of record objects. A database may hold many classes of record objects, so answer a is incorrect. An instance may contain many databases, so answer b is incorrect. A record is a collection of attributes and represents one instance of the class within a table, and an attribute represents only a single item of data. Therefore, answers c and d are also incorrect.

Question 3

Which of the following are system databases? [Check all correct answers]

❑ a. Primary files

❑ b. Secondary files

❑ c. Northwind

❑ d. Master

❑ e. Enterprise

Answer d is correct. The four system databases are **master, modal, tempdb,** and **msdb.** Primary and secondary files are physical files that hold a database's data, so answers a and b are incorrect. The Northwind database is a sample user database, so answer c is incorrect. SQL Server 2000 Enterprise Edition is a fully functional production database management system (DBMS). Therefore, answer e is also incorrect.

Question 4

Which tier is responsible for user access and presentation of data in the multitiered architecture?

○ a. Client

○ b. Middle

○ c. Server

Answer a is correct. The client tier handles the details of the user interface. The middle tier provides for transaction handling and business rules enforcement, whereas the server tier provides data storage and access. Therefore, answers b and c are incorrect.

Question 5

> Place the following items in ascending order by scope:
>
> Instance
>
> Table
>
> Attribute
>
> Database
>
> Record

The correct order for these items in ascending scope is:

Attribute

Record

Table

Database

Instance

An attribute is a specific datum. Records are collections of attributes related to a single item. Tables may be formed of many records. Databases may contain many tables. Each instance of SQL Server 2000 may contain several databases.

Question 6

> Which system database serves as the template for newly created databases?
>
> ○ a. **master**
> ○ b. **template**
> ○ c. **pubs**
> ○ d. **modal**
> ○ e. **msdb**

Answer d is correct. The **modal** database serves as the template for newly created databases. The **master** database stores state and object information, whereas the **msdb** database allows for task scheduling by the SQL System Agent, so answers a and e are incorrect. There is no **template** database in a default installation. Therefore, answer b is incorrect. The **pubs** database is one of the two sample user databases installed with SQL Server 2000. Therefore, answer c is also incorrect.

Question 7

> Which file extension is associated with a database file type that may not be present?
>
> ○ a. .ndf
>
> ○ b. .mdf
>
> ○ c. .mdb
>
> ○ d. .ldf

Answer a is correct. The .ndf file extension is associated with secondary data files, which may not be present for a database. The .mdf file extension is associated with primary data files, and the .ldf file extension is associated with log files, both of which will be present for each database. Therefore, answers b and d are incorrect. The extension .mdb is associated with Microsoft Access databases and is not a SQL Server 2000 extension, so answer c is also incorrect.

Question 8

> Which of the following versions of SQL Server 2000 could be used to test a workgroup-sized DBMS solution over a 60-day test period? [Check all correct answers]
>
> ❑ a. Enterprise
>
> ❑ b. Standard
>
> ❑ c. Standalone
>
> ❑ d. Master
>
> ❑ e. Enterprise Evaluation

Answers a, b, and e are correct. The Enterprise version is capable of scaling far beyond a workgroup solution but could be used, and the Enterprise Evaluation version has the same features and a 120-day trial period. The Standard version is designed for use up to a workgroup-sized implementation. Answer c is incorrect because there is no "standalone" version of SQL Server 2000. The Personal version can operate as a standalone option, but its limitation on concurrent cached processes makes its use very limited in a test at this scale. There is no Master version of SQL Server 2000, so answer d is also incorrect.

Question 9

> Which of the following are features of client/server database models? [Check all correct answers]
>
> ❏ a. Greater scalability
>
> ❏ b. Ease of modification
>
> ❏ c. Load balancing
>
> ❏ d. Ease of multiplatform migration
>
> ❏ e. Distributed processing

Answers a, b, c, d, and e are all correct. Client/server database models enjoy greater scalability than do monolithic solutions. Multitiered solutions offer ease in modification and multiplatform migration, while also allowing for distributed processing that can aid in load balancing in large-scale implementations.

Question 10

> There are several versions of SQL Server 2000, including:
>
> Enterprise
>
> Developer
>
> Personal
>
> Match the following definitions and statements with the appropriate versions of SQL Server 2000. (Note: some items may be used more than once.):
>
> Full-featured version of SQL Server 2000
>
> Has a limit of five concurrent batch processes
>
> Licensed for development and not as a production server

The correct answer is:

Enterprise

Full-featured version of SQL Server 2000

Developer

Full-featured version of SQL Server 2000

Licensed for development and not as a production server

Personal

Has a limit of five concurrent batch processes

Need to Know More?

 Dalton, Patrick, and Paul Whitehead. *SQL Server 2000 Black Book*. The Coriolis Group: Scottsdale, AZ, 2001. ISBN 1-57610-770-1. An excellent reference to keep close at hand during installation of SQL Server 2000. This is a good reference for a DBA's library, as it has many solutions to commonly experienced issues.

 Delaney, Kalen. *Inside Microsoft SQL Server 2000*. Microsoft Press: Redmond, WA, 2000. ISBN 0-7356-0998-5. A good review of SQL Server 2000 components including white papers and articles on a broad range of topics.

 Garcia, Marci, Jamie Reding, Edward Whalen, and Steve DeLuca. *Microsoft SQL Server 2000 Administrator's Companion*. Microsoft Press: Redmond, WA, 2000. ISBN 0-7356-1051-7. Detailed information about planning an installation including information on the differing versions of SQL Server 2000. An excellent reference during installation as well.

 Iseminger, David. *Microsoft SQL Server 2000 Reference Library with CD-ROM*. Microsoft Press: Redmond, WA, 2000. ISBN 0-7356-1280-3. An exhaustive library covering detailed information on all aspects of SQL Server 2000 implementations. A necessary reference for IT departments supporting Microsoft SQL Server 2000 implementations.

 http://support.microsoft.com/support/Access/Content/reldesign.asp. A good collection of resources dealing with relational database design. Some information applies to earlier versions of Microsoft SQL Server, but the articles on normalization and understanding relational database design provides prospective database administrators with a better understanding of these concepts.

Installation Planning

Terms you'll need to understand:

✓ Default instance
✓ Named instance
✓ Server Components
✓ Management Tools
✓ Development Tools
✓ Client Connectivity Components
✓ English Query
✓ Analysis Services
✓ Multiprotocol Network Library
✓ AppleTalk

✓ Banyan VINES
✓ Named Pipes
✓ NWLink IPX/SPX
✓ TCP/IP Sockets
✓ Collations
✓ Unicode
✓ Code page
✓ Windows authentication
✓ Mixed Mode authentication

Techniques you'll need to master:

✓ Recognizing default and named instances of SQL Server 2000
✓ Identifying basic requirements for installing the various editions of SQL Server 2000
✓ Selecting an installation type and desired components

✓ Understanding the file path structure used by SQL Server 2000
✓ Identifying the network libraries used for connection to an instance of SQL Server
✓ Determining the authentication mode for an instance of SQL Server 2000

Thorough planning before performing an installation of SQL Server 2000 will prevent many difficulties later. This chapter provides a review of the minimum hardware requirements for installing SQL Server 2000, the various editions and components that may be installed, and configuration details such as service accounts and file paths to be used.

 Pay close attention to the specifics of network library and authentication mode selection, as these topics apply to many scenarios presented in the certification exam.

The details provided in this chapter cover the basic requirements for planning a SQL Server 2000 installation and are not intended as an exhaustive review of all possible items and options involved in Enterprise-level database implementations. Additional references listed at the end of this chapter provide information beyond that required for the certification exam.

Instances

Multiple databases may be supported by a single instance of SQL Server 2000. Multiple instances of SQL Server 2000 on a single powerful machine provide a separate development environment and improved compartmentalization of secure information. Additionally, *named instances* of SQL Server 2000 allow multiple versions of SQL Server to exist on a single machine, providing continued legacy support of data maintained within older versions.

Many possible combinations are possible using named instances of SQL Server 2000. SQL Server 2000 introduces the concept of a *default instance*, which is identified by the network name of its server. Additional instances of SQL Server 2000 may be installed, each identified by a unique name. The naming conventions for named instances of SQL Server 2000 are as follows:

➤ Any names except the reserved names *Default* and *MSSQLServer* may be used.

➤ Instance names are limited to 16 characters.

➤ The first character of an instance name must be a letter (A-Z, a-z), an ampersand (&), or an underscore (_).

➤ Only letters, numbers, ampersands, and underscores may be used for instance naming. Punctuation marks, dashes, asterisks, and spaces are not allowed.

➤ The instance name is not case sensitive.

Enterprise implementations require planning when creating named instances to avoid having multiple instances of generic terms such as *local*. Make sure that instance-naming schemes provide for multiple unique names in a simple, scalable format that identifies the instances by their function or other meaningful description.

Default Instance

The default instance is a new concept to SQL Server 2000, which allows multiple named instances on a single server machine. Default instances are identified by the network name of the server computer and may be accessed by applications using client software from earlier versions of SQL Server.

An instance of SQL Server 6.5, SQL Server 7.0, or SQL Server 2000 may be installed as the default instance, and only one default instance may exist on each machine. There may be no default instance if only named instances of SQL Server 2000 are installed.

Named Instances

SQL Server 2000 named instances may be installed before, after, or instead of a default instance. Named instances are identified by the network name of the server along with the name of the instance. This identification may be accessed by applications utilizing SQL Server 2000 client components, using the format \servername\instancename.

Each named instance has its own set of services, registry structures, and directory structures, allowing each to be maintained independently of any others on the same machine. Options settings may be completely different for each instance.

Separate system resources are utilized for each instance, requiring a more robust system if multiple instances are to be run on a single machine.

Multiple Versions

Multiple instances of SQL Server 2000 may run on a single machine, and multiple versions of SQL Server may run on a single machine as well. SQL Server 6.5 may exist alongside an instance of SQL Server 7.0 or SQL Server 2000 using *version switching*. If SQL Server 7.0 is installed as the default instance, additional named instances of SQL Server 2000 may also be installed alongside the default installation.

If version switching is to be used between SQL Server 6.5 and a default instance of SQL Server 2000, the default instance of SQL Server 2000 should be upgraded from the default instance of SQL Server 7.0 that had been installed alongside of the SQL Server 6.5 instance. Version switching must be enabled.

It is possible to have three versions of SQL Server on a single machine. However, instances of SQL Server 6.5 and SQL Server 7.0 must be installed to allow version switching, and named instances of SQL Server 2000 must be used.

Options

Before installing an instance of SQL Server 2000, you should be familiar with the options available in each of the SQL Server 2000 editions, as well as the components that may be selected during the installation.

 When taking the test, carefully read the question details for specified editions of SQL Server and the operating system platform used in the scenario. This will help you eliminate incorrect answers.

Editions

SQL Server 2000 is distributed in three primary editions: Enterprise, Developer, and Standard. Also available are the SQL Server 2000 CE (used for Windows CE devices), Personal, and Desktop Engine editions.

The Enterprise Edition provides all available features of SQL Server 2000. The Developer version provides the same features; however, it is only licensed for development, not for a production implementation. A 120-day Evaluation version of the Enterprise Edition is also available and provides full functionality during its trial period.

The Standard edition lacks features designed for enterprise database solutions such as *fail-over clustering*, *federated databases*, and *log shipping*. Standard edition SQL Server instances are sufficient for standalone installations and are often used for small-office database implementations.

A detailed comparison of the possible combinations of SQL Server 2000 editions and operating systems goes far beyond the scope of this book. Tables 3.1 through 3.3 provide a brief comparison of the various editions of SQL Server 2000 when installed on a Microsoft Windows 2000 Advanced Server (see Table 3.1), a Datacenter Server (see Table 3.2), and a Microsoft Windows NT 4 Server Enterprise (see Table 3.3). Additional information may be found in the references listed at the end of this chapter.

Table 3.1   Capability comparison of SQL Server 2000 editions installed on a Windows 2000 Advanced Server.

Edition	Maximum Datastore Memory Supported	Maximum Number of CPUs
Enterprise	8GB	8
Enterprise Evaluation	8GB	8
Developer	8GB	8
Standard	2GB	4
Personal	2GB	2
Desktop Engine	2GB	2

Table 3.2   Capability comparison of SQL Server 2000 editions installed on a Windows 2000 Datacenter Server.

Edition	Maximum Datastore Memory Supported	Maximum Number of CPUs
Enterprise	64GB	32
Enterprise Evaluation	64GB	32
Developer	64GB	32
Standard	2GB	4
Personal	2GB	2
Desktop Engine	2GB	2

Table 3.3   Capability comparison of SQL Server 2000 editions installed on a Windows NT 4.0 Server Enterprise.

Edition	Maximum Datastore Memory Supported	Maximum Number of CPUs
Enterprise	3GB	8
Enterprise Evaluation	3GB	8
Developer	3GB	8
Standard	2GB	8
Personal	2GB	2
Desktop Engine	2GB	2

All editions of SQL Server 2000 dynamically configure user connections automatically, unlike previous versions of SQL Server that limited the number of concurrent user connections. Each connection requires additional system resources. Therefore, if a large number of concurrent connections are expected, system resources must be planned accordingly.

Installation

During installation of Enterprise or Standard editions of SQL Server 2000, several options are available:

➤ Full Server and Client Tools installations perform a complete installation of SQL Server 2000.

➤ Selecting the Client Tools Only option installs only the Management Tools and SQL Server 2000 Books Online.

➤ Other options under the Server and Client Tools installation include code samples and development tools, which may be installed if the system is intended for use as a development server.

➤ Personal Edition installations provide a full SQL Server 2000 database with some limitations. This is only recommended for testing or for implementations requiring five connections or less.

➤ Connectivity Only installations include the Data Access Components (DAC) and network libraries necessary for client applications to connect to SQL Server 2000.

Components

Many components are available during an installation of SQL Server 2000. A number of options are accessible on the Select Components screen, including the following:

➤ *Server Components*—Installed when the option for Server and Client Tools is selected. Server Components includes:

  ➤ *SQL Server*—Installs the SQL Server 2000 database engine

  ➤ *Full-text Search*—Installs the full-text search engine

  ➤ *Replication*—Installs the scripts and binary files for database replication

  ➤ *Upgrade Tools*—Installs the Upgrade Wizard (necessary for SQL 6.5 upgrades).

➤ *Performance Counters*—Installs the components for use in performance diagnostics.

➤ *Debug Symbols*—Installs the debug symbols for SQL Server 2000.

➤ *Management Tools*—Installed when the option Client Tools Only is selected or during Server and Client Tools setup. Management Tools includes:

 ➤ *SQL Server Enterprise Manager*—Provides Microsoft Management Console (MMC) interface for database administration.

 ➤ *Query Analyzer*—Provides graphical query analysis and an interactive Transact-SQL interface.

 ➤ *Profiler*—Provides auditing support for database activity.

 ➤ *Conflict Viewer*—Displays synchronization conflicts.

 ➤ *DTC Client*—Provides Distributed Transaction Coordinator (DTC) for use in multiple server transactions.

➤ *Development Tools*—Installed through a Custom Installation in the Setup Type screen. Development Tools includes:

 ➤ *Libraries*—Installs library and header files to allow for C language support.

 ➤ *Backup and Restore API*—Provides samples and documentation for custom backup and restore application development.

 ➤ *Debug Viewer*—Displays information for stored procedure debugging.

➤ *MDAC SDKs*—Contains software development kits for Microsoft Data Access Components (MDAC) and Extensible Markup Language (XML).

➤ *Client Connectivity Components*—Installed when Connectivity Only is selected or as an option in the Select Components option during Setup.

➤ *SQL Server 2000 Books Online*—Installs the complete online documentation for SQL Server 2000.

➤ *Code Samples*—Installs sample files for use by developers writing applications to access SQL Server 2000.

➤ *English Query*—An optional package that allows for plain English querying of the database (for example, "How many products contain paper?").

➤ *Analysis Services*—An optional package for online analytical processing (OLAP) of large data structures, used for data warehousing and data mining projects.

Note: Many of the foregoing components will be discussed in greater detail in Chapters 4 and 5.

File Paths

Installing an instance of SQL Server 2000 involves storing a number of files on the server. Files installed into the Windows system directory cannot be moved, but both SQL Server program files and SQL Server data files may be directed to locations defined by the system administrator performing the installation.

 Program files generally stay around the same size; however, data files usually become larger. Therefore, data files should be located in an NTFS volume capable of supporting expected development and expansion. They may not be placed in a compressed volume. Additionally, to optimize disk performance and provide *fault tolerance*, log files should be located on a drive other than that used for the primary and secondary database files.

The system administrator installing SQL Server 2000 may specify alternate locations for the program and data files beyond the default options.

Table 3.4 details the default file paths for SQL Server 2000 instances.

Network Libraries

SQL Server 2000 installs a number of *dynamic link libraries (DLLs)* that provide access to network *interprocess communication (IPC)* mechanisms. These network libraries provide communication avenues between client/server applications and multiple server distributed databases.

Each server can monitor multiple network libraries simultaneously. During installation, all network libraries are copied onto the destination server but must first be configured before they become accessible to the server for communication. Configurations may be changed after installation.

Table 3.4 Default installation file paths.		
File Type	Default Instance	Named Instance*
Program Files	\Program Files\Microsoft SQL Server \Mssql\Binn	\Program Files\Microsoft SQL Server\MSSQL$*MyInstance*\Binn
Data Files	\Program Files\Microsoft SQL Server \Mssql\Data	\Program Files\Microsoft SQL Server\MSSQL$*MyInstance*\Data

* Example instance is named MyInstance. Other named instances would have their own names in the place of MyInstance, according to service naming conventions.

Many questions on the exam deal with this topic. Be sure to know these libraries.

Named instances do not allow access to *Multiprotocol*, *AppleTalk*, or *Banyan VINES* libraries; clustered servers allow only *Named Pipes* and *TCP/IP* library access. The AppleTalk network library only supports the AppleTalk protocol. Additional information on each library option is as follows:

➤ *Multiprotocol*—Provides communication through most Windows NT/2000 IPC mechanisms, but may not be used by named instances of SQL Server 2000. This protocol is not available to named instances.

   ➤ May provide encryption for user password authentication and data if the Enable Multiprotocol Encryption option is selected. This should be used only for compatibility with legacy implementations. Secure Socket Layer (SSL) encryption provides a more secure solution.

   ➤ The only protocols within the Multiprotocol library that are considered fully supported are Named Pipes, NWLink IPX/SPX, and TCP/IP.

   ➤ Server network library DLLs: ssnetlib.dll and ssmsrpc.dll.

   ➤ Client network library DLLs: dbnetlib.dll and dbmsrpcn.dll.

➤ *Named Pipes*—Required for all Windows NT and Windows 2000 installations of SQL Server 2000.

   ➤ Default instance pipe: *servername*\pipe\sql\query.

   ➤ Named instance pipe: *servername*\pipe\MSSQL$*MyInstance*\sql\query.

   ➤ Server network library DLLs: ssnetlib.dll and ssnmpn70.dll (Windows NT).

   ➤ Client network library DLLs: dbnetlib.dll and dbnmpntw.dll.

➤ *NWLink IPX/SPX*—Allows communication using the NWLink IPX/SPX protocol utilized by Novell networks.

   ➤ Default Novell Bindery service name is the same as the server computer.

   ➤ Default instance IPX port: 33854.

   ➤ Named instance port(s): First available port after the default port.

   ➤ Server network library DLL: ssnetlib.dll.

   ➤ Client network library DLL: dbnetlib.dll.

➤ *TCP/IP Sockets*—Allows communication using standard Windows Sockets across the TCP/IP protocol. This is the default network library for all SQL Server 2000 installations.

  ➤ UDP port used for establishing connections: 1434.

  ➤ Default instance port: 1433.

  ➤ Named instance port(s): Dynamically assigned at startup.

  ➤ Server network library DLL: ssnetlib.dll.

  ➤ Client network library DLL: dbnetlib.dll.

➤ *AppleTalk*—Provides communication with Apple Macintosh clients using native AppleTalk protocols. This protocol will not be supported by future versions of SQL Server. It does not work on named instances.

  ➤ Default AppleTalk service object name: Assigned by the system administrator.

  ➤ Default AppleTalk zone: The network library uses the local zone.

  ➤ Server network library DLLs: ssnetlib.dll and ssmsad70.dll (Windows NT).

  ➤ Client network library DLLs: dbnetlib.dll and dbmsadsn.dll.

➤ *Banyan VINES*—Provides communication over the Banyan VINES IP protocol. This protocol will not be supported by future versions of SQL Server. It does not work on named instances.

  ➤ Default StreetTalk service name: Assigned by the system administrator.

  ➤ Server network library DLLs: ssnetlib.dll and ssmsvi70.dll.

  ➤ Client network library DLLs: dbnetlib.dll and dbmsvinn.dll.

Multiprotocol encryption may be selected during installation by selecting the Enable Multiprotocol Encryption option. If a *certificate* is installed on the server, the Enable Protocol Encryption For All Libraries option is available during installation. Otherwise, the desired encryption must be configured after installation using the Server Network Utility.

Collations

Multinational database enterprise implementations may require additional character sets to be supported by an instance of SQL Server 2000. Extended character sets provide any number of possible language-specific characters, including accented versions of some common A-Z characters. The order in which character sets are sorted may also vary between languages (for example, determining if "a" is less than or greater than "b" when sorted).

To allow improved functionality in multinational settings, SQL Server 2000 includes the capability to use specified *collations* (collections of alphabetic character sets and rules for proper use of certain characters in a language). The default collation for an instance is chosen during setup but may be changed later. Each new database created uses this setting as its default unless otherwise specified. The database default collation is used unless otherwise specified when defining new character columns, variables, or parameters.

Data may be stored as a *Unicode* data type using the two-byte character set defined by the International Organization for Standardization (ISO) and the Unicode Consortium to facilitate multinational data compatibility. Data may also be stored as a non-Unicode data type that uses one or two bytes for each character set. Non-Unicode data types have an associated *code page*, which provides the basis for the sort order of the character set.

Collations within SQL Server implementations specify three properties for character data:

➤ The sort order for Unicode data types

➤ The sort order for non-Unicode data types

➤ The code page for non-Unicode data types

If all users of a database use a single language, the collation installed should match that of the language. However, if the users of a database require multiple languages, the collation chosen should provide support for all of those languages, such as the **Latin1_General** collation that is used for western European languages.

The Unicode character sets should be used for globally accessible character data exchange. The ability to avoid translations between collations often offsets the additional database storage requirements for a two-byte character set.

When choosing data types during database creation, Unicode and non-Unicode data types may be selected. These character data types are as follows:

➤ *Unicode*—**nchar, nvarchar,** and **ntext**

➤ *Non-Unicode*—**char, varchar,** and **text**

Requirements

SQL Server 2000 does not have a hardware compatibility list (HCL) of its own. If a server meets certain basic requirements for the Windows operating system and hardware, SQL Server 2000 can be installed.

Hardware

When planning a database implementation, it is crucial to plan for later scalability. The minimum requirements for an installation of SQL Server 2000 are as follows:

➤ *CPU*—Intel-compatible, 166MHz or higher

➤ *RAM*—64MB (128MB recommended for the Enterprise edition)

➤ *Hard Disk*—250MB for a typical SQL Server database installation (130MB for Analysis Components and 80MB for English Query)

➤ *Monitor*—VGA or higher (800×600 minimum for graphical tools)

➤ *Mouse*—Microsoft-compatible

➤ *Other*—CD-ROM (required for installation)

Software

Installations of other software on a server supporting SQL Server 2000 may potentially interfere with its proper functioning. If possible, the server on which SQL Server 2000 is installed should be dedicated to SQL Server 2000 alone. The minimum requirements that must be met for an installation of SQL Server 2000 are as follows:

➤ *Enterprise*—NT Server 4.0 Server, NT Server Enterprise edition 4.0 (SP5 or later required on any NT Server versions), or any versions of Windows 2000 Server (required for Active Directory SQL Server features)

➤ *Developer*—Same as for Enterprise edition, plus NT 4.0 Workstation and Windows 2000 Professional

➤ *Standard*—Same as for Enterprise edition

➤ *Personal*—Same as for Enterprise edition, plus NT 4.0 Workstation, Windows 2000 Professional, Windows ME, and Windows 98

Additionally, Internet Explorer (IE) 5.0 or higher is required for all installations of SQL Server 2000. Internet Information Server (IIS) 4.01 or higher is required for writing XML applications.

Services

Instances of SQL Server 2000 run as services on Windows NT and Windows 2000 operating systems. Each instance requires two services for operation: *SQL Server* and *SQL Server Agent*.

Table 3.5 details the service naming conventions for default and named instances.

Service Accounts

During installation of an instance of SQL Server 2000, you can customize the service account information to specify the *Local System Account* or a *Domain User Account*. The Local System Account does not require a password but may restrict access to other database servers and to the SQL Mail service.

Domain user accounts use *Windows authentication*, which allows the same name and password to be used for connecting to both the operating system and the instance of SQL Server. This is the preferred type of service account because many multiserver operations can only be performed with a domain user account, such as the following:

➤ Joins involving remote data sources

➤ Server replication

➤ Remote drive backups

➤ SQL Mail and SQLAgentMail (if using Microsoft Exchange)

➤ Remote Procedure Calls (RPCs)

The same domain user account many be used for multiple instances of SQL Server 2000. This is recommended to simplify replication.

Table 3.5 SQL Server 2000 service naming conventions.		
Service	**Default Instance**	**Named Instance***
SQL Server	MSSQLSERVER	MSSQ$*MyInstance*
SQL Server Agent	SQLSERVERAGENT	SQLAgent$*MyInstance*

* Example instance is named MyInstance. Other named instances would have their own names in the place of MyInstance, according to service naming conventions.

To be used as a service account, a Domain User Account must be granted a number of permissions, including permission to do the following (see Chapter 11 for more information):

➤ Log on as a service

➤ Access and change permissions to the SQL Server directory as well as the database files (.mdf, .ndf, and .ldf)

➤ Access and change permissions to the registry keys corresponding to the server and its related services

In some cases, additional functionality may require the service account to be a member of the local Administrators group or local Power Users group on the server.

Authentication

During installation of SQL Server 2000, the *authentication mode* must be selected. The authentication mode determines how user logon attempts are validated. Two authentication modes are available in SQL Server 2000 (further details will be given in Chapter 11):

➤ *Windows authentication*—Provides access to SQL Server through a logon using Windows user accounts that have been granted access.

➤ *Mixed Mode authentication*—Allows users to connect to SQL Server using Windows user account validation or SQL Server authentication, providing backward compatibility with earlier versions of SQL Server and access capability from non-Windows platforms.

 Many questions on the exam deal with this topic. Remember that Windows authentication requires a Windows NT or Windows 2000 user account for logon attempts.

When connecting to an instance of SQL Server via the Named Pipes network library, the user must have Access The Computer From The Network permission or have permission to connect to the IPC pipe (*servername*\IPC$).

Practice Questions

Question 1

> Which of the following are valid names for instances of SQL Server 2000? [Check all correct answers]
>
> ❑ a. New Instance
>
> ❑ b. AccountingRecords
>
> ❑ c. *MyInstance*
>
> ❑ d. Default
>
> ❑ e. Local
>
> ❑ f. 2001Data

Answers c and e are correct. *MyInstance* and *Local* are allowable names for instances of SQL Server 2000, although Local is not a good choice for enterprise database implementations. Answer a is incorrect because *New Instance* includes a space, which is not an allowable character. *AccountingRecords* exceeds the 16-character limit, and *2001Data* does not begin with one of the allowable characters. Therefore, answers b and f are also incorrect. Answer d is incorrect because *Default* is a reserved term used to denote the default instance.

Question 2

> Which of the following versions of SQL Server may be installed on a single server? [Check all correct answers]
>
> ❑ a. SQL Server 2000 and SQL Server 6.5
>
> ❑ b. SQL Server 2000 and SQL Server 7.0
>
> ❑ c. SQL Server 6.5 and SQL Server 7.0
>
> ❑ d. SQL Server 6.5, SQL Server 7.0, and SQL Server 2000

Answers a, b, c, and d are all correct. SQL Server 6.5 and either SQL Server 7.0 or SQL Server 2000 may coexist using version switching. Named instances of SQL Server 2000 may coexist with an instance of SQL Server 7.0.

Question 3

> During database creation, character sets of two data types may be selected:
>
> Unicode
>
> Non-Unicode
>
> Match the following character variable types with the appropriate data types:
>
> **char**
>
> **nchar**
>
> **nvarchar**

The correct answer is:

Unicode

    char

Non-Unicode

    nchar

    nvarchar

Question 4

> Which of the following platforms allow an instance of SQL Server 2000 Enterprise to support 4GB of RAM? [Check all correct answers]
>
> ❏ a. Windows 2000 Advanced Server
>
> ❏ b. Windows 2000 Datacenter Server
>
> ❏ c. Windows NT4 Server Enterprise edition
>
> ❏ d. Windows Legacy edition

Answers a and b are correct. SQL Server 2000 Enterprise supports up to 8GB of RAM on Windows 2000 Advanced Server and up to 64GB of RAM on Windows 2000 Datacenter Server. Answer c is incorrect because SQL Server 2000 Enterprise supports only up to 3GB of RAM on the Windows NT4 Server Enterprise edition. Answer d is incorrect because Windows Legacy edition does not exist.

Question 5

Two authentication modes are offered during installation:

Windows authentication

Mixed Mode authentication

Match the following methods of authentication with the appropriate authentication mode. (Note: some items may be used more than once.):

Provides access to SQL Server through a logon using Windows account validation

Used for backward compatibility with earlier versions of SQL Server

Provides access capability from non-Windows platforms

The correct answer is:

Windows authentication

Provides access to SQL Server through a logon using Windows account validation

Mixed Mode authentication

Provides access to SQL Server through a logon using Windows account validation

Used for backward compatibility with earlier versions of SQL Server

Provides access capability from non-Windows platforms

Question 6

Which of the following component options install the SQL Server Enterprise Manager?

○ a. Server Components

○ b. Management Tools

○ c. Development Tools

○ d. Code Samples

Answer b is correct. The SQL Server Enterprise Manager is one of the components installed when the Management Tools option is selected, along with the Query Analyzer, Profiler, Conflict Viewer, and DTC Client. The Server Components installation includes SQL Server, Full-text Search, Replication, Upgrade Tools, Performance Counters, and Debug Symbols. Therefore, answer a is incorrect. Answer c is incorrect because the Development Tools installation includes C language Libraries, Backup and Restore API documentation, Debug Viewer, and MDAC Software Development Kits. Answer d is also incorrect, because the Code Samples installation loads only the sample files used for development.

Question 7

> Which protocols are fully supported by the Multiprotocol network library?
> [Check all correct answers]
>
> ❑ a. Named Pipes
>
> ❑ b. NWLink IPX/SPX
>
> ❑ c. TCP/IP Sockets
>
> ❑ d. AppleTalk
>
> ❑ e. Banyan VINES

Answers a, b, and c are correct. Answers d and e are incorrect because only Named Pipes, NWLink IPX/SPX, and TCP/IP Sockets are considered to be tested and fully supported.

Question 8

> Unicode collations are required for users in multiple countries to connect to an instance of SQL Server 2000.
>
> ○ a. True
>
> ○ b. False

Answer b is correct. Unicode character sets are used to ensure compatibility across multiple language types, but many countries may share a common character set and sort order (for example, Mexico and Spain both use the Spanish character set). Collations have rules for the sort order of both Unicode and non-Unicode character data types.

Question 9

> You are a system administrator responsible for installing SQL Server 2000
> for a developer in the programming department as quickly as possible. The
> developer has a Pentium Pro 200 machine with 128MB of RAM, 500MB of
> free disk space, and is running Windows NT 4.0 Server (SP6). The monitor
> supports only up to 1280×1024 resolution, and the mouse is an older, MS-
> compatible, three-button mouse. You decide to install Windows 2000 Pro-
> fessional and load SQL Server 2000 Developer edition on this machine. Is
> this the fastest way to accomplish this task?
>
> ○ a. Yes
>
> ○ b. No

Answer b is correct. The developer's system is capable of supporting an installation of SQL Server 2000 Developer edition just as it is. It is not necessary to
install Windows 2000 Professional first, provided that the service pack version
on NT 4 Server installations is SP5 or higher. The fastest way to accomplish this
task is to install SQL Server 2000 Developer on the system as it is now.

Question 10

> You are a system administrator managing a global enterprise network that
> has Windows 2000 and Windows NT Enterprise edition servers accessed by
> Windows NT Workstation, Windows 2000 Professional, Windows ME, and
> Windows 98 client computers. All user accounts are located in a single user
> domain, and all of the database servers are located in a resource domain.
> Which authentication modes will allow domain users on the client comput-
> ers to connect to instances of SQL Server 2000 located on servers within
> the resource domain? [Check all correct answers]
>
> ❏ a. Windows authentication
>
> ❏ b. Mixed Mode
>
> ❏ c. Named Pipes

Answers a and b are correct. Windows authentication mode requires the use of a
valid user account that has been granted access rights to the instance of SQL
Server 2000. Mixed Mode authentication also allows SQL Server authentication, which provides backward compatibility and access from non-Windows platforms. Answer c is incorrect because Named Pipes is a network library that may
be used for communication between servers or clients and servers running SQL
Server 2000; it does not provide logon and password authentication.

Need to Know More?

 Dalton, Patrick, and Paul Whitehead. *SQL Server 2000 Black Book*. The Coriolis Group: Scottsdale, AZ, 2001. ISBN 1-57610-770-1. An excellent reference to keep close at hand during installation of SQL Server 2000. This is a necessary book in any DBA's library, as it has many solutions to commonly experienced issues.

 Delaney, Kalen. *Inside Microsoft SQL Server 2000*. Microsoft Press: Redmond, WA, 2000. ISBN 0-7356-0998-5. A good review of SQL Server 2000 components including white papers and articles on a broad range of topics.

 Iseminger, David. *Microsoft SQL Server 2000 Reference Library with CD-ROM*. Microsoft Press: Redmond, WA, 2000. ISBN 0-7356-1280-3. An exhaustive library covering detailed information on all aspects of SQL Server 2000 implementations. A necessary reference for IT departments supporting Microsoft SQL Server 2000 implementations.

 Stanek, William. *Microsoft SQL Server 2000 Administrator's Pocket Consultant*. Microsoft Press: Redmond, WA, 2000. ISBN 0-7356-1129-7. A condensed reference for SQL Server 2000 that provides ready access to important tips for database administrators.

Basic Installation

· ·

Terms you'll need to understand:

✓ Database server installation

✓ Typical installation

✓ Minimal installation

✓ Custom installation

✓ Client Tools Only

✓ Connectivity Only

✓ Analysis Services

✓ English Query

✓ Uninstallation

✓ Add/Remove Programs

Techniques you'll need to master:

✓ Installing a default instance of SQL Server 2000

✓ Identifying Typical, Minimal, and Custom installation types

✓ Installing a named instance of SQL Server 2000

✓ Enacting Client Tools Only or Connectivity Only installations

✓ Adding and removing components on existing installations of SQL Server 2000

✓ Installing SQL Server 2000 Analysis Services

✓ Installing Microsoft English Query 2000 components

✓ Uninstalling an instance of SQL Server 2000

After planning is completed, you are now ready to install an instance of SQL Server 2000. Options chosen during installation will provide access to various components of SQL Server as well as tools that the database administrator (DBA) will use for maintenance and development. The installations may be either a default instance of SQL Server or named instances using SQL Server 2000, which allow multiple instances to exist on a single server machine.

This chapter covers basic installation procedures and options for both default and named instance installations of SQL Server 2000. In all cases, it is assumed that the minimum hardware requirements (outlined in Chapter 3) have been met for an installation of SQL Server 2000 Enterprise on a Windows 2000 server platform. Additional references are listed at the end of this chapter.

Before You Begin

Just as a carpenter first assembles all of the tools and materials necessary to create a cabinet before beginning construction, a DBA must also assemble the tools and materials necessary to perform an installation of SQL Server 2000 before beginning. Certain steps should be followed to ensure an optimal environment during the installation.

After the necessary hardware has been prepared and the operating system loaded, the final items required for installation should be collected. In all cases, make sure that all service packs and patches have been successfully installed before beginning an installation of SQL Server 2000. In addition, the following items should be verified before beginning:

➤ Both the SQL Server 2000 Installation CD-ROM and CD Key should be available. Installation will prompt for this required information.

➤ In some cases, antivirus (AV) software can interfere with the installation process. Make certain that the AV software is not scheduled for a system scan during the installation period. Disable the AV software until the process is completed to avoid possible conflict.

➤ A number of *Registry keys* are written during the installation process. Avoid running any other processes that may alter or access the Registry during installation to minimize potential difficulties.

➤ Because the installation process writes a number of events to the *Event Log* during setup, Microsoft recommends that the *Event Viewer* be closed during installation.

➤ Close any services that are dependent on SQL Server or that use *data source names (DSN)* or *open database connectivity (ODBC) application programming interface (API)* access.

➤ Decide on locations for program and data files, keeping in mind that program files do not generally increase in storage requirements, but data files will over the lifetime of the database instance.

➤ Determine the authentication mode required based on expected access requirements.

➤ Log on using a User account with local Administrator permissions.

 Domain Controllers do not have local accounts, so a domain-level Administrator account will be necessary for the installation. Member servers will have local Administrators groups. Installation of SQL Server 2000 should be performed using an account that is a member of this group on the appropriate server.

➤ When installing SQL Server 2000 on a computer that is already running another instance of SQL Server, always perform a complete backup before beginning the installation.

Default Instance

Only one default instance can exist on a server. This instance is accessed using the network name of the server on which it resides. The default instance may be SQL Server 6.5, SQL Server 7.0, or SQL Server 2000. If an instance of an earlier version of SQL Server exists, SQL Server 2000 should not be installed as the default instance without removing the earlier edition or performing an upgrade if the information is to be maintained.

Installation

To perform a basic installation of the default instance of SQL Server 2000, take the following steps:

1. Insert the SQL Server 2000 disc in the CD-ROM drive. If Autorun has been disabled, it may be necessary to double-click the Autorun.exe file in the root directory of the disc.

2. Select SQL Server 2000 Components (see Figure 4.1).

Figure 4.1 The SQL Server Autorun screen.

> ➤ If installing SQL Server 2000 on a Windows 95 platform, select SQL Server 2000 Prerequisites and then Install Common Controls Library Update before selecting SQL Server 2000 Components.

3. Select Install Database Server to open the Installation Wizard (see Figure 4.2).

> ➤ At this time, install Analysis Services and English Query components by selecting Install Analysis Services or Install English Query. These are discussed in detail later in this chapter.

4. Click Next at the Welcome screen.

5. Click Next on the Computer Name screen to install an instance on the local computer (see Figure 4.3).

> ➤ An alternative to a local installation can be selected at this time using the options on the Computer Name screen. Remote installations are covered in Chapter 5.

6. Select Create A New Instance Of SQL Server, Or Install Client Tools on the Installation Selection screen (the default), and click Next to begin creating a new instance of SQL Server (see Figure 4.4).

> ➤ The Upgrade, Remove, or Add Components to an Existing Instance of SQL Server options and Advanced Options (such as creating an unattended installation file) can be selected on the Installation Selection screen. These options are covered later in this chapter.

Figure 4.2 The Install Components screen.

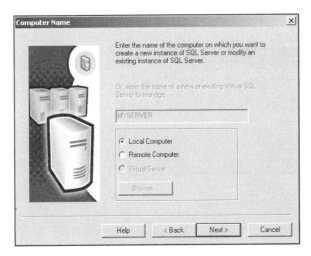

Figure 4.3 The Computer Name screen.

7. Enter a Name and Company name in the appropriate boxes on the User Information screen. Click Next at the Welcome prompt (see Figure 4.5).

8. Read the Microsoft Licensing Agreement, and click Yes to accept the Agreement. Selecting No at this point terminates the installation. Input your CD-Key when prompted.

9. Select Server And Client Tools on the Installation Definition screen (the default). Click Next to continue the installation (see Figure 4.6).

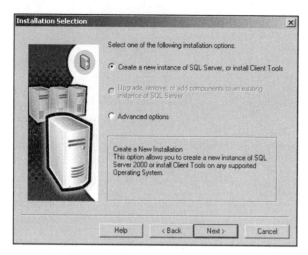

Figure 4.4 The Installation Selection screen.

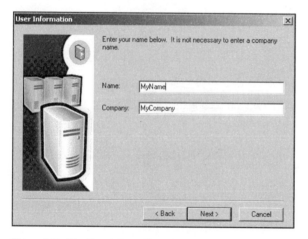

Figure 4.5 The User Information screen.

➤ Installation options for Client Tools Only or Connectivity Only can be selected on this screen. These options are covered later in this chapter.

10. Leave the Default option checked on the Instance Name screen (the default). Click Next to continue the installation (see Figure 4.7).

➤ To create a named instance of SQL Server 2000, the Default option should be deselected on this screen. This option is covered later in this chapter.

11. Select Typical on the Setup Type screen (the default), accept the default settings for program and data file locations, and click Next to continue the installation (see Figure 4.8).

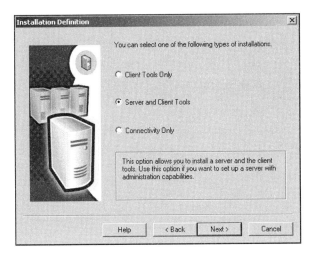

Figure 4.6 The Installation Definition screen.

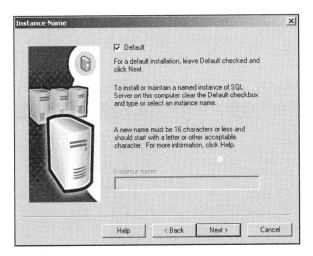

Figure 4.7 The Instance Name screen.

➤ Typical, Minimum, or Custom installations can be selected on the Setup Type screen. A comparison of these types appears later in this chapter.

➤ To select an alternate destination folder location for the program or data files, select the Browse option for the appropriate file type. Navigate to the alternate destination, and select OK to return to the Setup Type screen.

12. Accept the default setting of Use The Same Account For Each Service. Auto Start SQL Server Service on the Services Accounts screen, and enter the account information for the appropriate Domain User service account. Click Next to continue the installation (see Figure 4.9).

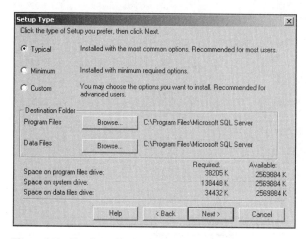

Figure 4.8 The Setup Type screen.

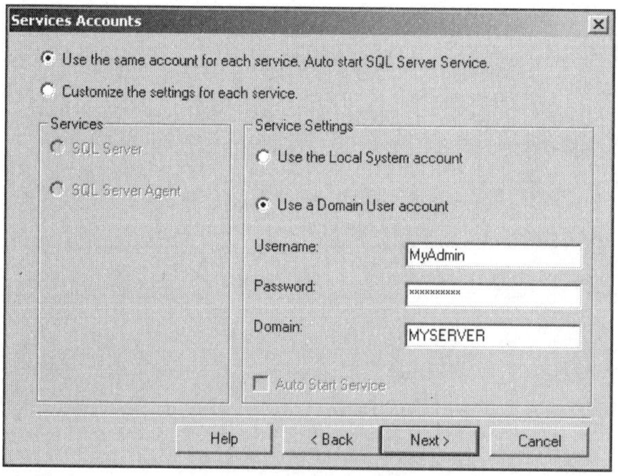

Figure 4.9 The Services Accounts screen.

➤ Alternate service accounts for the SQL Server and SQL Server Agent services can be selected on this screen. The Auto Start option for each can also be configured at this time.

➤ The Local System account can be selected as the service account for these services instead of a Domain User account. However, this may limit the accessibility of databases located on other servers.

13. Select the appropriate authentication mode on the Authentication Mode screen. Enter the system administrator (SA) password if Mixed Mode is selected. Click Next to continue the installation (see Figure 4.10).

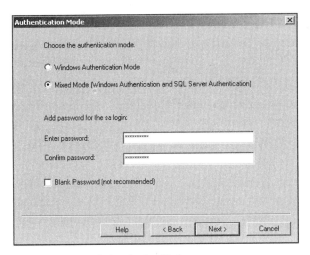

Figure 4.10 The Authentication Mode screen.

> ➤ Windows Authentication Mode (the default) may be used if Windows authentication is the only method required. Mixed Mode authentication provides for both Windows authentication and SQL Server authentication.

> ➤ If Mixed Mode is selected, a Blank Password option can be selected for the SA. This is not recommended because it reduces the security of the SQL Server installation.

14. At this point, you can select Back if you need to revise any of the previous options. If not, click Next on the Start Copying Files screen. This begins the process of copying files from the installation disc to the destination locations selected during configuration.

15. Click Finish if prompted to complete the installation of the MDAC and continue with the installation process.

> ➤ The Installation Wizard may detect active tasks that are in use but need to be altered by the installation of SQL Server 2000. Click Next to continue the installation.

16. Click Finish on the Setup Complete screen after selecting the option to restart (the default) the computer following installation. After the computer restarts, the default instance of SQL Server 2000 is accessible for use.

Typical, Minimum, and Custom Installations

The options during selection of Setup Type allow the DBA to configure the installation of SQL Server 2000 according to the requirements dictated by available hard drive space and required components.

Table 4.1 details the storage capacity requirements for default selections of Typical, Minimum, and Custom installation types. Data file storage will increase over time, but system and program file sizes usually remain stable unless new components are added later.

The Typical installation is usually sufficient for most production installations. It does not include Code Samples or most Development Tools (Debugger only), but it does provide items not included in a Minimum installation, such as Upgrade Tools, Client Tools, and Books Online. Custom installations allow for selecting components and subcomponents according to need or for changing collations settings or network libraries.

 Knowing which components are installed in the Typical and Minimum installations will help to identify potential answers in certain types of scenario questions that list possible solutions for experienced problems.

Named Instance

Named instances of SQL Server 2000 may be installed before, after, or instead of a default database instance. These instances each require their own program and data file storage as well as separate services.

To perform a basic installation of a named instance of SQL Server 2000 called "MyInstance," take the following steps:

1. Insert the SQL Server 2000 disc in the CD-ROM drive. If Autorun has been disabled, it may be necessary to double-click the Autorun.exe file in the root directory of the disc.

Table 4.1	Storage requirements by installation type.		
Type	System Files	Program Files	Data Files
Typical	182,917K	38,205K	34,432K
Minimum	75,116K	12,127K	25,600K
Custom*	182,917K	38,205K	34,432K

* Custom installations begin with the same components as those for Typical installations. Components added or removed will affect storage capacity requirements.

2. Select SQL Server 2000 Components.

   ➤ To install SQL Server 2000 on a Windows 95 platform, select SQL Server 2000 Prerequisites and then Install Common Controls Library Update before selecting SQL Server 2000 Components.

3. Select Install Database Server to open the Installation Wizard.

   ➤ The Analysis Services and English Query components can be selected at this time by selecting Install Analysis Services or Install English Query. These components are discussed in detail later in this chapter.

4. Click Next at the Welcome screen.

5. Click Next on the Computer Name screen to install an instance on the local computer.

   ➤ An alternative to a local installation can be selected at this time using the options on the Computer Name screen. Remote installations are covered in Chapter 5.

6. Select Create A New Instance Of SQL Server, Or Install Client Tools on the Installation Selection screen (the default). Click Next to begin creating a new instance of SQL Server.

   ➤ The Upgrade, Remove, Or Add Components To An Existing Instance Of SQL Server options and Advanced options (such as creating an unattended installation file) can be selected on this Installation Selection screen. These options are covered later in this chapter.

7. Enter a Name and Company name in the appropriate boxes on the User Information screen. Click Next at the Welcome prompt.

8. Read the Microsoft Licensing Agreement, and click Yes to accept the Agreement. Selecting No at this point terminates the installation. Input your CD-Key when prompted.

9. Select Server And Client Tools on the Installation Definition screen (the default). Click Next to continue the installation.

   ➤ Installation options for Client Tools Only or Connectivity Only can be selected on the Installation Definition screen. These options are covered later in this chapter.

10. Enter the appropriate Instance Name in the appropriate box (in this example, MyInstance) on the Instance Name screen (this is the only option if another instance is already installed). Click Next to continue the installation (see Figure 4.11).

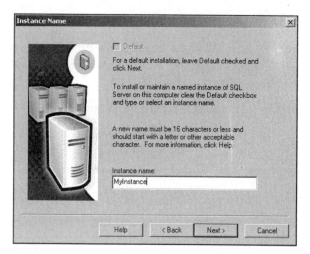

Figure 4.11   The Instance Name screen showing a named instance installation.

11. Select Typical on the Setup Type screen (the default), accept the default settings for program and data file locations, and click Next to continue the installation.

   ➤ To select an alternate destination folder location for the program or data files, select the Browse option for the appropriate file type. Navigate to the alternate destination, and select OK to return to the Setup Type screen.

12. Accept the default setting of Use The Same Account For Each Service. Auto Start SQL Server Services on the Services Accounts screen, enter the account information for the appropriate Domain User service account, and click Next to continue the installation.

   ➤ Alternate service accounts for the SQL Server and SQL Server Agent services can be selected on this screen. The Auto Start option for each can also be configured at this time.

   ➤ The Local System account can be selected as the service account for these services instead of a Domain User account. However, this may limit the accessibility of databases located on other servers.

13. Select the appropriate authentication mode on the Authentication Mode screen, enter the SA password if Mixed Mode is selected, and click Next to continue the installation.

   ➤ Windows Authentication Mode (the default) can be used if Windows authentication is the only method required. Mixed Mode authentication provides for both Windows authentication and SQL Server authentication.

➤ If Mixed Mode is selected, a Blank Password option can be selected for the SA. This is not recommended because it reduces the security of the SQL Server installation.

14. At this point, you can select Back if you need to revise any of the previous options. If not, click Next on the Start Copying Files screen. This begins the process of copying files from the installation disc to the destination locations selected during configuration.

15. Click Finish if prompted to complete the installation of the MDAC and continue with the installation process.

➤ The Installation Wizard may detect active tasks that are in use but need to be altered by the installation of SQL Server 2000. Click Next to continue the installation beyond this point.

16. Click Finish on the Setup Complete screen after selecting the option to restart (the default) the computer following installation. After the computer restarts, the default instance of SQL Server 2000 is accessible for use.

The process is the same for each additional named instance. Remember that each additional instance increases the system capacity requirements.

Subinstallations

If full functionality is not needed, two subsets of the full installation—Client Tools Only and Connectivity Only—are possible. These additional options are available through the Installation Definition screen.

Client Tools Only

An installation of Client Tools Only provides the Management Tools necessary for administration of SQL Server database instances.

To perform a basic installation of the SQL Server 2000 Client Tools Only, take the following steps:

1. Insert the SQL Server 2000 CD in the CD-ROM drive. If Autorun has been disabled, double-click the Autorun.exe file in the root directory of the disc.

2. Select SQL Server 2000 Components.

➤ If installing SQL Server 2000 on a Windows 95 platform, select SQL Server 2000 Prerequisites and Install Common Controls Library Update before selecting SQL Server 2000 Components.

3. Select Install Database Server to open the Installation Wizard.

➤ The Analysis Services and English Query components can be selected at this time by selecting Install Analysis Services or Install English Query. Installation of these components are detailed later in this chapter.

4. Click Next at the Welcome screen.

5. Click Next on the Computer Name screen to install an instance on the local computer.

➤ An alternative to a local installation can be selected at this time using the options on the Computer Name screen. Remote installations are covered in Chapter 5.

6. Select Create A New Instance Of SQL Server, Or Install Client Tools on the Installation Selection screen (the default). Click Next to begin creating a new instance of SQL Server.

➤ The Upgrade, Remove, Or Add Components To An Existing Instance Of SQL Server options and Advanced Options (such as creating an un-attended installation file) can be selected on this screen. These options are covered later in this chapter.

7. Enter a Name and Company name in the appropriate boxes on the User Information screen, and click Next at the Welcome prompt.

8. Read the Microsoft Licensing Agreement, and click Yes to accept the Agreement. Selecting No at this point terminates the installation.

9. Select Client Tools Only on the Installation Definition screen, and click Next to continue the installation (see Figure 4.12).

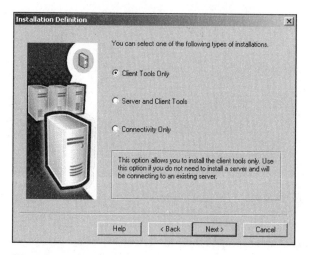

Figure 4.12 The Installation Definition screen with Client Tools Only selected.

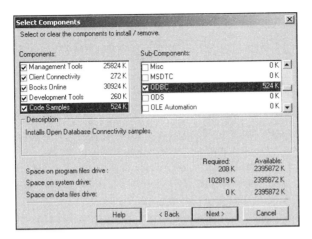

Figure 4.13   The Select Components screen.

10. Add or remove any desired components or subcomponents on the Select Components screen. Click Next to continue the installation (see Figure 4.13).

11. Click Next on the Start Copying Files screen unless you wish to select Back to revise any of the previous options. This begins the process of copying files from the installation disc to the destination locations selected during configuration.

12. Click Finish if prompted to complete the installation of the MDAC and continue with the installation process.

    ➤ The Installation Wizard may detect active tasks that are in use but need to be altered by the installation of SQL Server 2000. Click Next to continue the installation.

13. Click Finish on the Setup Complete screen, and restart the computer following installation. The installation of SQL Server Client Tools is now complete.

Connectivity Only

Installing Connectivity Only provides the Data Access Components (DAC) and Network Libraries so that applications can connect to SQL Server instances.

To perform a basic installation of SQL Server 2000 Connectivity Only, take the following steps:

1. Insert the SQL Server 2000 disc in the CD-ROM drive. If Autorun has been disabled, it may be necessary to double-click the Autorun.exe file in the root directory of the disc.

2. Select SQL Server 2000 Components.

   ➤ To install SQL Server 2000 on a Windows 95 platform, you must select SQL Server 2000 Prerequisites and then Install Common Controls Library Update before selecting SQL Server 2000 Components.

3. Select Install Database Server to open the Installation Wizard.

   ➤ Selecting Install Analysis Services or Install English Query at this time installs these components. The Analysis Services and English Query components are covered in detail later in this chapter.

4. Click Next at the Welcome screen.

5. Click Next on the Computer Name screen to install an instance on the local computer.

   ➤ An alternative to a local installation can be selected at this time using the options on this screen. Remote installations are covered in Chapter 5.

6. Select Create A New Instance Of SQL Server, Or Install Client Tools on the Installation Selection screen (the default). Click Next to begin creating a new instance of SQL Server.

   ➤ The Upgrade, Remove, Or Add Components To An Existing Instance Of SQL Server options and Advanced Options (such as creating an unattended installation file) can be selected on this screen. These options are covered later in this chapter.

7. Enter a Name and Company name in the appropriate boxes on the User Information screen, and click Next at the Welcome prompt.

8. Read the Microsoft Licensing Agreement, and click Yes to accept the Agreement. Selecting No at this point terminates the installation.

9. Select Connectivity Only on the Installation Definition screen, and click Next to continue the installation (see Figure 4.14).

10. Click Next on the Start Copying Files screen unless you wish to select Back to revise any of the previous options. This begins the process of copying files from the installation disc to the destination locations selected during configuration.

11. Click Finish if prompted to complete the installation of the MDAC and continue with the installation process.

   ➤ The Installation Wizard may detect active tasks that are in use but need to be altered by the installation of SQL Server 2000. Click Next to continue the installation.

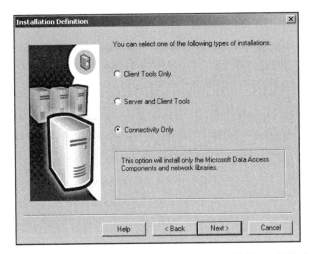

Figure 4.14 The Installation Definition screen with Connectivity Only selected.

12. Click Finish on the Setup Complete screen, and restart the computer following installation. The installation of SQL Server Connectivity support is now complete.

Adding Components

Components and subcomponents may be added after the initial installation of SQL Server 2000 by selecting Upgrade, Remove, or Add Components to an Existing Instance of SQL Server on the Installation Selection screen.

 It is not always necessary to restart the server after installations of additional components, but it is recommended to allow the server to update any settings that may have changed during installation.

Adding or Removing Components

Components and subcomponents may be added or removed after an installation of SQL Server 2000 has been completed.

To add or remove components to a previously installed instance of SQL Server 2000, take the following steps:

1. Insert the SQL Server 2000 disc in the CD-ROM drive. If Autorun has been disabled, it may be necessary to double-click the Autorun.exe file in the root directory of the disc.

2. Select SQL Server 2000 Components.

   ➤ To install SQL Server 2000 on a Windows 95 platform, you must select SQL Server 2000 Prerequisites and then Install Common Controls Library Update before selecting SQL Server 2000 Components.

3. Select Install Database Server to open the Installation Wizard.

   ➤ Selecting Install Analysis Services or Install English Query at this time installs these components. The Analysis Services and English Query components are covered in detail later in this chapter.

4. Click Next at the Welcome screen.

5. Click Next on the Computer Name screen to install an instance on the local computer.

   ➤ An alternative to a local installation can be selected at this time using the options on this screen. Remote installations are covered in Chapter 5.

6. Select Upgrade, Remove, Or Add Components To An Existing Instance Of SQL Server on the Installation Selection screen, and click Next to continue (see Figure 4.15).

7. Leave the Default option checked on the Instance Name screen (the default), and click Next to continue the installation.

   ➤ To add or remove products from a named instance of SQL Server 2000, the Default option should be deselected on this screen and the named instance selected in the appropriate box before selecting Next.

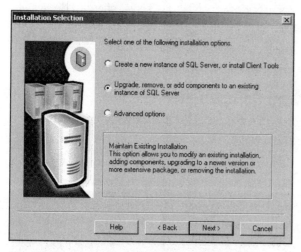

Figure 4.15   The Installation Selection screen.

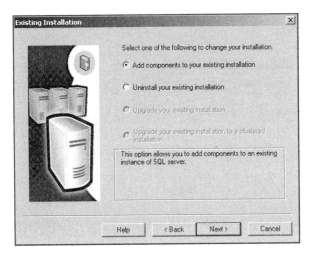

Figure 4.16 The Existing Installation screen.

8. Select the Add Components To Your Existing Installation option on the Existing Installation screen, and click Next to continue (see Figure 4.16).

➤ The Uninstall Your Existing Installation, Upgrade Your Existing Installation, and Upgrade Your Existing Installation To A Clustered Installation options are also available for selection on this screen. Details on clustered servers are covered in Chapter 5. Uninstalling an instance of SQL Server 2000 is covered later in this chapter.

➤ The Uninstall Your Existing Installation option completely removes an installation of SQL Server 2000 from the server. Do not use it to remove components. Use the Add Components to Your Existing Installation option for both addition and removal of components and subcomponents.

9. Add or remove any desired components or subcomponents on the Select Components screen. Click Next to continue the installation (see Figure 4.17).

10. Click Next on the Start Copying Files screen unless you wish to select Back to revise any of the previous options. This begins the process of copying files from the installation disc to the destination locations selected during configuration.

11. Click Finish on the Setup Complete screen, and restart the computer following installation. The alteration of installed SQL Server components is now complete.

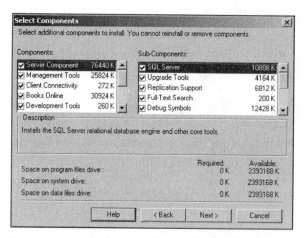

Figure 4.17 The Select Components screen.

Upgrading Installed Components

As new versions of SQL Server 2000 components and subcomponents become available, the installed version may be upgraded to include new information. This option also allows for the upgrade of the SQL Server 2000 instance to a more robust version. To accomplish this, select the Upgrade Your Existing Installation option on the Existing Installation screen and then proceed according to the type of upgrade being performed.

Installing Additional Components

In addition to a full installation of SQL Server 2000 and its components, two additional options are available: Analysis Services and English Query.

Analysis Services

The Analysis Services installation provides components for online analytical processing (OLAP) and data mining applications.

To perform an installation of SQL Server 2000 Analysis Services, take the following steps:

1. Insert the SQL Server 2000 disc in the CD-ROM drive. If Autorun has been disabled, it may be necessary to double-click the Autorun.exe file in the root directory of the disc.

2. Select SQL Server 2000 Components.

➤ To install SQL Server 2000 on a Windows 95 platform, you must select SQL Server 2000 Prerequisites and then Install Common Controls Library Update before selecting SQL Server 2000 Components.

3. Select Install Analysis Services to open the Installation Wizard (see Figure 4.18).

4. Click Next at the Welcome screen.

5. Read the Software Licensing Agreement, and click Yes to accept the Agreement. Selecting No at this point terminates the installation.

6. Add or remove any desired components on the Select Components screen. Click Next to continue the installation using the default folder location (see Figure 4.19).

➤ To select an alternate destination folder location for the selected Analysis Services components, select the Browse option for the appropriate file type and then navigate to the alternate destination. Select OK to return to the Select Components screen.

7. Click Next on the Data Folder Location screen to continue the installation using the default data folder location (see Figure 4.20).

Figure 4.18 The Install Components screen with Install Analysis Services selected.

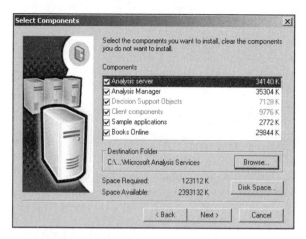

Figure 4.19 The Select Components screen.

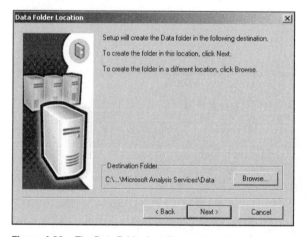

Figure 4.20 The Data Folder Location screen.

➤ To select an alternate destination data folder location for the SQL Server 2000 Analysis Services, select the Browse option for the appropriate file type and then navigate to the alternate destination. Select OK to return to the Data Folder Locations screen.

8. Click Next on the Select Program Folder screen to continue the installation using the default Program Folder name (see Figure 4.21).

➤ To select an alternate destination Program Folder for the SQL Server 2000 Analysis Services, select one of the existing folders from the available list or enter an alternative in the Program Folders box. Select Next to continue the installation.

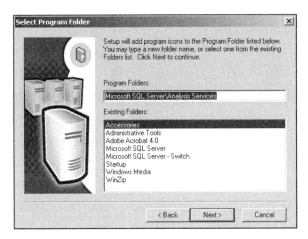

Figure 4.21 The Select Program Folder screen.

9. Click Finish on the Setup Complete screen. The installation of SQL Server 2000 Analysis Services is now complete.

English Query

The English Query installation provides the components necessary for applications to accept English questions instead of SQL language queries.

To install the SQL Server 2000 English Query component, take the following steps:

1. Insert the SQL Server 2000 disc in the CD-ROM drive. If Autorun has been disabled, it may be necessary to double-click the Autorun.exe file in the root directory of the disc.

2. Select SQL Server 2000 Components.

   ➤ To install SQL Server 2000 on a Windows 95 platform, you must select SQL Server 2000 Prerequisites and then Install Common Controls Library Update before selecting SQL Server 2000 Components.

3. Select Install English Query to open the Installation Wizard (see Figure 4.22).

4. Click Continue at the Microsoft English Query 2000 Setup screen to continue installation. Selecting Exit Setup terminates the installation (see Figure 4.23).

5. Read the Licensing Agreement, and click I Agree to accept the agreement. Selecting I Do Not Agree at this point terminates the installation. A Print License option is also available on this screen.

6. Select Complete when prompted to install all subcomponents for development using the English Query component of SQL Server 2000. Select

Figure 4.22   The Install Components screen with Install English Query selected.

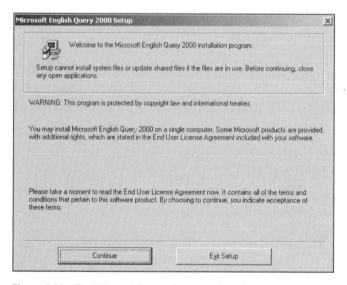

Figure 4.23   The Microsoft English Query 2000 Setup screen.

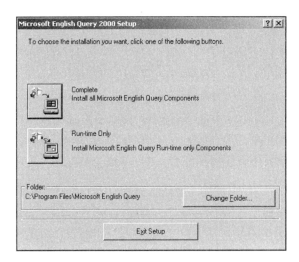

Figure 4.24 The Install Components screen.

Run-Time Only if only the runtime subcomponents are desired during the installation (see Figure 4.24).

➤ To select an alternate installation folder location for the English Query files, select the Browse option for the appropriate file type and then navigate to the alternate destination. Select OK to return to the Microsoft English Query 2000 Setup screen.

7. Click OK when prompted. The SQL Server 2000 English Query installation is now complete.

Uninstalling

Instances of SQL Server 2000 may be uninstalled later through the SQL Server 2000 Setup process or by using Add/Remove Programs. Each instance of SQL Server must be removed separately.

SQL Server 2000 Uninstallation

A complete uninstallation of an SQL Server 2000 instance may be performed using the Uninstall Your Existing Installation option on the Existing Installation screen.

To uninstall an existing installation of SQL Server 2000, take the following steps:

1. Insert the SQL Server 2000 disc in the CD-ROM drive. If Autorun has been disabled, it may be necessary to double-click the Autorun.exe file in the root directory of the disc.

2. Select SQL Server 2000 Components.

3. Select Install Database Server to open the Installation Wizard.

4. Click Next at the Welcome screen.

5. Click Next on the Computer Name screen to install an instance on the local computer.

   ➤ An alternative to a local uninstallation can be selected at this time using the options on this screen. Remote uninstallations are covered in Chapter 5.

6. Select Upgrade, Remove, Or Add Components To An Existing Instance Of SQL Server on the Installation Selection screen. Click Next to continue (see Figure 4.25).

7. Leave the Default option checked on the Instance Name screen (the default), and click Next to continue the installation.

   ➤ To uninstall a named instance of SQL Server 2000, the Default option should be deselected on this screen and the named instance selected in the appropriate box before selecting Next.

8. Select the option to Uninstall Your Existing Installation on the Existing Installation screen, and click Next to begin the removal process (see Figure 4.26).

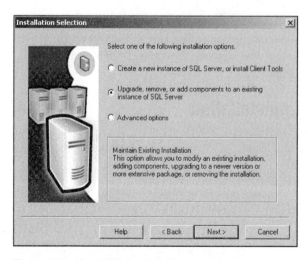

Figure 4.25 The Installation Selection screen.

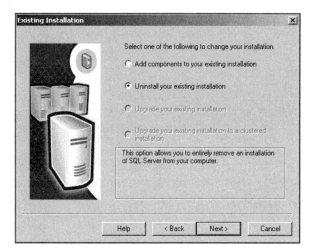

Figure 4.26 The Existing Installation screen.

9. Click Next when prompted.

10. Click Finish on the Setup Complete screen. The uninstallation of the SQL Server 2000 instance is now complete.

This process may be repeated for each additional instance to be removed. The server should be restarted to complete the uninstallation process.

Add/Remove Programs Uninstallation

Uninstallation of an SQL Server 2000 instance may be performed using the Add/Remove Programs component of Windows.

On the Windows 2000 platform, Add/Remove Programs may be used to remove an instance of SQL Server 2000 using the following steps:

1. Open the Windows 2000 Control Panel by selecting Start|Settings|Control Panel.

2. Double-click the Add/Remove Programs icon.

3. Under the Change Or Remove Programs option, highlight the instance or component of SQL Server 2000 to be removed (see Figure 4.27).

4. Click the Change/Remove option.

5. Click Yes when prompted to Confirm File Deletion (see Figure 4.28).

6. Click OK when file removal has completed.

This process may be repeated for each additional instance or component to be removed. The server should be restarted to complete the uninstallation process.

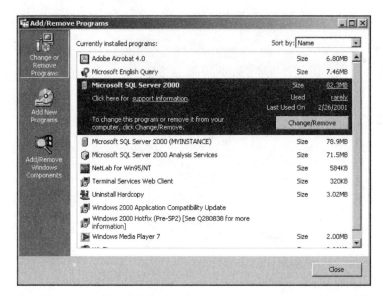

Figure 4.27 The Change Or Remove Programs screen with the SQL Server 2000 default instance selected.

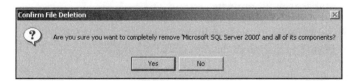

Figure 4.28 The Confirm File Deletion screen.

Practice Questions

Question 1

> Which of the following preparations are necessary for installing SQL Server 2000? [Check all correct answers]
>
> ❏ a. Obtaining the CD-ROM media and CD Key for SQL Server 2000.
>
> ❏ b. Disabling antivirus-scanning software during installation.
>
> ❏ c. Closing Registry editing tools.
>
> ❏ d. Closing Event Viewer.
>
> ❏ e. Closing services dependent on SQL Server, data source names (DSN), or open database connectivity (ODBC) application programming interface (API) calls.
>
> ❏ f. Choosing file locations capable of supporting installation type requirements as well as eventual increased data file sizes.
>
> ❏ g. Selecting the proper authentication mode.
>
> ❏ h. Logging on with a User account that is granted local Administrator permissions.
>
> ❏ i. Performing a backup of any other instances of SQL Server already installed.

Answers a, b, c, d, e, f, g, h, and i are all correct. In addition to these preparations, it is also best to avoid performing any unnecessary tasks on a server during installation. Also, the DBA should be familiar with what to expect during a normal installation to recognize any potential problems.

Question 2

> Arrange the following steps in order for a named instance installation of SQL Server 2000:
>
> Select Server and Client Tools on the Installation Definition screen.
>
> Input *MyServer* as the Instance Name.
>
> Select Local Computer on the Computer Name screen.
>
> Deselect Default on the Instance Name screen.

The correct answer is:

> Select Local Computer on the Computer Name screen.
>
> Select Server and Client Tools on the Installation Definition screen.
>
> Deselect Default on the Instance Name screen.
>
> Input *MyServer* as the Instance Name.

Question 3

> Which of the following are options on the Installation Definition screen during a default installation of SQL Server 2000? [Check all correct answers]
>
> ❑ a. Typical
>
> ❑ b. Minimum
>
> ❑ c. Custom
>
> ❑ d. Client Tools Only
>
> ❑ e. Mixed Mode
>
> ❑ f. Connectivity Only

Answers d and f are correct. The options presented on the Installation Definition screen are Server And Client Tools, Client Tools Only, and Connectivity Only. Answers a, b, and c are incorrect because Typical, Minimum, and Custom installations are options presented on the Setup Type screen. Answer e is also incorrect, because Mixed Mode is an option on the Authentication Mode screen.

Question 4

> You are the SA responsible for installing an instance of SQL Server 2000 Enterprise on a Windows 2000 Advanced Server. The server has 256MB of RAM and three drives (C:, D:, and E:), having 185MB, 1.5GB, and 35MB of available space, respectively. System files are stored on D: drive, program files are stored on C: drive, and data files are stored on E: drive. You plan to perform a Typical installation of SQL Server 2000 using the current configuration. Can this installation succeed?
>
> ○ a. Yes
>
> ○ b. No

Answer a is correct. The minimum storage requirements for a Typical installation are 183MB of system file storage, 38MB of program file storage, and 35MB of data file storage. However, this installation provides no additional space for expanding data files and is an example of what not to do. In this scenario, the data files should be located on D: drive to provide the greatest possible capacity.

Question 5

You are the DBA responsible for installing an instance of SQL Server 2000 on a Windows 2000 Advanced Server to be used for development of new database applications. The server has 512MB of RAM, two CPUs, and three 4GB drives that are less than 50 percent utilized. You plan a Typical installation of SQL Server 2000 placing the system, program, and data files each on a separate disk. Will this plan complete the installation as specified?

○ a. Yes

○ b. No

Answer b is correct. Although the server hardware is certainly capable of supporting the installation of SQL Server 2000, a Typical installation does not include the Code Samples and Development Tools (other than Debugger) that are required for a development server. The correct installation would be a Custom installation in which the additional subcomponents for development are selected in addition to the default options.

Question 6

> You are the DBA responsible for installing a named instance of SQL Server 2000 on a server already running SQL Server 7. During the installation, you performed the following steps:
>
> 1. Selected Install Database Server.
>
> 2. Selected the Create a New Instance of SQL Server or Install Client Tools options.
>
> 3. Entered MyName and MyCompany and agreed to the Licensing Agreement.
>
> 4. Selected Server and Client Tools.
>
> 5. Entered the name Default in the Instance Name box.
>
> 6. Selected the Minimal installation type.
>
> 7. Accepted the default settings for service accounts and entered the password for the local Administrator account.
>
> 8. Selected Windows Authentication Mode.
>
> Will this installation run without affecting the existing instance of SQL Server 7?
>
> ○ a. Yes
>
> ○ b. No

Answer b is correct. A named instance of SQL Server 2000 may not use the reserved word Default, so the installation will not run as desired. If a Default installation had been selected instead of a Named installation, the installation would overwrite or upgrade the SQL Server 7 instance because there can only be one Default installation on a server. To leave the existing SQL Server 7 instance as it is and install SQL Server 2000, you can create a named instance of SQL Server 2000 (using a name other than Default or MSSQLServer), which can coexist with the Default instance.

Question 7

> You are the SA of a Windows 2000 Advanced Server that does not have much available space remaining on its hard drive. Database applications are to be run on this computer that will access SQL Server instances on two other servers. What is the minimum installation that will provide the necessary components for this?
>
> ○ a. Typical
>
> ○ b. Minimum
>
> ○ c. Custom
>
> ○ d. Default
>
> ○ e. Client Tools Only
>
> ○ f. Connectivity Only

Answer f is correct. The Connectivity Only subinstallation provides the DAC and Network Libraries necessary for applications to connect to instances of SQL Server. Answers a, b, and c are incorrect because Typical, Minimum, and Custom installations are types of SQL Server installations. Answer d is incorrect because Default is an instance type, not an installation type. Answer e is wrong as well because the Client Tools Only installation includes Management Tools and additional subcomponents unnecessary for simple connectivity.

Question 8

You are a database administrator responsible for a default installation of SQL Server 2000 on a server configured with three drives available for installation (Drive 1, 200MB; Drive 2, 120MB; Drive 3, 500MB). Management has approved three installation scenarios:

Scenario 1: system files (Drive 1), program files (Drive 2), data files (Drive 3)

Scenario 2: system files (Drive 2), program files (Drive 1), data files (Drive 3)

Scenario 3: system and program files (Drive 1), data files (Drive 2)

Management has further stated that only the following installation options are available in order to ease documentation of the network. Match the following Setup Types with the approved scenarios capable of supporting them (note: some answers may be used more than once):

Minimum

Typical

Custom (with no changes to the default selections—management simply copied this from a book)

The correct answer is:

Scenario 1: system files (Drive 1), program files (Drive 2), data files (Drive 3)

Minimum

Typical

Custom (with no changes to the default selections)

Senario 2: system files (Drive 2), program files (Drive 1), data files (Drive 3)

Minimum

Scenario 3: system and program files (Drive 1), data files (Drive 2)

Minimum

Question 9

Which of the following options may be selected from the SQL Server 2000 Components menu? [Check all correct answers]

❑ a. Analysis Services

❑ b. Management Tools

❑ c. Client Tools

❑ d. Database Server

❑ e. English Query

Answers a, d, and e are correct. The options presented on the SQL Server 2000 Components screen are to Install Database Server, Install Analysis Services, and Install English Query. Answers b and c are incorrect because Management Tools is a subcomponent of the Client Tools component available on the Installation Definition screen.

Question 10

You are an SA managing a global enterprise network that has Windows 2000 and Windows NT Enterprise edition servers accessed by Windows NT Workstation, Windows 2000 Professional, Windows ME, and Windows 98 client computers. You have three database servers running SQL Server 2000 Enterprise with a default instance and two named instances on each server.

All data has been removed from the two named instances on two of the servers. You have been charged with removing the unnecessary instances to free up available disk space. You have performed the following steps on both machines:

1. Opened the Control Panel.

2. Double-clicked the Add/Remove Programs icon.

3. Highlighted the first named instance of SQL Server, and clicked the Change/Remove option.

4. Confirmed file deletion, and clicked OK after the removal was completed.

5. Closed the Add/Remove Programs screen and Control Panel.

6. Restarted the servers.

Will this process complete the task as defined?

○ a. Yes

○ b. No

Answer b is correct. Each instance of SQL Server 2000 must be removed separately. The listed process must be repeated for the remaining named instance on each of the two servers to complete the removal of both named instances from these machines.

Need to Know More?

 Dalton, Patrick, and Paul Whitehead. *SQL Server 2000 Black Book.* The Coriolis Group: Scottsdale, AZ, 2001. ISBN 1-57610-770-1. An excellent reference to keep close at hand during installation of SQL Server 2000. This is a good reference for a DBA's library, as it has many solutions to commonly experienced issues.

 Iseminger, David. *Microsoft SQL Server 2000 Reference Library with CD-ROM.* Microsoft Press: Redmond, WA, 2000. ISBN 0-7356-1280-3. An exhaustive library covering detailed information on all aspects of SQL Server 2000 implementations. A necessary reference for IT departments supporting Microsoft SQL Server 2000 implementations.

 Shapiro, Jeffrey. *SQL Server 2000—The Complete Reference.* Osborne/McGraw-Hill: Berkeley, CA, 2001. ISBN 0-07-212588-8. A detailed, if somewhat lengthy, reference for SQL Server 2000 administration.

 http://msdn.microsoft.com/library/default.asp?URL=/library/psdk/sql/portal_7ap1.htm. *Microsoft SQL Server 2000 Books Online.* A complete online copy of the documentation for SQL Server 2000. This is an SQL Server 2000 database administrator's best friend because it is included on the installation CD-ROM.

Advanced
Installation and Upgrade

. . . .

Terms you'll need to understand:

✓ Remote installation

✓ Unattended installation

✓ Failover clustering

✓ Node

✓ Virtual server

✓ Upgrade

Techniques you'll need to master:

✓ Performing a remote installation of SQL Server 2000

✓ Creating an unattended installation file for deployment on multiple servers

✓ Modifying a sample template to create a custom unattended installation file manually

✓ Adding and removing nodes from a virtual server

✓ Configuring alternate services accounts for instances of SQL Server 2000

✓ Configuring network libraries for instances of SQL Server 2000

✓ Performing SQL Server 2000 upgrades

Basic installations of SQL Server 2000 are often used for new implementations and development servers. In many real-world applications, a more customized implementation is required. Advanced options include remote installations, unattended installation file creation and deployment, custom installation configuration, and clustered server setup. Planning configuration issues such as the creation of service accounts, linked server setup, and network library configuration are also important for more advanced installations. Advanced planning is also necessary when upgrading older versions of SQL Server (such as SQL Server 6.5 and SQL Server 7.0) to SQL Server 2000.

This chapter covers advanced installation procedures, configuration options, and upgrade implementations of SQL Server 2000, all of which might be included on the exam. It is not intended to be an exhaustive review of all possible options. In all cases, it is assumed that the minimum hardware requirements (outlined in Chapter 3) have been met for an installation of SQL Server 2000 Enterprise on a Windows 2000 server platform. Additional references are listed at the end of this chapter.

Before You Begin

The same preparation steps used for basic installations are needed for advanced installations. Please review these steps (listed in Chapter 4) before proceeding.

After the necessary hardware has been prepared and the operating system loaded, you should collect the final items required for installation. In all cases, make sure that all service packs and patches have been successfully installed before beginning an installation.

Note: Always remember to create a complete backup of any previously installed instances before performing an installation or upgrade of SQL Server instances.

Advanced Installation

Many advanced installation options are used to improve accessibility and to ease deployment across a domain or enterprise network. As in basic installations, only one default instance can exist on a server. However, you can install multiple named instances if sufficient system resources are available to support them.

Remote Installation

You can deploy SQL Server 2000 from a central location using the Remote Installation option. Both default and named instances can be deployed in this manner, as well as Connectivity Only and Client Only installations (see Chapter 4). To perform a remote installation, the user account used for the installation must have administrative privileges to access both the source share and destination server. To perform a remote installation of the default instance of SQL Server 2000, take the following steps:

1. Insert the SQL Server 2000 disc in the CD-ROM drive. If Autorun has been disabled, it might be necessary to double-click the Autorun.exe file in the root directory of the disc.

2. Select SQL Server 2000 Components from the main menu.

   ➤ If installing SQL Server 2000 on a Windows 95 platform, perform the SQL Server 2000 Prerequisites installation and Install Common Controls Library Update on the destination server itself.

3. Select Install Database Server on the next screen to open the Installation Wizard.

   ➤ Analysis Services and English Query components are not intended for remote installation in this manner.

4. Click Next at the Welcome screen.

5. Select Remote Computer on the Computer Name screen, and enter the name of the destination server (see Figure 5.1).

   ➤ You may also select the Browse button to open the Select Computer screen (see Figure 5.2), where you may select a server from those available before returning to the Computer Name screen.

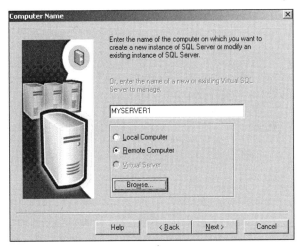

Figure 5.1   The Computer Name screen with MYSERVER1 selected for the remote installation.

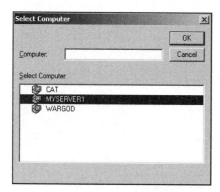

Figure 5.2 The Select Computer screen with MYSERVER1 selected from the server options available.

6. Select Create A New Instance Of SQL Server, Or Install Client Tools on the Installation Selection screen (the default), and click Next to begin creating a new instance of SQL Server (see Figure 5.3).

   ➤ The Upgrade, Remove, or Add Components to an Existing Instance of SQL Server options and Advanced Options are not intended for remote installation.

7. Enter a Name and Company Name in the appropriate boxes on the User Information screen.

8. Read the Microsoft Licensing Agreement, and click Yes to accept the Agreement. Selecting No at this point terminates the installation. Input your CD-Key when prompted.

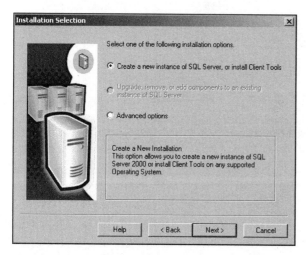

Figure 5.3 The Installation Selection screen showing the installation options available.

9. Input the Username, Password, and Domain information in the appropriate locations on the Remote Setup Information screen. Verify the Target Computer information as well as the Universal Naming Convention (UNC) Target Path and the location of the Setup Source Files. Click Next to continue the installation (see Figure 5.4).

   ➤ Note that the Setup Source Files location does not have to be on the server being used for the remote installation. It may be on a centralized file server in order to ease large-scale deployment.

10. Select Server And Client Tools on the Installation Definition screen (the default). Click Next to continue the installation (see Figure 5.5).

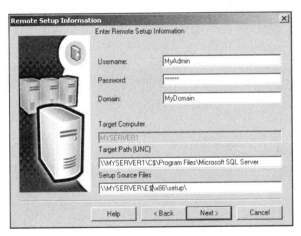

Figure 5.4   The Remote Setup Information screen for completing information needed to access the remote server.

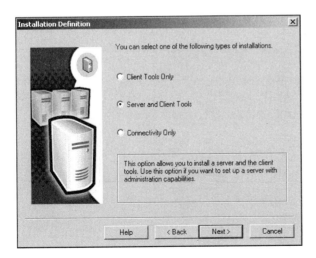

Figure 5.5   The Installation Definition screen is used for selecting the type of installation you want.

➤ Installation options for Client Tools Only or Connectivity Only can be selected on this screen as well and can be remotely installed.

11. Leave the Default option checked on the Instance Name screen (the default). Click Next to continue the installation (see Figure 5.6).

➤ To create a named instance of SQL Server 2000, deselect the Default option on this screen, and input the Instance Name into the appropriate location.

12. Select Typical on the Setup Type screen (the default), accept the default settings for program and data file locations, and click Next to continue the installation (see Figure 5.7).

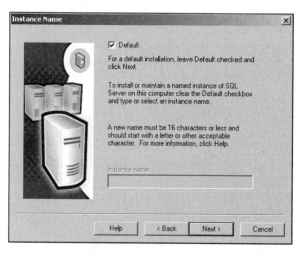

Figure 5.6 The Instance Name screen on which you can select a default instance or create a new named instance for the installation.

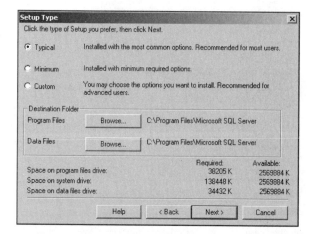

Figure 5.7 The Setup Type screen showing the types of installations available.

➤ Select from among Typical, Minimal, or Custom installations on the Setup Type screen.

➤ To select an alternate destination folder location for the program or data files, select the Browse option for the appropriate file type. Navigate to the alternate destination, and select OK to return to the Setup Type screen.

13. Accept the default setting of Use The Same Account For Each Service. Auto Start SQL Server Service on the Services Accounts screen, and enter the account information for the appropriate Domain User service account. Click Next to continue the installation (see Figure 5.8).

➤ Alternate service accounts for the SQL Server and SQL Server Agent services can be selected on this screen. You also can configure the Auto Start option for each at this time.

➤ You can select the Local System account on the destination server, instead of a Domain User account, as the service account for these services. However, this could limit the accessibility of databases on other servers.

14. Select the appropriate authentication mode on the Authentication Mode screen. Enter the System Administrator (SA) password if Mixed Mode is selected. Click Next to continue the installation (see Figure 5.9).

➤ Windows Authentication Mode (the default) can be used if Windows authentication is the only method required. Mixed Mode Authentication provides for both Windows authentication as well as SQL Server authentication.

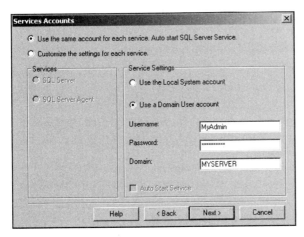

Figure 5.8   The Services Accounts screen on which you can enter the service settings you want.

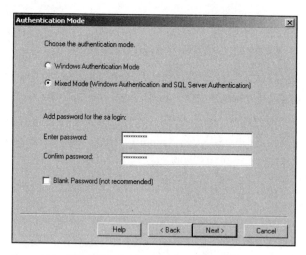

Figure 5.9   The Authentication Mode screen gives the options of either Windows Authentication Mode or Mixed Mode authentication.

➤ If you select Mixed Mode, you can select a Blank Password option for the SA. This is not recommended because it reduces the security of the SQL Server installation.

15. You may select Back if you need to revise any of the previous options. If not, click Next on the Setup Information screen to proceed to the Choose Licensing Mode screen.

16. Select the appropriate licensing mode on the Choose Licensing Mode screen, and enter the appropriate number of devices or processors as appropriate. Click Continue to continue the installation (see Figure 5.10).

➤ Per Seat licensing (the default) requires that each device accessing SQL Server 2000 must have its own Client Access License (CAL).

➤ Processor licensing requires that each processor on the server must have its own Processor License. This is often used for servers that will be accessed by Internet portals and online storefront applications where the number of concurrent connections may vary widely.

17. Click Finish on the Setup Complete screen. This starts the process of copying files from the installation disc to the destination locations selected during configuration. A popup message is displayed during the installation process to indicate that installation has commenced. Another message is displayed when the remote installation has been completed successfully.

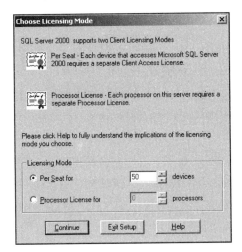

Figure 5.10 The Choose Licensing Mode screen where you can select from two types of licenses: Per Seat and Processor.

18. Click OK on the Setup Complete popup message to complete the installation. It is a good idea to reboot the destination server after the installation is completed to ensure that the instance of SQL Server 2000 will be accessible for use.

Remote Uninstallation

You cannot uninstall SQL Server 2000 remotely without using a remote access software package such as Microsoft's Systems Management Server (SMS). Perform uninstallation actions on the appropriate server itself.

Unattended Installation

When deploying instances with identical setup configuration choices on multiple servers or when a remote setup must be performed using distributed media rather than network installations, you can create an unattended installation setup initialization (.iss) file. This file includes all information necessary to complete an installation without intervention.

 Failover clustering setup may not be performed using an unattended installation.

The .iss file includes a copy of the SQL Server 2000 CD-Key information. Always remove this when the installation has been completed to safeguard the registration key. To create an unattended installation file of the named instance *MyInstance* of SQL Server 2000, take the following steps:

1. Insert the SQL Server 2000 disc in the CD-ROM drive. If Autorun has been disabled, it might be necessary to double-click the Autorun.exe file in the root directory of the disc.

2. Select SQL Server 2000 Components.

3. Select Install Database Server to open the Installation Wizard.

   ➤ Analysis Services and English Query components are not intended for unattended installations.

4. Click Next at the Welcome screen.

5. Select Local Computer on the Computer Name screen, and enter the name of the destination server.

   ➤ Unattended installations are meant to run locally to the destination server. Therefore, select the Local Computer option at this point.

6. Select Advanced Options on the Installation Selection screen, and click Next to begin configuring the new unattended installation file (see Figure 5.11).

7. Select Record Unattended .ISS file (the default) on the Advanced Options screen. Click Next to continue the installation (see Figure 5.12).

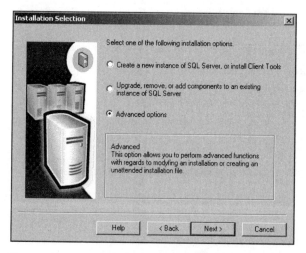

Figure 5.11   The Installation Selection screen explains what Advanced Options are available.

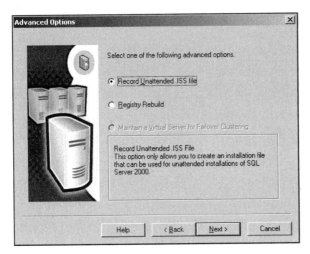

Figure 5.12 The Advanced Options screen explains what selecting Record Unattended .ISS File means.

➤ The Registry Rebuild and Maintain a Virtual Server For Failover Clustering options are discussed later in this chapter.

8. Enter a Name and Company Name in the appropriate boxes on the User Information screen.

9. Read the Microsoft Licensing Agreement, and click Yes to accept the Agreement. Selecting No at this point terminates the installation. Input your CD-Key when prompted.

10. Select Server And Client Tools on the Installation Definition screen (the default). Click Next to continue the installation.

➤ You can select Options for Client Tools Only or Connectivity Only on this screen as well and can configure it for unattended installation.

11. Enter an Instance Name in the appropriate box (in this example, *MyInstance*) on the Instance Name screen (this is the only option if another instance is already installed). Click Next to continue the installation (see Figure 5.13).

12. Select Typical on the Setup Type screen (the default), accept the default settings for program and data file locations, and click Next to continue the installation.

➤ You can select Typical, Minimum, or Custom installations on the Setup Type screen.

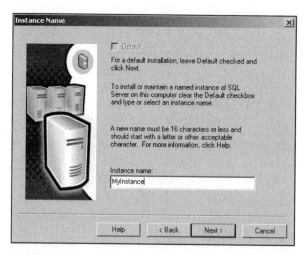

Figure 5.13 The Instance Name screen showing a Named Instance installation.

> ➤ To select an alternate destination folder location for the program or data files on the destination server, input the alternate destination, and select OK to return to the Setup Type screen.

13. Accept the default setting of Use the Same Account for Each Service-Auto start SQL Server Service on the Service Accounts screen, and enter the account information for the appropriate Domain User service account. Click Next to continue the installation.

> ➤ You can select alternate service accounts for the SQL Server and SQL Server Agent on this screen. You can also configure the Auto Start option for each at this time.

> ➤ You can select the Local System account on the destination server as the service account for these services instead of a Domain User account. However, this could limit the accessibility of databases on other servers.

14. Select the appropriate authentication mode on the Authentication Mode screen. Enter the System Administrator (SA) password if Mixed Mode is selected. Click Next to continue the installation.

> ➤ You may use Windows Authentication Mode (the default) if Windows authentication is the only method required. Mixed Mode Authentication provides for both Windows authentication as well as SQL Server authentication.

> ➤ If Mixed Mode is selected, a Blank Password option can be selected for the SA. This is not recommended because it reduces the security of the SQL Server installation.

15. You may select Back if you need to revise any of the previous options. If not, click Next on the Setup Information screen to proceed to the Choose Licensing Mode screen.

16. Select the appropriate licensing mode on the Choose Licensing Mode screen, and enter the appropriate number of devices or processors. Click Continue to continue the installation.

    ➤ Per Seat licensing (the default) requires that each device accessing SQL Server 2000 must have its own Client Access License (CAL).

    ➤ Processor licensing requires that each processor on the server must have its own Processor License. This is often used for servers that will be accessed by Internet portals and online storefront applications where the number of concurrent connections may vary widely.

17. Click Finish on the Setup Complete screen. This begins the process of copying files from the installation disc to the destination locations selected during configuration.

18. Once the configuration is complete, the new unattended installation setup initialization file, setup.iss, will be located in the C:\WINNT\ folder. This file should be copied to a new location and given a meaningful name to distinguish it from other files of the same type (for example, SqlSetupMyInstance.iss). Options available for the manual configuration within this file are covered in greater detail in the Custom Installation section later in this chapter.

19. A batch file (.bat) can be created to begin the installation process using the new unattended installation file. Options available for the configuration of this batch file are covered in greater detail in the Custom Installation section later in this chapter.

20. You should copy the .iss and .bat files to the distribution media (such as a floppy disk) or to a folder on the destination server. The media and SQL Server 2000 CD-ROM should be inserted into the destination server or made available on a network file share.

21. Begin the unattended installation by executing the batch file or executing the appropriate command-line installation sequence. The unattended installation file will then proceed through the installation process, providing previously selected user configuration details directly to the installation wizard. This allows the installation to proceed without further interaction from the user (see Figure 5.14).

Figure 5.14 An unattended installation of the sqlins.iss file with the SQL Server 2000 CD-ROM located in D: drive.

➤ It is a good idea to reboot the destination server after the installation is completed to ensure that the instance of SQL Server 2000 will be accessible for use.

Custom Installation

An unattended installation file is generally used to install a default instance of SQL Server 2000, but it also can be used to deploy named instance installations. Many other configuration options are possible by manually editing the .iss and .bat files used for deployment. Microsoft's Systems Management Server can also be used to perform an automated deployment of SQL Server 2000 using the Smssqins.bat file included on the SQL Server media.

You can edit the unattended installation files manually using any text editor, such as the Microsoft Notepad utility included in most Windows 2000 Server installations. The easiest method for manually creating an unattended installation file for a custom installation of SQL Server 2000 is to modify a copy of the sample unattended installation files included with SQL Server 2000. Table 5.1 details these sample files.

Table 5.1 Sample unattended installation setup initialization files.		
Installation Type	**Batch File***	**Setup Initialization File***
Default typical installation of SQL Server 2000	sqlins.bat	sqlins.iss
Custom installation with all components	sqlcst.bat	sqlcst.iss
Client Tools Only installation (no server)	sqlcli.bat	sqlcli.iss

* These files cannot be edited directly on the SQL Server 2000 CD-ROM. Copy the appropriate files to another location and then edit the copied files.

It is very simple to edit the batch file that executes an unattended installation. Open the file using a text editor, make any necessary changes to the file, and save the file again using a meaningful name so that you can later identify the file easily. An example of an unattended installation batch file follows (Listing 5.1).

Listing 5.1   Sample sqlsetup.bat unattended installation batch file for an unattended installation of the sqlsetup.iss file with the SQL Server 2000 CD-ROM located in D: drive.

```
@echo off
rem    SQL Server 2000 Unattended Installation File
cls
echo    Beginning unattended installation.
@echo on
start /wait D:\x86\setup\setupsql.exe -SMS -f1 "sqlsetup.iss"
@echo off
```

Table 5.2 details the installation options included in the sample unattended installation batch file.

Manual configuration of the unattended installation setup initialization file is accomplished in the same manner as its batch file counterpart. The .iss file is formatted in the Microsoft initialization file (.ini) format and can be edited using any text editor. An example of an unattended installation setup initialization file follows (Listing 5.2).

Note: All password and CD-Key information has been replaced using asterisks (*). This information must be edited and replaced with valid values before this file can be executed successfully.

Table 5.2 Sample batch file installation options.	
Option*	**Purpose**
cls	Clears the terminal display of previous activity
echo	Displays a message to the user
start /wait	Returns command-line control to the user after installation completion (with **-SMS**)
-f1 "sqlsetup.iss"	Selects the unattended installation setup initialization file, sqlsetup.iss

* Additional installation options are available. See the sample .bat files for examples.

Listing 5.2 Sample sqlsetup.iss unattended installation setup initialization file for an unattended installation of the SQL Server 2000 named instance *MYINSTANCE*.

```
[InstallShield Silent]
 Version=v5.00.000
 File=Response File

[File Transfer]
 OverwriteReadOnly=NoToAll

[DlgOrder]
 Dlg0=SdWelcome-0
 Count=15
 Dlg1=DlgMachine-0
 Dlg2=DlgInstallMode-0
 Dlg3=DlgAdvanced-0
 Dlg4=SdRegisterUser-0
 Dlg5=SdLicense-0
 Dlg6=DlgClientServer-0
 Dlg7=DlgInstanceName-0
 Dlg8=SetupTypeSQL-0
 Dlg9=DlgServices-0
 Dlg10=DlgSQLSecurity-0
 Dlg11=DlgCollation-0
 Dlg12=DlgServerNetwork-0
 Dlg13=SdStartCopy-0
 Dlg14=SdFinish-0

[SdWelcome-0]
 Result=1

[DlgMachine-0]
 Type=1
 Result=1

[DlgInstallMode-0]
 Type=32
 Result=1

[DlgAdvanced-0]
 AdvType=4
 Result=1

[SdRegisterUser-0]
 szName=MyName
 Result=1
```

```
[SdLicense-0]
 Result=1

[DlgCDKey-0]
 Result=1
 CDKey=*****-*****-*****-*****-*****

[DlgClientServer-0]
 Type=2
 Result=1

[DlgInstanceName-0]
 InstanceName=MYINSTANCE
 Result=1

[SetupTypeSQL-0]
 szDir=%PROGRAMFILES%\Microsoft SQL Server
 Result=301
 szDataDir=%PROGRAMFILES%\Microsoft SQL Server

[DlgServices-0]
 Local-Domain=61680
 AutoStart=15
 SQLDomain=MYSERVER
 SQLDomainAcct=MYADMIN
 SQLDomainPwd=**************
 AgtDomain=MYDOMAIN
 AgtDomainAcct=MYADMIN
 AgtDomainPwd=**************
 Result=1

[DlgSQLSecurity-0]
 LoginMode=1
 Result=1

[DlgCollation-0]
 collation_name=SQL_Latin1_General_CP1_CI_AS
 Result=1

[DlgServerNetwork-0]
 NetworkLibs=255
 TCPPort=0
 TCPPrxy=Default
 NMPPipeName=\\.\pipe\MSSQL$MYINSTANCE\sql\query
 Result=1

[SdStartCopy-0]
 Result=1
```

```
[License]
 LicenseMode=PERDEVICE
 LicenseLimit=2

[SdFinish-0]
 Result=1
 bOpt1=0
 bOpt2=0
```

Table 5.3 details the purpose of the sections in the sample unattended installation setup initialization file. For more information about the meaning of each field that appears in the table, see the Web sites for SQL Books Online listed at the end of this chapter.

Table 5.3	Sample setup initialization file sections.
Section*	Purpose
[InstallShield Silent]	Required InstallShield information. Do not alter.
[File Transfer]	Option to overwrite read-only files during installation.
[DlgOrder]	Lists the screens in their attended-installation order. Each corresponds to another section of the installation file.
[SdWelcome-0]	Provides a response to the Welcome screen.
[DlgMachine-0]	Provides responses to the Computer Name screen.
[DlgInstallMode-0]	Provides responses to the Installation Selection screen.
[DlgAdvanced-0]	Provides responses to the Advanced Options screen.
[SdRegisterUser-0]	Provides responses to the User Information screen.
[SdLicense-0]	Provides a response to the Software License Agreement screen.
[DlgCDKey-0]	Provides the necessary CD-Key for the installation.
[DlgClientServer-0]	Provides responses to the Installation Definition screen.
[DlgInstanceName-0]	Provides responses to the Instance Name screen.
[SetupTypeSQL-0]	Provides responses to the Setup Type screen.
[DlgServices-0]	Provides responses to the Service Accounts screen.
[DlgSQLSecurity-0]	Provides responses to the Authentication Mode screen.
[DlgCollation-0]	Provides responses to the Collation Settings screen.
[DlgServerNetwork-0]	Provides responses to the Network Libraries screen.
[SdStartCopy-0]	Provides a response to the Start Copying Files screen.
[License]	Provides responses to the Licensing Mode screen.
[SdFinish-0]	Provides a response to the Setup Complete screen.

* Additional installation options are possible. See the sample .iss files for examples.

Listing 5.3 is an example of an unattended installation setup initialization file based on the sample default typical installation setup initialization file, sqlins.iss. This file was modified to include the user name JaneDoe, the CD-Key *ABCDE-FGHIJ-KLMNO-PQRST-UVWXY*, the alternate file location of *%PROGRAMFILES%\Microsoft SQL2000*, and Per-Server licensing for 500 users.

Note: The CD-Key ABCDE-FGHIJ-KLMNO-PQRST-UVWXY is not valid for installation of SQL Server 2000. It has been used here as an example only.

Listing 5.3   Sample based on the sqlins.iss unattended installation setup initialization file with highlighted user input entries.

```
[InstallShield Silent]
Version=v5.00.000
File=Response File

[File Transfer]
OverwriteReadOnly=NoToAll

[DlgOrder]
Dlg0=SdWelcome-0
Count=14
Dlg1=DlgMachine-0
Dlg2=DlgInstallMode-0
Dlg3=SdRegisterUser-0
Dlg4=SdLicense-0
Dlg5=DlgClientServer-0
Dlg6=DlgInstanceName-0
Dlg7=SetupTypeSQL-0
Dlg8=DlgServices-0
Dlg9=DlgSQLSecurity-0
Dlg10=DlgCollation-0
Dlg11=DlgServerNetwork-0
Dlg12=SdStartCopy-0
Dlg13=SdFinish-0

[SdWelcome-0]
Result=1

[DlgMachine-0]
Type=1
Result=1

[DlgInstallMode-0]
Type=1
Result=1
```

```
[SdRegisterUser-0]
 szName=JaneDoe
 Result=1

[SdLicense-0]
 Result=1

[DlgCDKey-0]
 Result=1
 CDKey=ABCDE-FGHIJ-KLMNO-PQRST-UVWXY

[DlgClientServer-0]
 Type=2
 Result=1

[DlgInstanceName-0]
 InstanceName=MSSQLSERVER
 Result=1

[SetupTypeSQL-0]
 szDir=%PROGRAMFILES%\Microsoft SQL2000
Result=301
 szDataDir=%PROGRAMFILES%\Microsoft SQL2000

[DlgServices-0]
 Local-Domain=3855
 AutoStart=15
 Result=1

[DlgSQLSecurity-0]
 LoginMode=-1
 Result=1

[DlgCollation-0]
 collation_name=' '
 Result=1

[DlgServerNetwork-0]
 NetworkLibs=255
 TCPPort=1433
 TCPPrxy=Default
 NMPPipeName=\\.\pipe\sql\query
 Result=1
```

```
[SdStartCopy-0]
 Result=1

[License]
 LicenseMode=PERSERVER
 LicenseLimit=500

[SdFinish-0]
 Result=1
 bOpt1=0
 bOpt2=0
```

Registry Rebuild

One of the available selections on the Advanced Options screen is Registry Rebuild. This selection is used to recover from a corrupted Registry without requiring a full reinstallation of SQL Server 2000.

To use this option, you must have a record of all of the choices used in the original installation configuration. This option is covered in greater detail in Chapter 8.

Note: If all installation information was not recorded in specific detail, you cannot use this option. A full reinstallation is necessary to recover from the corrupted Registry settings.

Failover Clustering

SQL Server 2000 provides support for high-availability configurations using Microsoft Cluster Service (MSCS)-configured server clusters. In a failover cluster, multiple servers maintain access to shared Small Computer Systems Interface (SCSI) storage (see Figure 5.15), providing automatic redirection of the processing for an instance from one node to another in the event of failure.

Each server in a cluster is referred to as a *node*. SQL Server 2000 Enterprise Edition may use either two-node (Windows NT 4.0 Enterprise or Windows 2000 Advanced Server) or four-node (Windows 2000 Datacenter Server) configurations. Shared storage resources are combined to form cluster groups, which are owned by one of the nodes but whose ownership may be transferred between nodes. All nodes should have identical hardware configurations so that transferring resource ownership will not result in performance loss due to hardware variations, such as the amount of available RAM.

Clustered nodes regularly send a network signal to one another, referred to as a *heartbeat message*. If the MSCS software fails to detect a node's heartbeat, the node is treated as a failed server. All cluster groups and application resources are

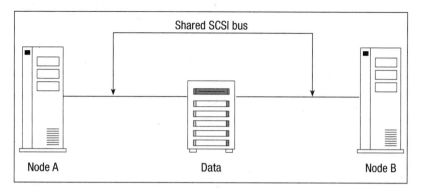

Shared SCSI bus

Node A

Data

Node B

Figure 5.15 A simplified two-node cluster.

transferred to the ownership of another node in the cluster, which then takes over control of processing network requests. This action is transparent to the client accessing these resources, although some traces might have to be restarted if some processes were uncompleted when the failure occurred.

MSCS must be installed and configured before you attempt to install SQL Server 2000 failover clustering. The details of MSCS installation go beyond the scope of this book and are not covered here. As a prospective database administrator, you should try to learn the process of installation and configuration of the MSCS to improve your troubleshooting ability.

Table 5.4 details some of the tools, features, and components of SQL Server 2000 and their compatibility with failover clustering.

An instance of SQL Server 2000 installed on a failover cluster is referred to as a *virtual server*.

Table 5.4 SQL Server 2000 support under failover clustering.	
Component	**Compatibility**
Multiple Instances	Supported.
SQL Server Enterprise Manager	Supported.
SQL Server Replication	Supported.
SQL Query Analyzer	Supported.
SQL Server Analysis Services	Not supported.
SQL Profiler	Supported.
SQL Mail	Supported, although the MAPI information must be configured carefully for all nodes.
Network Libraries	TCP/IP Sockets and Named Pipes are supported, although TCP/IP Sockets is the recommended library for clustered server access.

New Virtual Server

To create a new failover cluster, you must first ensure that MSCS has been configured and that at least one cluster disk resource has been created. NetBIOS should be disabled for the nodes in a cluster, all event logs should be cleared, all errors should be resolved before installation begins, and all service accounts on all nodes in the cluster should be given administrative privileges.

To create a new virtual server, take the following steps:

1. Insert the SQL Server 2000 disc in the CD-ROM drive. If Autorun has been disabled, it might be necessary to double-click the Autorun.exe file in the root directory of the disc.

2. Select SQL Server 2000 Components.

3. Select Install Database Server to open the Installation Wizard.

4. Click Next at the Welcome screen.

5. Select Virtual Server on the Computer Name screen, and input a virtual server name where appropriate. Click Next to continue the installation.

6. Enter a Name and Company Name in the appropriate boxes on the User Information screen. Click Next to continue the installation.

7. Read the Microsoft Licensing Agreement, and click Yes to accept the Agreement. Selecting No at this point terminates the installation.

8. Enter one IP address for each client access network supported by the failover cluster on the Failover Clustering screen. After all IP addresses are added, click Next to continue the installation.

9. On the Cluster Disk Selection screen, select the cluster disk group where the data files will reside. Click Next to continue the installation.

10. On the Cluster Management screen, remove any nodes that should not be part of the cluster definition for the new virtual server. Click Next to continue the installation.

11. Enter the logon information on the Remote Information screen, and click Next to continue the installation.

    ➤ This account must have administrative privileges on all nodes in the cluster.

12. Enter an Instance Name in the appropriate box (in this example, *MyInstance*) on the Instance Name screen (this is the only option if another instance is already installed) or accept the Default instance. Click Next to continue the installation.

13. Select Typical on the Setup Type screen (the default), accept the default settings for program and data file locations (the first available cluster disk resource by default), and click Next to continue the installation.

    ➤ To select an alternate destination folder location for the program or data files, select the Browse option under Data Files. Navigate to the alternate clustered drive resource owned by the node on which Setup is being performed, and select OK to return to the Setup Type screen.

14. Accept the default setting of Use the Same Account for Each Service-Auto start SQL Server Service on the Service Accounts screen, enter the account information for the appropriate Domain User service account, and click Next to continue the installation.

15. Select the appropriate authentication mode on the Authentication Mode screen, enter the SA password if Mixed Mode is selected, and click Next to continue the installation.

16. At this point, you can select Back if you need to revise any of the previous options. If not, click Next on the Start Copying Files screen. This starts the process of copying files from the installation disc to the destination locations selected during configuration.

17. Click Finish on the Setup Complete screen, and restart the computer and any other nodes following installation as directed. Carefully read any messages following installation, and follow any instructions. After the computer restarts, the default instance of SQL Server 2000 is accessible for use.

Adding a Node

SQL Server 2000 can support as many nodes in a cluster as are supported by the operating system.

To add a node to an existing virtual server, take the following steps:

1. Insert the SQL Server 2000 disc in the CD-ROM drive. If Autorun has been disabled, it might be necessary to double-click the Autorun.exe file in the root directory of the disc.

2. Select SQL Server 2000 Components.

3. Select Install Database Server to open the Installation Wizard.

4. Click Next at the Welcome screen.

5. Select Virtual Server on the Computer Name screen, and input the name of the virtual server where you want to add the node. Click Next to continue the installation.

6. Select Advanced Options on the Installation Selection screen, and click Next to continue the installation.

7. Select Maintain a Virtual Server for Failover Clustering on the Advanced Options screen. Click Next to continue the installation.

8. Click Next on the Failover Clustering screen.

9. On the Cluster Management screen, select the node you wish to add to the virtual server, and select Add. Click Next to continue the installation.

10. Enter the logon information on the Remote Information screen, and click Next to continue the installation.

11. Click Finish on the Setup Complete screen, and follow any instructions as directed.

Removing a Node

If a node fails, it must be removed before another is added in its place.

To remove a node from an existing virtual server, take the following steps:

1. Insert the SQL Server 2000 disc in the CD-ROM drive. If Autorun has been disabled, it might be necessary to double-click the Autorun.exe file in the root directory of the disc.

2. Select SQL Server 2000 Components.

3. Select Install Database Server to open the Installation Wizard.

4. Click Next at the Welcome screen.

5. Select Virtual Server on the Computer Name screen, and input the name of the virtual server from which you wish to remove a node. Click Next to continue the removal.

6. Select Advanced Options on the Installation Selection screen, and click Next to continue the removal.

7. Select Maintain a Virtual Server for Failover Clustering on the Advanced Options screen. Click Next to continue the removal.

8. Click Next on the Failover Clustering screen.

9. On the Cluster Management screen, select the node you wish to remove from the virtual server and select Remove. Click Next to continue the removal.

10. Enter the logon information on the Remote Information screen, and click Next to continue the removal.

11. Click Finish on the Setup Complete screen, and follow any instructions. Restart any nodes as directed.

Virtual Server Uninstallation

To remove a failover cluster instance, take the following steps:

1. Insert the SQL Server 2000 disc in the CD-ROM drive. If Autorun has been disabled, it might be necessary to double-click the Autorun.exe file in the root directory of the disc.

2. Select SQL Server 2000 Components.

3. Select Install Database Server to open the Installation Wizard.

4. Click Next at the Welcome screen.

5. Select Virtual Server on the Computer Name screen, and input the name of the virtual server from which you wish to remove the instance. Click Next to continue the uninstallation.

6. Select Upgrade, Remove or Add Components to an Existing Instance of SQL Server on the Installation Selection screen. Click Next to continue the uninstallation.

7. Enter the appropriate Instance Name to be uninstalled in the appropriate box on the Instance Name screen, or accept the Default instance. Click Next to continue the uninstallation.

8. Select Uninstall Your Existing Installation on the Existing Installation screen. Click Next to continue the uninstallation.

9. Enter the logon information on the Remote Information screen, and click Next to continue the uninstallation.

10. Click OK on the Setup screen when the uninstallation is complete.

11. Click Finish on the Setup Complete screen, and follow any instructions. Restart any nodes as directed.

Configuration

You can configure many options during installation of SQL Server 2000, either through direct selection or through unattended installation files. A few of these items require special attention, as they will probably be encountered in most production environments eventually. A prospective database administrator should be familiar with the configuration of alternate service accounts and network libraries.

Configuring Services Accounts

On the Services Accounts screen, you can select options that allow you to configure local or domain accounts for the two SQL Server 2000 services: SQL Server and SQL Server Agent. Each instance requires its own set of these two services, and you can configure the service accounts for each instance independently.

 The services accounts used in a failover cluster must be members of the Administrators local group on each node in the cluster.

Several options for configuring the services accounts are available:

➤ Select the Use The Same Account For Each Service. Auto Start SQL Server Service option. Select Use The Local System Account (see Figure 5.16).

Note: You may encounter authentication problems if you try to use the Local System account to access another server elsewhere in the Domain.

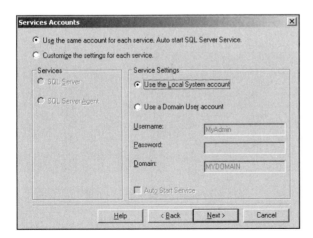

Figure 5.16 The Services Accounts screen configured to use the same Local Systems account for both services. Auto Start is set for both services.

➤ Select the Use The Same Account For Each Service. Auto Start SQL Server Service option. Select Use A Domain User Account (see Figure 5.17). The user account selected must have administrative privileges on the installation server.

➤ Select the option to Customize The Settings For Each Service. Select either Use The Local Systems Account or Use A Domain User Account for each service.

Note: If you want the SQL Server service to auto start at system boot, you must select the Auto Start Service option (see Figure 5.18). If you have not selected Auto Start for the SQL Server service, the option will be unavailable for the configuration of the dependent SQL Server Agent service (see Figure 5.19).

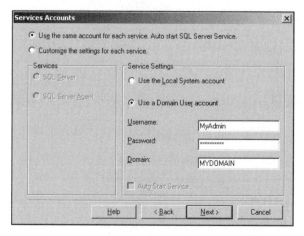

Figure 5.17 The Services Accounts screen configured to use the same Domain User account for both services. Auto Start is set for both services.

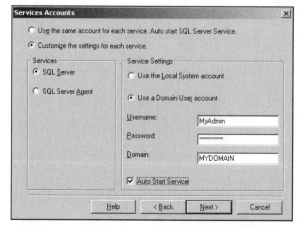

Figure 5.18 The Services Accounts screen configured to use customized settings for each service. Configuration is being performed for the SQL Server service using a Domain User account. Auto Start is set for this service.

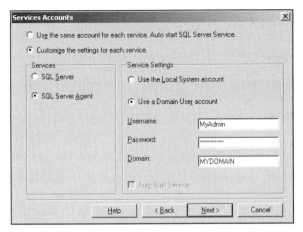

Figure 5.19   The Services Accounts screen configured to use customized settings for each service. Configuration is being performed for the SQL Server Agent service using a Domain User account. Auto Start is unavailable here as it was not selected in the SQL Server service configuration.

Configuring Network Libraries

All of the server network libraries are installed during installation, although only the TCP/IP Sockets (Windows NT 4.0, Windows 2000, and Windows 98) and Named Pipes (Windows NT 4.0 and Windows 2000 only) libraries are initially enabled. You must use the SQL Server Network Utility if you want to enable or disable other network libraries at a later time (see Figure 5.20). You can access this package via the shortcut in the Microsoft SQL Server Startup folder.

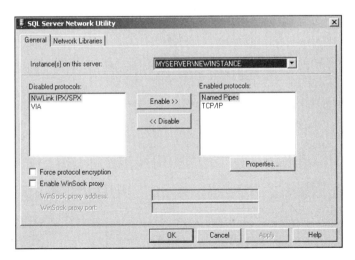

Figure 5.20   SQL Server Network Utility screen with the General tab selected. You can enable or disable protocols on this screen.

Each instance may be configured separately to listen on its own set of network libraries. You can configure network libraries by highlighting the enabled protocol desired and selecting the Properties tab (see Figure 5.21).

The Network Libraries tab displays the current files and file locations used for the installed network libraries available (see Figure 5.22).

Upgrades

As with any new release of a product, Microsoft SQL Server 2000 will eventually replace previous versions of SQL Server in the production environment. Following are the most common:

➤ SQL Server 7.0

➤ SQL Server 7.0 Databases using the Copy Database Wizard

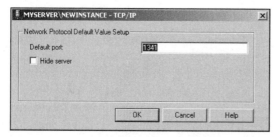

Figure 5.21   The Properties screen for the TCP/IP network library of the *NewInstance* SQL Server 2000 instance on the *MyServer* server.

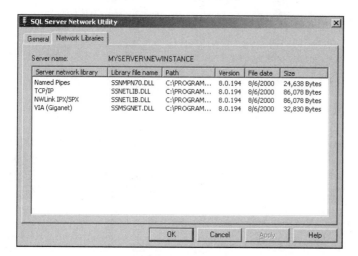

Figure 5.22   The SQL Server Network Utility screen with the Network Libraries tab selected. You can set the Network Protocol default value on this screen.

> ➤ SQL Server 6.5 Databases using the Upgrade Wizard

> ➤ Earlier versions of SQL Server 2000

 When upgrading versions before SQL Server 6.5, you must first upgrade the previous installation to SQL Server 6.5 or SQL Server 7.0 before performing the final upgrade to SQL Server 2000.

Before performing any upgrade, always perform a complete backup of all current databases, install the most recent service packs for all software, and stop any unnecessary tasks on the server, such as antivirus applications.

Upgrading Existing SQL Server 7.0 Installations

The most commonly encountered scenario in a production environment is the direct upgrade of an existing instance of SQL Server 7.0 to SQL Server 2000. No additional temporary file space is required for this type of installation. Although named instances of SQL Server 2000 may exist along with an instance of SQL Server 7.0 (see Chapter 4 for details on installing named instances), you should replace the earlier version if you want to preserve your database information during an upgrade to SQL Server 2000.

An in-place upgrade from SQL Server 7.0 to SQL Server 2000 preserves SQL Server Books Online for SQL Server 7.0 as well as the data stored in the instance's databases. However, the upgrade replaces SQL Server 7.0 tools and program files with SQL Server 2000 versions. Performing a version upgrade of this type is a one-way process. Once completed, the only way to restore the previous SQL Server 7.0 instance is to uninstall SQL Server 2000, reinstall SQL Server 7.0, and restore from the most recent SQL Server 7.0 backup.

You can upgrade an instance of SQL Server 7.0 by selecting the option to Upgrade, Remove, or Add Components to an Existing Instance of SQL Server on the Installation Selection screen.

After responding Next to several screens, the upgrade process begins. After the upgrade is completed, you should restart the server as directed.

Upgrading SQL Server 7.0 Databases

Databases contained in an instance of SQL Server 7.0 may also be upgraded by using the Copy Database Wizard from a named instance of SQL Server 2000 on the same server or from a default or named instance of SQL Server 2000 on another server.

You can also use the Copy Database Wizard to move databases between SQL Server 2000 instances.

This type of upgrade enables you to upgrade only selected databases while leaving others available in their original SQL Server 7.0 location and to minimize server downtime. You can use the Copy Database Wizard to perform an upgrade in a production environment on a server in use; however, you should not update databases during the upgrading process.

You can access the Copy Database Wizard from within the SQL Server Enterprise Manager by expanding the appropriate Server Group, right-clicking the Server, and expanding All Tasks to provide access to the Copy Database Wizard (see Figure 5.23).

After the Welcome screen, you are prompted for the source and destination server identification and logon credentials (see Figure 5.24).

You are then presented with a listing of available databases that you may select to copy or move from the source server (see Figure 5.25).

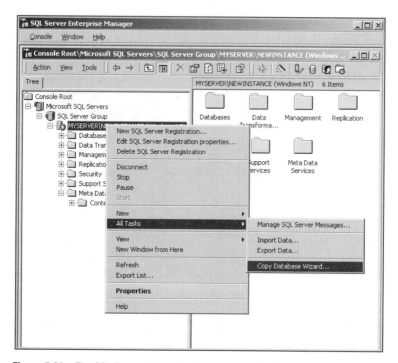

Figure 5.23   The SQL Server Enterprise Manager showing the expansion of menus to reveal access to the Copy Database Wizard.

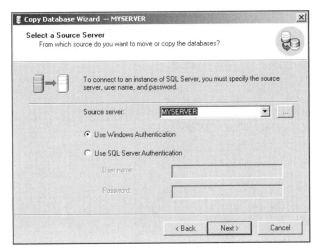

Figure 5.24   The Select a Source Server screen is used to select the source server for the database you want to move or copy.

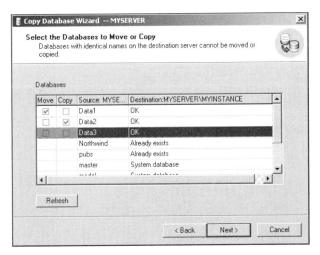

Figure 5.25   The database selection screen showing databases selected for Move and Copy operations.

After selecting the databases desired, you are prompted with the new file locations designated for them (see Figure 5.26). If file location conflicts are indicated, select the Modify option. This option brings up a screen allowing for the
selection of new file locations.

After the Copy Database Wizard finishes, you should review the generated log
file and resolve any configuration issues that remain pending (see Figure 5.27).

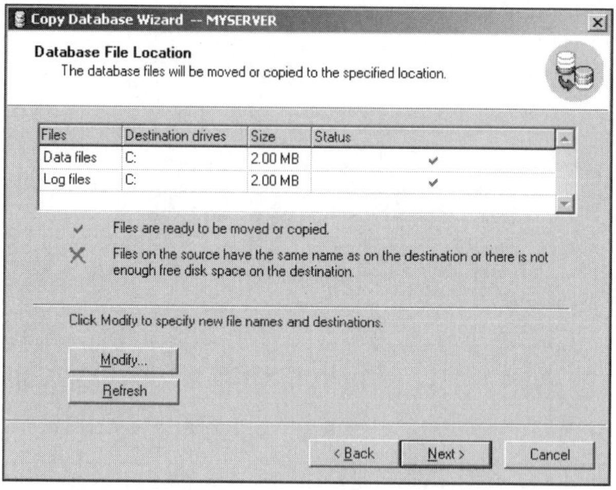

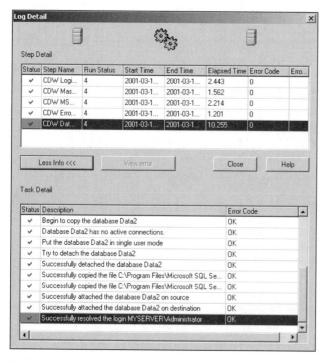

Figure 5.26 The Database File Location screen lists the type of files to be moved or copied, the destination drive, the size of the files, and the status of the request.

Figure 5.27 The Log Detail screen gives a status of the Copy Database Wizard processes.

Upgrading SQL Server 6.5 Databases

Databases contained in an instance of SQL Server 6.5 can be upgraded by using the SQL Server Upgrade Wizard from a named instance of SQL Server 2000 on the same server or from a default or named instance of SQL Server 2000 on another server.

 Upgrading an instance of SQL Server 6.5 requires additional file space of approximately 1.5 times the size of the databases being migrated.

This type of upgrade stops the MSSQL Server service during the data export. The upgrade attempt may fail if users access the database during this procedure. The SQL Server Upgrade Wizard is used for this operation. You can access this package via the shortcut in the Microsoft SQL Server-Switch Startup folder.

Upgrades from SQL 6.5 require database information to be exported via a specified data transfer method—either Named Pipe or Tape methods (see Figure 5.28). Tape transfers are often used in single-server upgrades on machines without adequate storage space for the exported files.

It is not necessary for the export and import server to have the same administrative password, as both sets of logon credentials are input separately (see Figure 5.29).

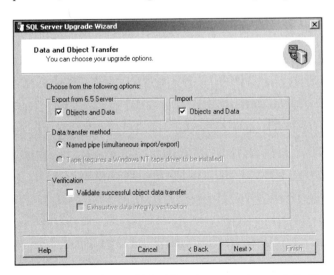

Figure 5.28   This Data and Object Transfer screen shows only the Named Pipe data transfer method available because no tape drives are present on this machine.

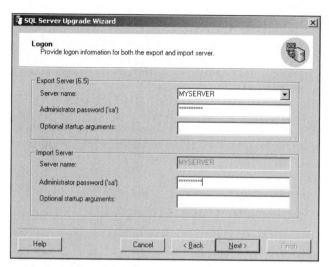

Figure 5.29 The Logon credentials screen where you enter logon information for the import and export servers.

 The SQL Server Update Wizard deletes all SQL Server 6.5 devices, not just those upgraded. Always perform a complete backup of all databases before beginning this upgrade.

Upgrading Existing SQL Server 2000 Instances

To upgrade an existing instance of SQL Server 2000, follow the same procedure as for an in-place upgrade of an existing installation of SQL Server 7.0. Select the Upgrade, Remove, or Add Components to an Existing Instance of SQL Server option on the Installation Selection screen.

This type of upgrade is used for upgrading the installed edition of SQL Server 2000 without affecting the data stored in the instance's databases. Often, this is used for upgrading from an Evaluation Edition or for upgrading a Personal or Standard Edition installation to an Enterprise Edition instance.

Practice Questions

Question 1

Several types of Advanced installation are possible:

Remote installation

Unattended installation

Virtual server

Match the following characteristics with the appropriate installation type:

Cannot be used for a failover cluster installations

Requires an installation setup initialization (.iss) file

Allows direct installation from one machine to a remote server

Exists on an MSCS-configured server cluster

Allows installation without user input required for each step of the installation

---

The correct answers are:

Remote installation

Allows direct installation from one machine to a remote server

Unattended installation

Cannot be used for a failover cluster installation

Requires an installation setup initialization (.iss) file

Allows installation without user input required for each step of the installation

Virtual server

Exists on an MSCS-configured server cluster

Question 2

> Which of the following are sample unattended installation setup initializa-
> tion files present on the SQL Server CD-ROM? [Check all correct answers]
>
> ❏ a. database_1.mdf
>
> ❏ b. sqlins.bat
>
> ❏ c. sqlcst.iss
>
> ❏ d. sqlcli.iss
>
> ❏ e. samplesql.iss

Answers c and d are correct. Both sqlcst.iss and sqlcli.iss are sample unattended installation setup initialization files included on the SQL Server 2000 CD-ROM. Answer a is incorrect because files ending in .mdf are primary data files. Answer b is incorrect because it is a sample unattended installation batch file, not an unattended installation setup initialization file. Answer e is incorrect because it is not one of the sample .iss files included on the SQL Server CD-ROM.

Question 3

> Which licensing mode is used in instances where a widely variable number
> of concurrent connections are required?
>
> ○ a. Mixed Mode
>
> ○ b. Per Seat
>
> ○ c. Processor
>
> ○ d. Clustered

Answer c is correct. Processor licensing is used in cases where a large or widely variable number of concurrent connections are required. Answer a is incorrect because Mixed Mode is an authentication mode, not a licensing mode. Answer b is incorrect because Per Seat licensing requires a separate Client Access License (CAL) for each concurrent connection. Finally, answer d is incorrect because there is no Clustered Licensing Mode.

Question 4

You are a database administrator responsible for configuring an unattended installation setup initialization file based on the sqlins.iss sample file, which has the following sections:

```
[InstallShield Silent]
[File Transfer]
[DlgOrder]
[SdWelcome-0]
[DlgMachine-0]
[DlgInstallMode-0]
[SdRegisterUser-0]
[SdLicense-0]
[DlgCDKey-0]
[DlgClientServer-0]
[DlgInstanceName-0]
[SetupTypeSQL-0]
[DlgServices-0]
[DlgSQLSecurity-0]
[DlgCollation-0]
[DlgServerNetwork-0]
[SdStartCopy-0]
[License]
[SdFinish-0]
```

Place the following values into the appropriate sections of the .iss file:

```
CDKey=ABCDE-FGHIJ-KLMNO-PQRST-UVWXY
InstanceName=MYINSTANCE
LicenseLimit=200
LicenseMode=PERSERVER
szName=MyUserName
```

The correct answer is:

```
[InstallShield Silent]
[File Transfer]
[DlgOrder]
[SdWelcome-0]
[DlgMachine-0]
[DlgInstallMode-0]
[SdRegisterUser-0]
    szName=MyUserName
[SdLicense-0]
[DlgCDKey-0]
    CDKey=ABCDE-FGHIJ-KLMNO-PQRST-UVWXY
[DlgClientServer-0]
[DlgInstanceName-0]
    InstanceName=MYINSTANCE
[SetupTypeSQL-0]
[DlgServices-0]
[DlgSQLSecurity-0]
[DlgCollation-0]
[DlgServerNetwork-0]
[SdStartCopy-0]
[License]
    LicenseMode=PERSERVER
    LicenseLimit=200
[SdFinish-0]
```

Question 5

Recording the exact choices made during installation is not important because the Registry can always be rebuilt at a later time if corruption occurs.

○ a. True

○ b. False

Answer b is correct. The Advanced option to Rebuild The Registry requires that all choices made during the original installation are known. Otherwise, a full installation is required to recover from a corrupted Registry.

Question 6

> Which of the following components and features of SQL Server 2000 are supported on a failover cluster installation? [Check all correct answers]
>
> ❏ a. Analysis Services
>
> ❏ b. Enterprise Manager
>
> ❏ c. Multiple Instances
>
> ❏ d. Profiler
>
> ❏ e. Query Analyzer
>
> ❏ f. Server Replication

Answers b, c, d, e, and f are correct. All of these options are supported on a failover cluster installation. Answer a is incorrect because Analysis Services is not supported.

Question 7

> If the Microsoft Cluster Service (MSCS) fails to detect the heartbeat message from a node, it treats that server as a failed node. Cluster groups and application resources owned by the failed server are transferred to another node, which takes over processing network requests.
>
> ○ a. True
>
> ○ b. False

Answer a is correct. In a failover cluster configuration, the failure of a single node results in the assumption of its role by another node. This allows for continued service in high-availability situations even if individual hardware failures occur.

Question 8

> You are the database administrator responsible for installing a named in-
> stance of SQL Server 2000. During the installation, you configured the Ser-
> vices Accounts as follows:
>
> - Customized the settings for each service
>
> - Configured the SQL Server service to use the Local Systems
>   account
>
> - Configured the SQL Server Agent service to use the Local Systems
>   account
>
> Can you successfully configure the SQL Server Agent service to auto start
> without making any other changes?
>
> ○ a. Yes
>
> ○ b. No

Answer b is correct. The SQL Server Agent service is dependent on the SQL
Server service, which must also be configured to auto start on server boot. By
using the Local Systems account, you may also run into difficulties in attempting
to connect to SQL Server instances on other servers.

Question 9

> You are the database administrator responsible for altering the configura-
> tion of the TCP/IP network library for a named instance of SQL Server 2000
> on a server that is also running a default instance of SQL Server 2000. This
> server has been upgraded from an instance of SQL Server 7.0 using an in-place
> direct upgrade. During the configuration, you performed the following tasks:
>
> - Opened the SQL Server Network Utility
>
> - Selected the named instance of SQL Server 2000
>
> - Disabled the Named Pipes network library
>
> - Modified the properties of the TCP/IP network library to run on port 8250
>
> After a later reboot of the server, your client software needs to connect to
> the default instance using the Named Pipes network library. If this func-
> tioned before your changes and no other alterations have been made, will
> the connection succeed?
>
> ○ a. Yes
>
> ○ b. No

Answer a is correct. The network libraries remain on the server after being disabled. All instances may have separately configured network libraries that do not affect other instances, provided the changes do not place the network libraries into conflict by selecting settings identical to those used by other instances such as an identical TCP/IP port.

Question 10

> Several options for upgrading are available:
>
> Copy Database Wizard
>
> Upgrade Wizard
>
> Upgrade option on the Installation Selection screen
>
> Match the following upgrade types with the appropriate option:
>
> SQL Server 6.5 to SQL Server 2000
>
> SQL Server 7.0 to SQL Server 2000
>
> SQL Server 7.0 Database to SQL Server 2000
>
> SQL Server 2000 Database to SQL Server 2000
>
> SQL Server 2000 Evaluation Edition to SQL Server 2000 Enterprise Edition

The correct answer is:

Copy Database Wizard

SQL Server 7.0 Database to SQL Server 2000

SQL Server 2000 Database to SQL Server 2000

Upgrade Wizard

SQL Server 6.5 to SQL Server 2000

Upgrade option on the Installation Selection screen

SQL Server 7.0 to SQL Server 2000

SQL Server 2000 Evaluation Edition to SQL Server 2000 Enterprise Edition

Need to Know More?

 Dalton, Patrick, and Paul Whitehead. *SQL Server 2000 Black Book.* The Coriolis Group: Scottsdale, AZ, 2001. ISBN 1-57610-770-1. An excellent reference to keep close at hand during installation of SQL Server 2000. This is a necessary book in any DBA's library, as it has many solutions to commonly experienced issues.

 Iseminger, David. *Microsoft SQL Server 2000 Reference Library with CD-ROM.* Microsoft Press: Redmond, WA, 2000. ISBN 0-7356-1280-3. An exhaustive library covering detailed information on all aspects of SQL Server 2000 implementations. A necessary reference for IT departments supporting Microsoft SQL Server 2000 implementations.

 Shapiro, Jeffrey. *SQL Server 2000—The Complete Reference.* Osborne/McGraw-Hill: Berkeley, CA, 2001. ISBN 0-07-212588-8. A detailed, if somewhat lengthy, reference for SQL Server 2000 administration.

 http://msdn.microsoft.com/library/default.asp?URL=/library/psdk/sql/portal_7api.htm. *Microsoft SQL Server 2000 Books Online.* A complete online copy of the documentation for SQL Server 2000. This is an SQL Server 2000 database administrator's best friend because it is included on the installation CD-ROM.

6

Creating Databases

. . . .

Terms you'll need to understand:

✓ Tables

✓ Views

✓ Stored procedures

✓ Filegroups

✓ Virtual log files

✓ Enterprise Manager

✓ Taskpad

✓ Query Analyzer

✓ **CREATE DATABASE** command

✓ **DROP DATABASE** command

Techniques you'll need to master:

✓ Planning proper data and log file placement for a new database

✓ Understanding how to create and use filegroups

✓ Creating and deleting a database using GUI and command-line methods

✓ Understanding the syntax and usage of the **CREATE DATABASE** and **DROP DATABASE** commands

✓ Creating and deleting new database objects, including tables, views, and stored procedures

A SQL Server 2000 instance begins with four databases installed (see Chapter 2): **master, modal, tempdb,** and **msdb.** In a default installation, two additional sample databases are also installed: **pubs** and **Northwind.** Additional user databases are then created using the **modal** database as a template. These databases can contain various types of objects, such as *tables, views,* and *stored procedures.* File storage requirements for these objects vary as objects are added, expanded, or removed.

This chapter covers the basic creation of databases and database objects within a SQL Server 2000 instance. The tools provided in SQL Server 2000 installations for creating these are the SQL Server Enterprise Manager, which is a graphical user interface (GUI) management tool, and the SQL Query Analyzer, which gives you the option of either using templates or command-line methods. An instance of SQL Server 2000 must already be installed (see Chapters 4 and 5) on a Windows 2000 server platform. Additional references are listed at the end of this chapter.

Basic Requirements

A SQL database requires several files to function. In its normal operations, the server uses primary and secondary data files as well as transaction log files. Follow these guidelines for placement and coordination of these files when setting up a production database:

➤ Place data and log files on local or directly accessible drives rather than on network file shares.

➤ Locate transaction log files and data files on separate physical disks.

➤ Separate files and filegroups among as many different local drives as possible to improve performance.

➤ Use filegroups to specify file placement on available disks.

➤ Do not put data and log files on file systems using compression.

Files

Most databases are capable of functioning properly using a single primary data file (.mdf) and a single transaction log file (.ldf). The use of secondary data files (.ndf) may improve performance by distributing tables onto multiple disks, which allows for parallel access; directing specific tables to particular locations, which minimizes fragmentation on available disks; and modeling the logical database design in physical storage.

Filegroups

Data files may be grouped into filegroups to allow for detailed allocation and placement of files and tables. If you create secondary data files (file1.ndf, file2.ndf, and file3.ndf) on separate physical drives (disk1, disk2, and disk3) and assign them to the filegroup "FILEGRP1," you can then create a table in the FILEGRP1 filegroup. Queries against this table can be distributed across the three drives, improving access performance. This is similar to the access accomplished using a RAID (redundant array of independent disks) stripe configuration, but this is accomplished through the software filegroup structure, making it easier to add new files on new disks and to expand total storage as requirements increase.

Considerations for filegroups include the following:

➤ Only primary and secondary data files can be part of a filegroup.

➤ Data files can only be assigned to one filegroup at a time.

➤ Files and filegroups cannot be shared between databases.

➤ Read-only filegroups may be used to prevent accidental modification of data included in the filegroup. Any filegroup other than the primary filegroup may be marked "read-only."

➤ Filegroups are usually not required for small databases (under 1GB). However, using filegroups may improve performance.

A database contains the primary filegroup, consisting of the primary file and any files not grouped into other filegroups, and any user-defined filegroups. All of the system tables are assigned to the primary filegroup. One filegroup is designated as the DEFAULT filegroup, to which any newly created objects are assigned if no filegroup is specified for them.

The primary filegroup is also the DEFAULT filegroup. If a user-defined filegroup is designated as the DEFAULT filegroup, new objects without a specific filegroup assignment will be created in the DEFAULT filegroup. System objects and tables are always in the primary filegroup, whether it is the DEFAULT filegroup or not.

Transaction Logs

In addition to data files, each SQL Server database maintains a serial record of all changes to the data. This record allows the server to roll back (undo) incomplete transactions or roll forward (apply) each in sequence. Transaction log files can be used to synchronize separate databases and to reapply sequential changes to the data files after performing disaster recovery operations.

Transaction logs are internally segmented into smaller portions, which are called virtual log files. Transaction checkpoints within the virtual log files mark where all transactions to that point have been applied to the database. When performing disaster recovery operations, it is unnecessary to roll forward any transactions prior to a checkpoint, because they have already been applied. Additional details of disaster recovery are covered in Chapter 8.

When determining the proper size of transaction logs, a good rule-of-thumb is that they should be approximately 25 percent of the size of all database data files combined.

Creating a Database

To create a new database within an instance of SQL Server, you must also create the primary data file, any secondary data files, and the transaction log. Considerations for database creation include the following:

➤ The permissions necessary to create a database are assigned to the **sysadmin** and **dbcreator** server roles by default. Roles and permissions will be covered in greater detail in Chapter 11.

➤ The creator of a database becomes the owner of the database.

➤ No more than 32,767 databases can exist on one server, each of which may contain over 2 billion objects.

➤ SQL Server 2000 automatically expands data files as required. It is best to assign a MAXSIZE value to prevent the file storage from overrunning available disk space.

➤ SQL Server 2000 databases may be created on "raw" partitions—ones without an NT File System (NTFS)- or File Allocation Table (FAT)-formatted partition.

Files located on raw partitions cannot be automatically expanded or backed up using the Windows Backup utility.

➤ After creating a new database, always back up the **master** database to preserve system settings related to the new database.

New databases are created using the **modal** database as a template. If you want certain properties or permissions on all new databases, make the changes to the **modal** database. All databases that you create will inherit the changes.

Creating a Database Using the Enterprise Manager

The easiest method to create a new database is by using SQL Server Enterprise Manager (EM), which is an included graphical user interface (GUI) utility. To create the new database **Data1** using the Enterprise Manager, take the following steps:

1. Open the SQL Server 2000 Enterprise Manager by selecting Start|Programs |Microsoft SQL Server|Enterprise Manager.

2. In the left panel, expand the desired server group by clicking the plus (+) sign.

3. Expand the configuration on the desired server by clicking the plus sign next to it, and enter authentication information if required.

4. Select the Databases folder by right-clicking the mouse, and choose New Database (see Figure 6.1).

5. On the new Database Properties screen, enter the name of the new database in the appropriate location on the General tab (see Figure 6.2).

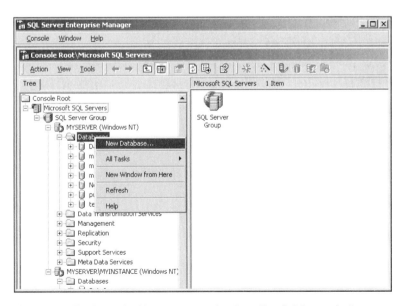

Figure 6.1   The Enterprise Manager screen showing a New Database selection.

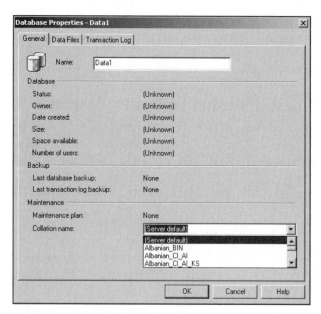

Figure 6.2 The Database Properties screen shows a new database, **Data1**, being created.

> You can also select a collation other than the database default here using the pull down list. (Refer to Chapter 3 for more information about collations.)

6. Modify any settings for the primary data file on the Data Files tab, and add any desired secondary data files. You can make associations with user-defined filegroups at this time (see Figure 6.3).

> Automatic file growth may be configured independently for each file, along with a maximum file size if desired.

7. Modify any settings for the transaction log file on the Transaction Log tab, and add any desired additional log files (see Figure 6.4).

> Automatic file growth may be configured independently for each file, along with maximum file size if desired.

8. Select OK to create the new database.

After the database has been created, it is listed in the Enterprise Manager. Click the new database, and select View|Taskpad to see an overview of its characteristics (see Figure 6.5).

Figure 6.3 The Data Files tab shows assignment of the secondary data file Data1_ExtraData to the user-defined filegroup "FGRP1."

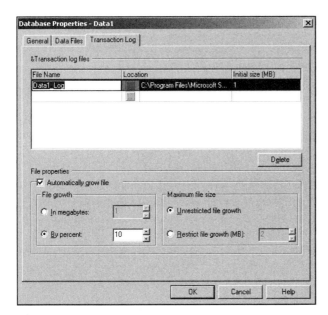

Figure 6.4 The Transaction Log tab shows the assignment of a transaction log file, Data1_Log.

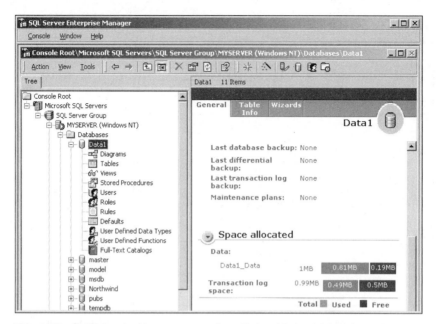

Figure 6.5 The Enterprise Manager screen shows Taskpad General details for the **Data1** database.

Creating a Database Using the Query Analyzer

Command-line database creation is also possible using the SQL Server Query Analyzer. This utility may be accessed from within the Enterprise Manager and contains a number of templates that make it easy to create a database. To create the **Data2** database using the Query Analyzer, take the following steps:

1. Open the SQL Server 2000 Enterprise Manager.

2. In the left panel, expand the desired server group by clicking the plus sign.

3. Click the desired server, and select View|Taskpad to see an overview of its characteristics, entering authentication information if required.

4 On the Wizards tab, under the General heading, select the Run SQL Query Analyzer option (see Figure 6.6).

5. After you have opened the SQL Query Analyzer, select the Templates tab on the left side, which allows access to the Create Database Templates. Double-clicking the appropriate template opens the template in the right panel (see Figure 6.7).

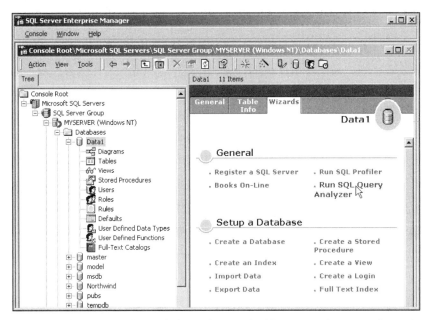

Figure 6.6 The Run SQL Query Analyzer is found on the Wizards tab of the server Taskpad.

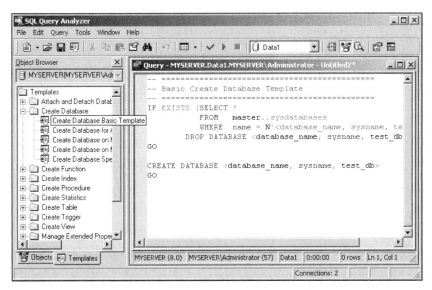

Figure 6.7 The SQL Query Analyzer Templates tab contains the Basic Create Database Template option.

6. You may edit Template parameters directly in the right pane or invoke the Replace Template Parameters screen by selecting Edit|Replace Template Parameters. Specify values for the parameters before clicking Replace All to apply your changes to the template (see Figure 6.8).

➤ Clicking Close returns you to the template without applying any changes.

7. After setting all of the parameters properly, execute the commands by selecting Query|Execute or using the F5 shortcut. Messages relating to the database creation are displayed in the lower-right pane.

8. After the creation process is completed, right-click the appropriate server in the left pane, and select Refresh to reveal the new database, **Data2** (see Figure 6.9).

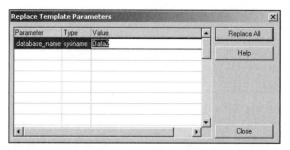

Figure 6.8   The Replace Template Parameters screen shows the new database, **Data2**.

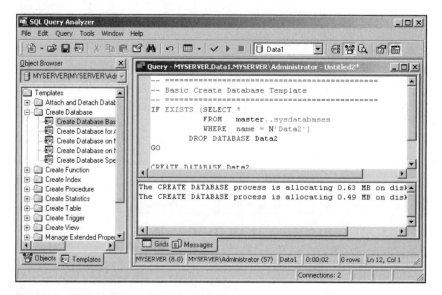

Figure 6.9   The SQL Query Analyzer screen shows the new database, **Data2**, and creation messages associated with it.

Many options beyond those used in the basic templates are available when using the **CREATE DATABASE** command-line option. Listing 6.1 details the options available for this command.

Listing 6.1   Syntax and usage of the CREATE DATABASE command.

```
CREATE DATABASE database_name
[ ON
[ < filespec > [ ,...n ] ]
[ , < filegroup > [ ,...n ] ]
]
[ LOG ON { < filespec > [ ,...n ] } ]
[ COLLATE collation_name ]
[ FOR LOAD | FOR ATTACH ]

< filespec > =
[ PRIMARY ]
( [ NAME = logical_file_name , ]
FILENAME = 'os_file_name'
[ , SIZE = size ]
[ , MAXSIZE = { max_size | UNLIMITED } ]
[ , FILEGROWTH = growth_increment ] ) [ ,...n ]

< filegroup > =
FILEGROUP filegroup_name < filespec > [ ,...n ]
```

Following are the arguments for the **CREATE DATABASE** command:

➤ *database_name*—The name of the new database. These should be meaningful, easily identifiable, unique within the server, and under 128 characters in length.

➤ **ON**—Indicates explicit definition of the disk files to be used for storing the data portions of the database. Comma-separated listings follow the keyword, defining the files to be used for primary and secondary data file storage.

➤ **LOG ON**—Indicates explicit definition of the disk files to be used for storing the transaction logs. Comma-separated listings follow this keyword, defining the files to be used. If LOG ON is not specified, a single transaction log file is created using an autogenerated name. This file is 25 percent of the size of all of the data files in the new database.

➤ **FOR LOAD**—Provides backward compatibility for earlier versions of SQL Server, creating a database with **dbo use only** turned on and a status of **loading**.

➤ **FOR ATTACH**—Attaches a database from an existing set of files. At least one primary data file must be specified, and the database must use the same code page and sort order as SQL Server. This command is often used for copying an existing database to another location and attaching the second copy as another database.

➤ *collation_name*—Specifies the default collation for the new database if it is other than the SQL Server instance default collation. (Refer to Chapter 3 for more information about collations.)

➤ **PRIMARY**—Associates the primary filegroup with the specified file. If this is not present, the first data file listed after **CREATE DATABASE** becomes the primary file.

➤ **NAME**—Provides a logical name assignment for the specified file. This is not required when the FOR ATTACH option is used.

➤ *logical_file_name*—Specifies the logical file name to be used in Transact-SQL statements for referencing the file. This name must be unique within the database.

➤ **FILENAME**—Specifies the operating system file name for the specified file.

➤ *'os_file_name'*—Specifies the operating system path and file name used in creating the physical file specified. This may not be a network file share or be located on a compressed file system.

➤ **SIZE**—Specifies the size for the specified new file. If this is not specified, new primary files are created using the size of the primary file in the **modal** database. The default size for unspecified new secondary files and log files is 1MB.

➤ *size*—A whole-number size for the specified file. Suffixes may be used (KB, MB, GB, and TB); MB (megabyte) is the default.

➤ **MAXSIZE**—Specifies the maximum size to which the specified file may expand. This prevents the database from attempting to overrun available physical drive space.

➤ *max_size*—A whole-number size for the specified file. Suffixes may be used here (KB, MB, GB, TB); MB (megabyte) is the default. If no number is specified, the file may expand until the disk is full.

➤ **UNLIMITED**—Specifies explicitly that a file may grow until the disk is full.

➤ **FILEGROWTH**—Specifies the increment at which the file may grow. This setting cannot exceed the value set in the MAXSIZE setting previously.

➤ *growth_increment*—Specifies how much space is added to a file each time that additional space is required. Suffixes may be used here (KB, MB, GB,

TB, and %); MB (megabyte) is the default. A value of zero indicates no growth ability. A specified percentage applies to the size of the file at the time of the growth. If this value is not specified, the default is 10 percent (with a minimum of 64KB).

Deleting a Database Using the Enterprise Manager

A database may be permanently deleted (also referred to as "dropping the database") using the Enterprise Manager. To delete a database using the Enterprise Manager, take the following steps:

1. Open the SQL Server 2000 Enterprise Manager by selecting Start|Programs |Microsoft SQL Server|Enterprise Manager.

2. In the left panel, expand the desired server group by clicking the plus sign.

3. Expand the configuration on the desired server by clicking the plus sign next to it, and enter authentication information if required.

4. Expand the Databases folder by clicking the plus sign next to it.

5. Select the database to be deleted by right-clicking it, and then select Delete from the drop-down menu.

6. Select the Yes button to remove the selected database.

   ➤ Selecting No at this time cancels the deletion.

   ➤ Check the Delete Backup and Restore History for the Database option to remove transaction log entries related to the specified database at this time.

Always back up the **master** database at this time to save the changes made as a result of deleting the database.

Deleting a Database Using the Query Analyzer

Command-line database deletion is also possible using the SQL Server Query Analyzer. To delete a database using the Query Analyzer, take the following steps:

1. Open the SQL Server 2000 Enterprise Manager.

2. In the left panel, expand the desired server group by clicking the plus sign.

3. Click the desired server, and select View|Taskpad to see an overview of its characteristics, entering authentication information if required.

4. On the Wizards tab, under the General heading, select the Run SQL Query Analyzer option.

5. In the right pane, enter the **DROP DATABASE** command, specifying one or several databases to be deleted or "dropped."

6. After you have set all parameters properly, execute the commands by selecting Query|Execute or using the F5 shortcut. Messages relating to the database deletion are displayed in the lower-right pane.

7. After the creation process is completed, right-click the appropriate server in the left pane, and select Refresh to verify the deletion.

The **DROP DATABASE** command is very simple. It has the following syntax:

```
DROP DATABASE database_name [,...n]
```

Following is the only argument for the **DROP DATABASE** command:

➤ *database_name*—The name of the database to be removed. A comma-separated list may be used if multiple databases are to be removed by a single command.

Creating an Object

The process for creating new database objects (such as tables, views, and stored procedures) is similar to that used to create a new database. The Enterprise Manager uses a convenient GUI-based method, whereas the SQL Query Analyzer provides command-line templates for creating objects.

Tables organize the data contained within a database in columnar form. A table can have no more than 1,024 columns. Each column requires a name unique to the table, a specified data type, and any additional constraints (for example, PRIMARY KEY designation, Uniqueness, and Nullability). DEFAULT values may also be specified for each column.

Views consist of data extracted from one or more tables. Views are used to aggregate data, restrict access to confidential or secure columns, and simplify subset extraction of available data.

Stored procedures are stored programmatic segments designed to allow multi-step scripted SQL language actions using runtime-specified parameters. Stored procedures can be used to extract data on a certain salesperson (for example, all invoices for a particular salesperson) by accepting a SalesID parameter at runtime.

Creating a Table Using the Enterprise Manager

The easiest method for creating a new table is the Table Designer GUI tool, which is accessible through the SQL Server Enterprise Manager utility. To create a new table using the Table Designer, take the following steps:

1. Open the SQL Server 2000 Enterprise Manager, by selecting Start|Programs |Microsoft SQL Server|Enterprise Manager.

2. In the left panel, expand the desired server group by clicking the plus sign.

3. Expand the configuration on the desired server by clicking the plus sign next to it, and enter authentication information if required.

4. Expand the desired database by clicking the plus sign next to it.

5. Select the Tables node by right-clicking the mouse, and choose New Table to open the Table Designer utility.

6. Each data element to be included in the table is represented by a column. As you input the data, set the data type and nullability (whether NULL values may be allowed for the field). Also insert any additional properties, such as a DE-FAULT value for columns that have no explicit value provided (see Figure 6.10).

7. Modify any necessary properties by clicking the Properties button for the table. Table name, ownership, permissions, relationships (PRIMARY KEY/ FOREIGN KEY relationships with existing tables), and indexes may be detailed here.

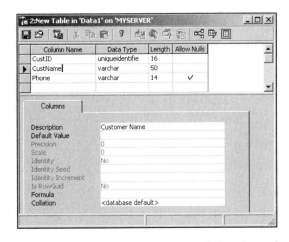

Figure 6.10   This Table Designer screen displays three columns in a new table.

➤ Indexes function like a book index, with an organized listing that allows for rapid searching for records matching specified criteria.

➤ Clustered indexes rearrange the data contained in the table and are useful for searches that include a range of values (such as searches for dates falling between two values). After the first value is located, additional values within the range will be physically located nearby within the database.

➤ Nonclustered indexes create an organized listing separate from the table itself, without rearranging the table's records. These indices are useful when searching for a unique value, such as a name or EmployeeID value.

8. Click Save to create the new table within the database.

The new table will be listed in the Tables node of the database in the Enterprise Manager.

Creating a View Using the Enterprise Manager

The easiest method for creating a new table is the GUI tool, accessible through the SQL Server Enterprise Manager utility. To create a new view, take the following steps:

1. Open the SQL Server 2000 Enterprise Manager by selecting Start|Programs |Microsoft SQL Server|Enterprise Manager.

2. In the left panel, expand the desired server group by clicking the plus sign.

3. Expand the configuration on the desired server by clicking the plus sign next to it, and enter authentication information if required.

4. Expand the desired database by clicking the plus sign next to it.

5. Select the Views node by right-clicking the mouse, and choose New View.

6. Add any desired source tables to the upper pane, then drag-and-drop desired columns into the View listing. Specify aliases, sort order, subset criteria, and any other constraints for each. The GUI tool presents the developing SQL **SELECT** clause, which may be tested by selecting the execution icon (a bold exclamation point located in the header). The extracted data is displayed in the bottom pane (see Figure 6.11).

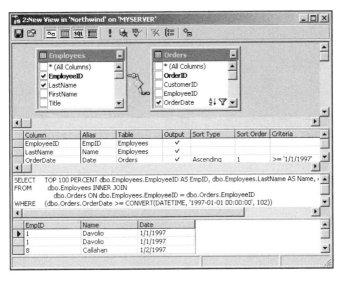

Figure 6.11   The View Designer displays aggregate data from two tables.

7. Modify any necessary properties by clicking the Properties button for the view. View name, ownership, extraction limitations (such as the TOP 100 records), and security measures such as view encryption and schema restriction may be detailed here.

8. Click Save to create the new view within the database.

The new view will be listed in the Views node of the database in the Enterprise Manager.

Creating a Stored Procedure Using the Enterprise Manager

The easiest method for creating a stored procedure is the GUI tool, accessible through the SQL Server Enterprise Manager utility. To create a new stored procedure, take the following steps:

1. Open the SQL Server 2000 Enterprise Manager by selecting Start|Programs |Microsoft SQL Server|Enterprise Manager.

2. In the left panel, expand the desired server group by clicking the plus sign.

3. Expand the configuration on the desired server by clicking the plus sign next to it, and enter authentication information if required.

4. Expand the desired database by clicking the plus sign next to it.

5. Select the Stored Procedures node by right-clicking the mouse, and choose New Stored Procedure.

6. Input the desired Transact-SQL code desired for the new stored procedure into the pane provided. To test the syntax of the newly input code without actually executing the procedure, select the Check Syntax button. If the new stored procedure will serve as a standard template, select the Save As Template button (see Figure 6.12).

7. Click OK to create the new stored procedure within the database. Selecting Cancel at this time will exit the Stored procedure creation tool, discarding all information from the input pane.

The new stored procedure will be listed in the Stored Procedures node of the database in the Enterprise Manager.

Deleting an Object Using the Enterprise Manager

Tables, views, and stored procedures may be permanently deleted using the Enterprise Manager. To delete an object using the Enterprise Manager, take the following steps:

1. Open the SQL Server 2000 Enterprise Manager by selecting Start|Programs |Microsoft SQL Server|Enterprise Manager.

2. In the left panel, expand the desired server group by clicking the plus sign.

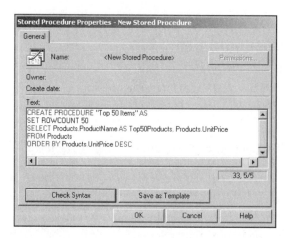

Figure 6.12 This new stored procedure will extract the 50 most expensive items from the Products table.

3. Expand the configuration on the desired server by clicking the plus sign next to it, and enter authentication information if required.

4. Expand the Databases folder by clicking the plus sign next to it.

5. Expand the appropriate database by clicking the plus sign next to it.

6. Select the node for the appropriate object type to be deleted by right-clicking it, and then select Delete from the drop-down menu.

7. Click Yes to remove the selected object.

Always back up the **master** database at this time to preserve the changes made as a result of deleting the object.

Practice Questions

Question 1

> You are a new database administrator responsible for a SQL Server 2000
> instance used by a regional furniture store chain. Your task is to create six
> new databases to be used for tracking sales information for individual stores
> within the chain. Inventory and sales staff members are moved from store
> to store so the required information for each store must be maintained in
> the same format. To create these databases in the most rapid manner pos-
> sible, which of the following items should you use? [Check all correct an-
> swers]
>
> ❑ a. SQL Query Analyzer
> ❑ b. SQL Server Enterprise Manager
> ❑ c. **modal** database
> ❑ d. **pubs** database
> ❑ e. **master** database
> ❑ f. **tempdb** database

Answers b and c are correct. The GUI Enterprise Manager is an easy-to-use
interface for rapidly creating new databases using the **modal** template. Because
all six stores use the same format, changes to the **modal** database are reflected in
all six newly created databases. Answer a is incorrect only because speed is necessary, and most new database administrators find GUI wizards faster than command-line options. However, the Query Analyzer is also a good tool for creating
the six new databases. Answer d is incorrect because the **pubs** database is simply
one of the sample databases included in SQL Server 2000. Answer e is incorrect
because the **master** database stores system variables and information rather than
user data. The **master** database should be backed up following the creation of the
new databases but is not used directly in the creation process. Answer f is incorrect because the **tempdb** database is used for temporary information storage rather
than long-term storage of user data.

Question 2

You are the database administrator responsible for a SQL Server 2000 instance used by a small gym to track membership. The server has storage available on a RAID array for the files used in a new database that you are to create, formatted as three striped volumes of 6GB each, mapped as D, E, and F. The C: drive is used for operating system and application files. You have decided on the following configuration:

- Primary data files are to be located on D: drive, secondary data files on E: drive, and log files on F: drive.

- Secondary data and transaction log files will be added to the user-defined filegroup FILEGRP1, and the primary data files will be left in the PRIMARY filegroup.

Will this configuration work?

O a. Yes

O b. No

Answer b is correct. The configuration as stated will not work. Although the separation of primary, secondary, and log files on the three drive shares will function, the transaction log files may not be included in a filegroup. Only primary and secondary data files may be assigned to filegroups. Excluding the transaction log files from FILEGRP1 would allow this configuration to be used. However, you can improve performance by reformatting the volumes and placing primary and secondary data files and transaction logs on separate physical disks.

Question 3

Which of the following databases may be dropped? [Check all correct answers]

❏ a. **master**

❏ b. **modal**

❏ c. **pubs**

❏ d. **tempdb**

❏ e. **msdb**

❏ f. **Northwind**

❏ g   **data1**

Answers c, f, and g are correct. The **pubs** and **Northwind** databases are samples included in the SQL Server installation, whereas **data1** is a user-defined database. Answers a, b, d, and e are incorrect because the four system databases (**master, modal, tempdb,** and **msdb**) may not be dropped from an instance of SQL Server 2000.

Question 4

Several file types may be used for each database:

Primary data files

Secondary data files

Transaction log files

Match the following characteristics with the appropriate file type (some may be used more than once):

Designated by the .ldf file extension

Designated by the .mdf file extension

Designated by the .ndf file extension

Allows roll forward and roll back actions

Can be associated with a filegroup

Required file type

Optional file type

The correct answer is:

Primary data files

Required file type

Can be associated with a filegroup

Designated by the .mdf file extension

Secondary data files

Optional file type

Can be associated with a filegroup

Designated by the .ndf file extension

Transaction log files

Required file type

Allows roll forward and roll back actions

Designated by the .ldf file extension

Question 5

> After creating a new database within an instance of SQL Server, you should always back up the **modal** database.
>
> ○ a. True
>
> ○ b. False

Answer b is correct. The **modal** database serves as the template for new databases and is not affected by changes made as the result of creating a new database. The **master** database should be backed up after a new database is created to preserve the changes made to the system files.

Question 6

> Many options are available when using the **CREATE DATABASE** command, including the following:
>
> *database_name*
>
> **FILEGROWTH**
>
> **FOR ATTACH**
>
> **MAXSIZE**
>
> **SIZE**
>
> Match the following characteristics with the appropriate option:
>
> Easily identifiable value under 128 characters
>
> Specifies a file's maximum size
>
> Unique within the database
>
> May be used to copy existing database files into the new database
>
> Specifies the initial file size for the new file
>
> Specifies the increment for growth of the file

The correct answer is:

database_name

Easily identifiable value under 128 characters

Unique within the database

FILEGROWTH

Specifies the increment for growth of the file

FOR ATTACH

May be used to copy existing database files into the new database

MAXSIZE

Specifies a file's maximum size

SIZE

Specifies the initial file size for the new file

Question 7

Which of the following objects may be created using the SQL Enterprise Manager utility? [Check all correct answers]

❏ a. Databases

❏ b. Tables

❏ c. Views

❏ d. Stored procedures

Answers a, b, c, and d are all correct. Both the SQL Enterprise Manager and SQL Query Analyzer may be used to create databases, tables, views, and stored procedures.

Question 8

> Two tools used to create databases and database objects within SQL Server 2000 are:
>
> SQL Enterprise Manager
>
> SQL Query Analyzer
>
> Match the following characteristics with the appropriate tool:
>
> Command-line interface
>
> Contains the Table Designer
>
> Graphical user interface (GUI)
>
> Includes command-line templates for common creation actions

The correct answers are:

SQL Enterprise Manager

Graphical user interface (GUI)

Contains the Table Designer

SQL Query Analyzer

Command-line interface

Includes command-line templates for common creation actions

Question 9

> Several steps are required to create a new Sales database that contains a table for Employee data and a view EmpID displaying only the EmployeeID and name of the employees to be input later. Arrange the following steps in the proper order:
>
> Back up the **master** database to preserve the changes to the system tables.
>
> Create a new Employee table in the Tables node in the Sales database.
>
> Create a new Sales database in the Databases node on the proper server.
>
> Create a new view EmpID in the Views node in the Sales database.
>
> Open the Enterprise Manager and navigate to the proper server.

The correct answer is:

Open the Enterprise Manager and navigate to the proper server.

Create a new Sales database in the Databases node on the proper server.

Create a new Employee table in the Tables node in the Sales database.

Create a new view EmpID in the Views node in the Sales database.

Back up the **master** database to preserve the changes to the system tables.

Question 10

Which of the following can be used to see a quick overview of a database's statistics?

○ a. Table Designer

○ b. Taskpad

○ c. Query Analyzer

Answer b is correct. The Taskpad view within the Enterprise Manager provides an overview of a database's statistics and access to a number of wizards including the SQL Query Analyzer. Answer a is incorrect because the Table Designer is used to create or modify tables and does not provide statistics on an entire database. Answer c is incorrect because the Query Analyzer is used to build and enact command-line SQL language actions.

Need to Know More?

 Dalton, Patrick, and Paul Whitehead. *SQL Server 2000 Black Book.* The Coriolis Group: Scottsdale, AZ, 2001. ISBN 1-57610-770-1. An excellent reference to keep close at hand during installation of SQL Server 2000. This is a necessary book in any DBA's library, as it has many solutions to commonly experienced issues.

 Delaney, Kalen. *Inside Microsoft SQL Server 2000.* Microsoft Press: Redmond, WA, 2000. ISBN 0-7356-0998-5. A good review of SQL Server 2000 components including white papers and articles on a broad range of topics.

 Iseminger, David. *Microsoft SQL Server 2000 Reference Library with CD-ROM.* Microsoft Press: Redmond, WA, 2000. ISBN 0-7356-1280-3. An exhaustive library covering detailed information on all aspects of SQL Server 2000 implementations. A necessary reference for IT departments supporting Microsoft SQL Server 2000 implementations.

 Shapiro, Jeffrey. *SQL Server 2000—The Complete Reference.* Osborne/McGraw-Hill: Berkeley, CA, 2001. ISBN 0-07-212588-8. A detailed, if somewhat lengthy, reference for SQL Server 2000 administration.

 http://msdn.microsoft.com/library/default.asp?URL=/library/psdk/sql/portal_7api.htm. *Microsoft SQL Server 2000 Books Online.* A complete online copy of the documentation for SQL Server 2000. This is an SQL Server 2000 database administrator's best friend because it is included on the installation CD-ROM.

Managing Databases

Terms you'll need to understand:

✓ Single-User Mode
✓ Detach operations
✓ Attach operations
✓ Expanding databases
✓ Shrinking databases
✓ Altering databases

Techniques you'll need to master:

✓ Restricting database access to Single-User Mode and restoring normal access
✓ Performing Attach and Detach operations on a database
✓ Expanding and shrinking database files
✓ Learning the syntax of the **ALTER DATABASE** command and using it correctly
✓ Using the Enterprise Manager to modify existing database objects, including tables, views, and stored procedures

Creating a database is only the beginning of a database administrator's job. Maintaining a SQL Server 2000 database is the rest of the job. This involves preserving data integrity and modifying existing structures to match changes in business data requirements. Modifications to preexisting objects are easily accomplished using both command-line and graphical user interface utilities, such as the Enterprise Manager.

This chapter covers the maintenance of SQL Server 2000 databases and database objects using the SQL Server Enterprise Manager and command-line functions available in the SQL Query Analyzer utility. An instance of SQL Server 2000 must already be installed (see Chapters 4 and 5) on a Windows 2000 server platform. Additional references are listed at the end of this chapter.

Getting Started

Review and familiarize yourself with the basic steps and commands used to create new databases and database objects (see Chapter 6). For database maintenance, you'll also need to learn how to modify existing database objects. You'll find that well-planned database objects and routine maintenance significantly reduce your workload as a database administrator.

Restricting Database Access

Before performing certain maintenance actions, you should have all existing users disconnect from the database and restrict database access to Single-User Mode. To restrict access for the **Data1** user database using the Enterprise Manager, take the following steps:

1. Open the SQL Server 2000 Enterprise Manager by selecting Start|Programs |Microsoft SQL Server|Enterprise Manager.

2. In the left panel, expand the desired server group by clicking the plus (+) sign.

3. Expand the configuration on the desired server by clicking the plus sign next to it, and enter authentication information if required.

4. Expand the Databases folder by clicking the plus sign next to it.

5. Select the appropriate database (**Data1** in this example) by right-clicking the mouse and choosing Properties.

6. Select the Options tab, enable the Restrict Access option, and select Single User (see Figure 7.1) in order to restrict access to the current logon.

   ➤ At other times you may need to restrict access only to members of the **db_owner, dbcreator,** and **sysadmin** roles. You do this by selecting the first Access Restriction option listed.

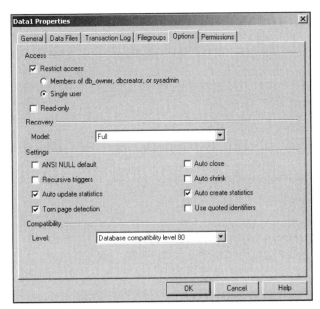

Figure 7.1   The Database Properties Options tab shows the settings for single-user restricted access.

Returning Database Access to Normal

After you have completed any maintenance tasks, take the following steps to return database access to its former state:

1. Open the SQL Server 2000 Enterprise Manager by selecting Start|Programs |Microsoft SQL Server|Enterprise Manager.

2. In the left panel, expand the desired server group by clicking the plus sign.

3. Expand the configuration on the desired server by clicking the plus sign next to it, and enter authentication information if required.

4. Expand the Databases folder by clicking the plus sign next to it.

5. Select the appropriate database by right-clicking the mouse and choosing Properties.

6. Select the Options tab, and disable the Restrict Access option.

Managing Databases

Basic maintenance involves the processes of copying, relocating, and adjusting the size of databases. Always back up the **master** database to preserve any changes made as a result of significant modifications or alterations to the database or its objects.

The Detach and Attach processes are used for copying an existing database as well as moving the location of database files. The Expand and Shrink processes are used for expanding or reducing (shrinking) the size of a database. Many database-level options are available through both the Enterprise Manager and command-line actions.

Attaching a Database

A detached database can be copied or moved before being attached again. Attaching a database creates a new database that uses existing data and transaction log files. To attach the detached **Data1** user database using the Enterprise Manager, take the following steps:

1. Open the SQL Server 2000 Enterprise Manager by selecting Start|Programs |Microsoft SQL Server|Enterprise Manager.

2. In the left panel, expand the desired server group by clicking the plus sign.

3. Expand the configuration on the desired server by clicking the plus sign next to it, and enter authentication information if required.

4. Select the Databases folder by right-clicking the mouse. Navigate to All Tasks, and select Attach Database.

5. On the Attach Database screen, navigate to the location of the current data and log files (see Figure 7.2). Input the name of the new database if different from its original name, and specify a database owner.

6. Click OK to complete the attachment of the database, or click Cancel to terminate the action without attaching the database.

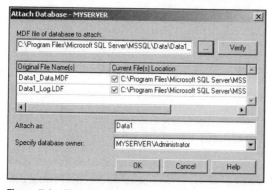

Figure 7.2 The Attach Database screen shows the **Data1** user database.

Detaching a Database

A detached database is disabled without deletion of the database files. This is typically used when moving a database to a new location. Detached databases are no longer listed in the Databases node of the Enterprise Manager and are not available to users.

System databases may not be detached. A database may not be detached while in use. You must have all users disconnect from the database. Viewing current user sessions is covered in Chapter 9.

To detach the **Data1** user database using the Enterprise Manager, take the following steps:

1. Open the SQL Server 2000 Enterprise Manager by selecting Start|Programs |Microsoft SQL Server|Enterprise Manager.

2. In the left panel, expand the desired server group by clicking the plus sign.

3. Expand the configuration on the desired server by clicking the plus sign next to it, and enter authentication information if required.

4. Expand the Databases folder by clicking the plus sign next to it.

5. Select the appropriate database by right-clicking the mouse. Navigate to All Tasks, and select Detach Database.

6. On the Detach Database screen, ensure that the status line indicates the database as being ready to be detached (see Figure 7.3).

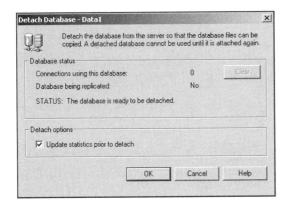

Figure 7.3 The Detach Database screen shows the status of the **Data1** user database.

➤ The Update Statistics Prior to Detach option is used mainly in the preparation of distributed read-only databases and is not generally required to move a database to another location.

7. Click OK to complete the detachment of the database, or click Cancel to terminate the Detach action without affecting the database.

Expanding a Database

If a database has been configured to expand automatically during creation, it is rarely necessary to expand a database manually. However, you may occasionally find it useful to perform a manual expansion of the database data or log files. You should be aware of the following restrictions before performing this action:

➤ The new file size must be larger than the original file size to expand a database. Shrinking a database is performed using a different utility and is covered later in this section.

➤ Performing this action on an active database file locks the file during the expansion. This action should be taken when the file is not in use.

To expand a data or transaction log file in the **Data1** user database using the Enterprise Manager, take the following steps:

1. Open the SQL Server 2000 Enterprise Manager by selecting Start|Programs |Microsoft SQL Server|Enterprise Manager.

2. In the left panel, expand the desired server group by clicking the plus sign.

3. Expand the configuration on the desired server by clicking the plus sign next to it, and enter authentication information if required.

4. Expand the Databases folder by clicking the plus sign next to it.

5. Select the appropriate database by right-clicking the mouse. Navigate to Properties.

6. Select the Data File or Transaction Log tab, as appropriate, and select the file to be expanded.

7. Increase the Space Allocated value for each file as required.

8. Click OK to complete the expansion of the file, or click Cancel to terminate the action without affecting the database.

Shrinking a Database

It is sometimes necessary to shrink a database at times when records are deleted or exported. You should be aware of the following restrictions before performing this action:

➤ Data files will shrink immediately. However, log files will not reduce in size until the next backup or truncation of the log.

➤ This action locks the affected database during operation and should be performed when the files are not in use.

➤ A database cannot generally be reduced smaller than the size of the **modal** template database.

To shrink the files in the **Data1** user database using the Enterprise Manager, take the following steps:

1. Open the SQL Server 2000 Enterprise Manager by selecting Start|Programs |Microsoft SQL Server|Enterprise Manager.

2. In the left panel, expand the desired server group by clicking the plus sign.

3. Expand the configuration on the desired server by clicking the plus sign next to it, and enter authentication information if required.

4. Expand the Databases folder by clicking the plus sign next to it.

5. Select the appropriate database by right-clicking the mouse. Navigate to All Tasks, and select Shrink Database.

6. Select the Maximum Free Space In Files After Shrinking option, and choose a percentage (see Figure 7.4).

➤ Select the Move Pages To Beginning Of File Before Shrinking option to compact the data pages. This is not advisable when pages are cached in

Figure 7.4 The Shrink Database screen for the **Data1** user database shows a weekly scheduled reduction of the database with defragmentation of the data pages selected.

the buffer for later access. Maintenance commands affecting table pin-
ning will be covered in Chapter 9.

➤ To enact this process at a time of minimum database usage, you can schedule the task for later action on this screen. Leave this option unselected if
you want to shrink the database immediately.

7. Click OK to complete the shrinking of the database, or click Cancel to terminate the action without affecting the database.

Altering Databases

The **ALTER DATABASE** command-line function can also be used for altering
a database. Listing 7.1 details the options available for this command.

It is not necessary to memorize the entire listing of options for the
ALTER DATABASE command for the exam. You just need to know the
basic capabilities of this command for modifying database files.

Listing 7.1   Syntax and usage of the **ALTER DATABASE** command.

```
ALTER DATABASE database
{ ADD FILE < filespec > [ ,...n ] [ TO FILEGROUP filegroup_name ]
| ADD LOG FILE < filespec > [ ,...n ]
| REMOVE FILE logical_file_name
| ADD FILEGROUP filegroup_name
| REMOVE FILEGROUP filegroup_name
| MODIFY FILE < filespec >
| MODIFY NAME = new_dbname
| MODIFY FILEGROUP filegroup_name {filegroup_property | NAME =
new_filegroup_name }
| SET < optionspec > [ ,...n ] [ WITH < termination > ]
| COLLATE < collation_name >
}

< filespec > =
( NAME = logical_file_name
    [ , NEWNAME = new_logical_name ]
    [ , FILENAME = 'os_file_name' ]
    [ , SIZE = size ]
    [ , MAXSIZE = { max_size | UNLIMITED } ]
    [ , FILEGROWTH = growth_increment ] )

< optionspec > =
    < state_option >
    | < cursor_option >
```

```
| < auto_option >
| < sql_option >
| < recovery_option >

< state_option > =
    { SINGLE_USER | RESTRICTED_USER | MULTI_USER }
    | { OFFLINE | ONLINE }
    | { READ_ONLY | READ_WRITE }

< termination > =
    ROLLBACK AFTER integer [ SECONDS ]
    | ROLLBACK IMMEDIATE
    | NO_WAIT

< cursor_option > =
    CURSOR_CLOSE_ON_COMMIT { ON | OFF }
    | CURSOR_DEFAULT { LOCAL | GLOBAL }

< auto_option > =
    AUTO_CLOSE { ON | OFF }
    | AUTO_CREATE_STATISTICS { ON | OFF }
    | AUTO_SHRINK { ON | OFF }
    | AUTO_UPDATE_STATISTICS { ON | OFF }

< sql_option > =
    ANSI_NULL_DEFAULT { ON | OFF }
    | ANSI_NULLS { ON | OFF }
    | ANSI_PADDING { ON | OFF }
    | ANSI_WARNINGS { ON | OFF }
    | ARITHABORT { ON | OFF }
    | CONCAT_NULL_YIELDS_NULL { ON | OFF }
    | NUMERIC_ROUNDABORT { ON | OFF }
    | QUOTED_IDENTIFIER { ON | OFF }
    | RECURSIVE_TRIGGERS { ON | OFF }

< recovery_option > =
    RECOVERY { FULL | BULK_LOGGED | SIMPLE }
    | TORN_PAGE_DETECTION { ON | OFF }
```

Following are the arguments for the **ALTER DATABASE** command:

➤ *Database*—The name of the database being altered.

➤ **ADD FILE**—Specifies that a new file is to be added.

➤ **TO FILEGROUP**—Specifies that the new file will be added to a filegroup.

➤ *filegroup_name*—Specifies the name of the filegroup for the new file.

➤ **ADD LOG FILE**—Specifies that a new log file is to be added to the database.

➤ **REMOVE FILE**—Specifies that a file is to be removed and deleted. This can only be performed if the file contains no data.

➤ **ADD FILEGROUP**—Specifies that a new filegroup will be added.

➤ *filegroup_name*—Specifies the name of the filegroup being added or dropped.

➤ **REMOVE FILEGROUP**—Specifies that the filegroup is to be removed and deleted. This can only be performed if the filegroup is empty.

➤ **MODIFY FILE**—Specifies that a file should be modified in some way. The options include **FILEGROWTH, FILENAME, MAXSIZE,** and **SIZE.** Following are some restrictions:

　➤ Only one of these may be modified at a time.

　➤ **SIZE** may only be used to increase file size.

➤ **MODIFY NAME** = *new_dbname*—Renames the specified database.

➤ **MODIFY FILEGROUP** *filegroup_name* { *filegroup_property* | **NAME** = *new_filegroup_name* }—Specifies a filegroup and the type of modification to be performed on it. The values for *filegroup_property* are as follows:

　➤ **READONLY**—Prevents updates to objects in the filegroup. This may not be enacted to the Primary filegroup.

　➤ **READWRITE**—Allows updates to objects in the filegroup.

　➤ **DEFAULT**—Sets the specified filegroup as the DEFAULT filegroup for new objects.

➤ **WITH** *<termination>*—Specifies when incomplete transactions should be rolled back during transition between states. The values for *<termination>* are as follows:

　➤ **ROLLBACK AFTER** *integer* [SECONDS]—Specifies a rollback after the specified number of seconds.

　➤ **ROLLBACK IMMEDIATE**—Specifies an immediate rollback.

　➤ **NO_WAIT**—Specifies that the transition will fail if all transactions cannot complete or roll back on their own immediately.

➤ **COLLATE** *<collation_name>*—Specifies a new collation for the database.

➤ *<filespec>*—Specifies the file properties. The values for *<*filespec*>* are as follows:

　➤ **NAME**—Specifies a logical file name.

➤ *logical_file_name*—The logical file name used by SQL Server to reference the file.

➤ FILENAME—Specifies the operating system file name.

➤ *'os_file_name'*—The path and operating system file name.

➤ SIZE—Specifies the file size.

➤ size—A whole-number size for the specified file. Suffixes may be used here (KB, MB, GB, and TB); MB (megabyte) is the default.

➤ MAXSIZE—Specifies the maximum size to which the specified file may expand.

➤ max_size—A whole-number size for the specified file. Suffixes may be used here (KB, MB, GB, and TB); MB (megabyte) is the default. If not specified, the file may grow until the disk is full.

➤ UNLIMITED—Specifies explicitly that file may grow until the disk is full.

➤ FILEGROWTH—Specifies the increment at which the file may grow. This setting may not exceed the value in the MAXSIZE setting.

➤ growth_increment—Specifies how much space is added to a file each time that additional space is required. Suffixes may be used here (KB, MB, GB, TB, and %); MB (megabyte) is the default. A value of zero indicates no growth ability. A specified percentage applies to the size of the file at the time of the growth. If this value is not specified, the default is 10 percent (with a minimum of 64KB).

➤ <*state_option*>—Specifies details of user access to the database. The values for <*state_option*> are as follows:

➤ SINGLE_USER—Specifies single-user restricted access.

➤ RESTRICTED_USER—Restricts access to members of the **db_owner**, **dbcreator**, and **sysadmin** roles.

➤ MULTI_USER—Returns access to the normal database settings.

➤ OFFLINE—Sets the database as offline.

➤ ONLINE—Sets the database as online.

➤ READ_ONLY—Prevents updates to the database.

➤ READ_WRITE—Allows updates to the database.

➤ **<cursor_option>**—Specifies details of cursor options. The values for **<cursor_option>** are as follows:

➤ **CURSOR_CLOSE_ON_COMMIT ON**—Specifies that any open cursors will be closed on rollback or commitment of a transaction.

➤ **CURSOR_CLOSE_ON_COMMIT OFF**—Specifies that cursors remain after a transaction is rolled back or committed.

➤ **CURSOR_DEFAULTLOCAL**—Sets cursor scope to Local.

➤ **CURSOR_DEFAULTGLOBAL**—Sets cursor scope to Global.

➤ **<auto_option>**—Specifies automatic options. The values for **<auto_option>** are as follows:

➤ **AUTO_CLOSE ON | OFF**—Specifies whether a database will shut down when the last user exits.

➤ **AUTO_CREATE_STATISTICS ON | OFF**—Specifies whether missing statistics will be automatically built for a query during optimization.

➤ **AUTO_SHRINK ON | OFF**—Specifies whether the database files should be periodically checked for automatic shrinking.

➤ **AUTO_UPDATE_STATISTICS ON | OFF**—Specifies whether out-of-date query statistics are to be automatically updated during optimization.

➤ **<sql_option>**—Specifies ANSI compliance options. The values for **<sql_option>** are as follows:

➤ **ANSI_NULL_DEFAULT ON | OFF**—Specifies whether **CREATE TABLE** follows SQL-92 rules for null value columns.

➤ **ANSI_NULLS ON | OFF**—Specifies whether comparisons including null values return a value of UNKNOWN.

➤ **ANSI_PADDING ON | OFF**—Specifies whether strings are padded (adding trailing spaces until the lengths match) before comparison.

➤ **ANSI_WARNINGS ON | OFF**—Specifies if warnings should be given for actions such as division by zero.

➤ **ARITHABORT ON | OFF**—Specifies whether a query should terminate on an arithmetic error.

➤ **CONCAT_NULL_YIELDS_NULL ON | OFF**—Specifies whether a concatenation operation involving a null value results in NULL or is treated as an empty character string (the default).

➤ QUOTED_IDENTIFIER ON | OFF—Specifies whether double quotation marks can be used to enclose delimited identifiers.

➤ NUMERIC_ROUNDABORT ON | OFF—Specifies if an error should be generated when loss of precision occurs in an expression.

➤ RECURSIVE_TRIGGERS ON | OFF—Specifies whether triggers are fired recursively (default is OFF).

➤ <recovery_options>—Specifies details of database recovery options. These modes are covered in greater detail in Chapter 8. The values for <recovery_options> are as follows:

➤ RECOVERY FULL—Specifies the Full Recovery Mode is to be used.

➤ RECOVERY BULK_LOGGED—Specifies the Bulk-Logged Recovery Mode.

➤ RECOVERY SIMPLE—Specifies the Simple Recovery Mode.

➤ TORN_PAGE_DETECTION ON | OFF—Specifies whether incomplete pages can be detected.

Managing Objects

Individual objects within an SQL Server 2000 database also require maintenance. Tables, views, and stored procedures require updates to match changing business data requirements. Simple creation and deletion of these items was covered in Chapter 6. Many object-level maintenance options are available through both the Enterprise Manager and command-line actions.

Modifying a Table Using the Enterprise Manager

The easiest method to modify an existing table is by using the Table Designer GUI tool accessible through the SQL Server Enterprise Manager utility. To modify an existing table using the Table Designer, take the following steps:

1. Open the SQL Server 2000 Enterprise Manager by selecting Start|Programs |Microsoft SQL Server|Enterprise Manager.

2. In the left panel, expand the desired server group by clicking the plus sign.

3. Expand the configuration on the desired server by clicking the plus sign next to it, and enter authentication information if required.

4. Expand the desired database by clicking the plus sign next to it.

5. Expand the Tables node by clicking the plus sign next to it.

6. Select the desired table by right-clicking the mouse and choosing Design Table to open the Table Designer utility.

7. Each data element to be included in the table is represented by a column. Add, delete, or modify columns here.

8. Modify any necessary properties by clicking the Properties button for the table. Table name, ownership, permissions, relationships (PRIMARY KEY/ FOREIGN KEY relationships with existing tables), and indexes may be detailed here.

➤ Indexes function like a book's index by creating an organized listing that allows for rapid searching for records matching specified criteria.

➤ Clustered indexes rearrange the data contained in the table and are useful for searches that include a range of values (such as searches for dates falling between two values). After the first value is located, additional values within the range will be physically located nearby within the database (see Figure 7.5).

➤ Nonclustered indexes create an organized listing separate from the table itself, without rearranging the table's records. These indexes are useful when searching for a unique value, such as a name or EmployeeID value.

9. Click Save to save the modified table within the database.

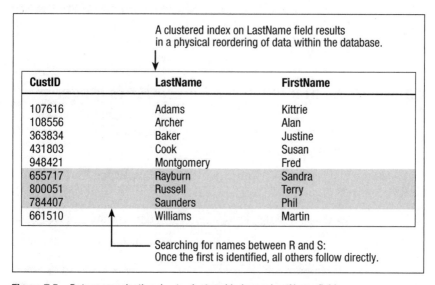

Figure 7.5 Data reorganization due to clustered index on LastName field.

Modifying a View Using the Enterprise Manager

The easiest method to modify an existing view is by using the GUI tool accessible through the SQL Server Enterprise Manager utility. To modify an existing view, take the following steps:

1. Open the SQL Server 2000 Enterprise Manager by selecting Start|Programs |Microsoft SQL Server|Enterprise Manager.

2. In the left panel, expand the desired server group by clicking the plus sign.

3. Expand the configuration on the desired server by clicking the plus sign next to it, and enter authentication information if required.

4. Expand the desired database by clicking the plus sign next to it.

5. Expand the Views node by clicking the plus sign next to it.

6. Select the desired View by right-clicking the mouse and choosing Design View.

7. Add any desired source tables to the upper pane, and drag-and-drop desired columns into the View listing. Specify aliases, sort order, subset criteria, and any other constraints for each. The GUI tool presents the altered SQL SELECT clause, which can be tested by selecting the execution icon, displaying the extracted data in the bottom pane.

8. Modify any necessary properties by clicking the Properties button for the view. View name, ownership, extraction limitations (such as the TOP 5 records), and security measures such as view encryption and schema restriction may be detailed here.

9. Click Save to save the modified view within the database.

Modifying a Stored Procedure Using the Enterprise Manager

The easiest method to modify an existing stored procedure is by using the GUI tool accessible through the SQL Server Enterprise Manager utility. To modify an existing stored procedure, take the following steps:

1. Open the SQL Server 2000 Enterprise Manager by selecting Start|Programs |Microsoft SQL Server|Enterprise Manager.

2. In the left panel, expand the desired server group by clicking the plus sign.

3. Expand the configuration on the desired server by clicking the plus sign next to it, and enter authentication information if required.

4. Expand the desired database by clicking the plus sign next to it.

5. Expand the Stored Procedures node by clicking the plus sign next to it.

6. Select the desired Stored Procedure by right-clicking the mouse and choosing Properties.

7. Modify the Transact-SQL code in the pane provided. To test the syntax of the modified code without actually executing the procedure, select Check Syntax.

8. Click OK to save the modified stored procedure within the database, or click Cancel to exit the creation tool, discarding all modifications to the stored procedure.

Modifying an Index Using the Enterprise Manager

The easiest method to modify the indexes on a table is by using the Manage Indexes GUI tool accessible through the SQL Server Enterprise Manager utility. To modify the index of an existing table using the Manage Indexes tool, take the following steps:

1. Open the SQL Server 2000 Enterprise Manager by selecting Start|Programs |Microsoft SQL Server|Enterprise Manager.

2. In the left panel, expand the desired server group by clicking the plus sign.

3. Expand the configuration on the desired server by clicking the plus sign next to it, and enter authentication information if required.

4. Expand the desired database by clicking the plus sign next to it.

5. Expand the Tables node by clicking the plus sign next to it.

6. Select the desired table by right-clicking the mouse and navigating to All Tasks. Select Manage Indexes to open the utility.

7. The existing indexes are displayed. Highlight the one you want, and select the Edit button to open the Edit Existing Index screen (see Figure 7.6).

   ➤ Select New to open the Create New Index screen.

8. Modify any necessary properties here. Select OK to save the modifications made to the index (see Figure 7.7).

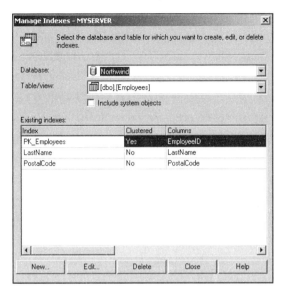

Figure 7.6   The Manage Indexes screen shows the Employees table in the **Northwinds**
sample database.

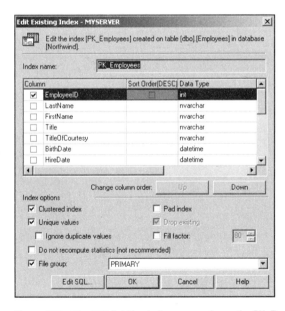

Figure 7.7   The Edit Existing Index screen shows the PK_Employees index for the Employees
table in the **Northwinds** sample database.

➤ Clustered indexes rearrange the data contained in the table and are useful for searches that include a range of values (such as searches for dates falling between two values). After the first value is located, additional values within the range will be physically located nearby within the database.

➤ Nonclustered indexes create an organized listing separate from the table itself, without rearranging the table's records. These indexes are useful when searching for a unique value such as a name.

Practice Questions

Question 1

You are a new database administrator responsible for an SQL Server 2000 instance. Your task is to modify two tables in the **Sales** database. You must complete these modifications before any users access the database in the morning. To prevent users from connecting before you have completed your modifications, arrange the following steps in the proper order:

Back up the **master** database to preserve the changes to the system tables.

Modify the tables in the **Sales** database.

Set **Sales** database access to Single-User Mode.

Set **Sales** database access to Unrestricted Mode.

Verify that all users are disconnected from the **Sales** database.

The correct answer is:

Verify that all users are disconnected from the **Sales** database.

Set **Sales** database access to Single-User Mode.

Modify the tables in the **Sales** database.

Back up the **master** database to preserve the changes to the system tables.

Set **Sales** database access to Unrestricted Mode.

Question 2

You are the database administrator responsible for a SQL Server 2000 instance. The server has storage available on a RAID (redundant array of independent disks) array for the files used for an **Employees** database into which you must import a large number of files. You must format it as three striped volumes of 6GB each, mapped as D, E, and F. The C: drive is used for operating system and application files and some lightly used files. Because you have insufficient space available for the data to be input, you decide to perform the following steps:

- Delete the **Northwind** and **pubs** database.

- Detach the **tempdb** database, and move it to the C: drive.

- Reattach the **tempdb** database.

- Shrink the **Employees** database.

- Save the **master** database to preserve the changes.

Will this configuration work?

○ a. Yes

○ b. No

Answer b is correct. The configuration as stated will not work. Although deleting the **Northwind** and **pubs** databases may free up sufficient space for the new data, the **tempdb** database is a system database and cannot be detached. Shrinking the **Employees** database may help somewhat by compacting the data pages.

Question 3

You are the database administrator responsible for several SQL Server 2000 instances in an Enterprise setting. Your boss asked you to get some work done early Saturday morning while the database was not being accessed, but it must be backed up before noon. You have just detached the **Inventory** database to move it to another server that has been prepared for it. The source server uses a set of mirrored IDE (Integrated Drive Electronics) drives to store the database files, and the new server uses a RAID configuration of SCSI drives. You detach the database and laboriously copy the huge files over an outdated 10MB network to the new server, which takes more than half of the available time.

Your boss calls you from the golf course and says that his son read in a magazine that you must select the Upgrade The Statistics Prior To Detaching The Database option or the move will fail. He says that you need to fix this before the board meeting at noon. Assuming all equipment, files, and SQL Server 2000 instances are fully functional, can you complete the move in time?

- ○ a. Yes
- ○ b. No

Answer a is correct. The Upgrade The Statistics Prior To Detaching The Database option is only necessary for read-only distributed databases. You will have enough time to attach the database to the new server so that the new application is available to run the Inventory reports for the board.

Question 4

You are the database administrator responsible for maintaining an existing Membership database using SQL Server 2000. You need to expand the Primary data file, MBRDAT.mdf, and remove the now-empty Secondary data file, MBRDAT_OLD.ndf. Which of the following tools may be used for these actions? [Check all correct answers]

- ❑ a. English Query
- ❑ b. Internet Explorer
- ❑ c. SQL Data Consolidator
- ❑ d. SQL Query Analyzer
- ❑ e. SQL Server Enterprise Manager

Answers d and e are correct. The SQL Query Analyzer command-line interface and the Enterprise Manager GUI utility may both be used to perform these tasks. Answer a is incorrect because the English Query package is not used for database maintenance. Answer b is incorrect because Internet Explorer is used to browse the web, not to modify an instance of SQL Server 2000. Answer c is incorrect because there is no SQL Data Consolidator utility at the time of this writing.

Question 5

You are the database administrator responsible for a SQL Server 2000 instance running on a dual-Pentium system using an expensive RAID drive array. After shrinking your **Sales** database, you examine the files on the drive and see that only the Sales.mdf file has reduced in size. The Sales.ldf file appears to be unchanged. A helpful member of the Sales team suggests that the drive in the RAID array containing the Sales.ldf file is failing and you should obtain a replacement from Purchasing. Is this the best option at this time?

○ a. Yes

○ b. No

Answer b is correct. After performing the Shrink database process, the data files (.mdf and .ndf) reduce in size immediately. The Transaction Log files (.ldf) will not reduce in size until the next truncation or backup of the logs. You should monitor the drives for possible failure and the size of the files following the next backup. Hardware replacement should not be your first option.

Question 6

You are the database administrator responsible for a SQL Server 2000 instance. A member of the programming group has released a new application that allows the CEO and his staff to access information in the **MasterSales** database. This was deployed overnight, replacing the previous, less capable application that had been in use for the last two years. You receive a panicked call from your boss. He says that the head of programming called and says that the database has crashed and the new application will not work. When you arrive, you check the database and can access it without problems, but you notice that the master **Sales** database is called **Sales**, not **MasterSales**. You perform the following **ALTER DATABASE** command:

```
ALTER DATABASE Sales
    MODIFY NAME = MasterSales
```

Will this change the name of the database?

○ a. Yes

○ b. No

Answer a is correct. The **ALTER DATABASE** command will change the name of the **Sales** database to **MasterSales**. Other configuration changes may be required if other applications still reference the **Sales** database, but the name of the database itself has been changed. Further problems should be referred back to the programming group.

Question 7

You are a new database administrator responsible for a SQL Server 2000 instance. Your task is to modify two tables in the **Sales** database. Which of the following tools should you use for this? [Check all correct anwers]

❑ a. ALTER DATABASE Wizard

❑ b. Enterprise Manager

❑ c. Shrink Database utility

❑ d. Table Designer utility

Answers b and d are correct. The Enterprise Manager GUI utility and Table Designer utility accessed from within the Enterprise Manager are used to perform this task. Answer a is incorrect because there is no ALTER DATABASE Wizard. The **ALTER DATABASE** command is used in command-line actions within an interface such as the Query Analyzer. Answer c is incorrect because the Shrink Database Wizard is not used in table-level maintenance.

Question 8

Which of the following databases may be detached? [Check all correct answers]

☐ a. **master**

☐ b. **modal**

☐ c. **pubs**

☐ d. **tempdb**

☐ e. **msdb**

☐ f. **Northwind**

☐ g. **data1**

Answers c, f, and g are correct. The **Northwind** and **pubs** databases are samples included in the SQL Server installation, and **data1** is a user-defined database. The four system databases (**master, modal, tempdb,** and **msdb**) may not be detached from an instance of SQL Server 2000.

Question 9

Several database maintenance actions may be taken:

Attaching a database

Detaching a database

Expanding a database

Restricting user access

Shrinking a database

Match the following characteristics with the appropriate action (some may be used more than once):

Can prevent user connections

Creates a new database using existing data and transaction log files

Decreases database file storage

Disables a database without deleting its files

Increases database file storage

Locks the database files while operating

Can be used to copy an existing database

Can only be performed on nonsystem databases

The correct answers are:

Attaching a database

Creates a new database using existing data and transaction log files

Can be used to copy an existing database

Detaching a database

Disables a database without deleting its files

Can be used to copy an existing database

Can only be performed on nonsystem databases

Expanding a database

Increases database file storage

Locks the database files while operating

Restricting user access

Can prevent user connections

Shrinking a database

Decreases database file storage

Locks the database files while operating

Question 10

After significantly modifying a database within an instance of SQL Server, you must always remember to back up the **master** database.

○ a. True

○ b. False

Answer a is correct. Backing up the **master** database preserves changes made to the system files during the modifications made to any databases.

Need to Know More?

 Dalton, Patrick, and Paul Whitehead. *SQL Server 2000 Black Book.* The Coriolis Group: Scottsdale, Arizona, 2001. ISBN 1-57610-770-1. An excellent reference to keep close at hand during installation of SQL Server 2000. This is a necessary book in any DBA's library, as it has many solutions to commonly experienced issues.

 Delaney, Kalen. *Inside Microsoft SQL Server 2000.* Microsoft Press: Redmond, WA, 2000. ISBN 0-7356-0998-5. A good review of SQL Server 2000 components including white papers and articles on a broad range of topics.

 Iseminger, David. *Microsoft SQL Server 2000 Reference Library with CD-ROM.* Microsoft Press: Redmond, WA, 2000. ISBN 0-7356-1280-3. An exhaustive library covering detailed information on all aspects of SQL Server 2000 implementations. A necessary reference for IT departments supporting Microsoft SQL Server 2000 implementations.

 Shapiro, Jeffrey. *SQL Server 2000—The Complete Reference.* Osborne/McGraw-Hill: Berkeley, CA, 2001. ISBN 0-07-212588-8. A detailed, if somewhat lengthy, reference for SQL Server 2000 administration.

 http://msdn.microsoft.com/library/default.asp?URL=/library/psdk/sql/portal_7ap1.htm. *Microsoft SQL Server 2000 Books Online.* A complete online copy of the documentation for SQL Server 2000. This is an SQL Server 2000 database administrator's best friend because it is included on the installation CD-ROM.

Disaster Recovery

Terms you'll need to understand:

✓ Backup

✓ Restore

✓ Full backup

✓ Differential backup

✓ Transaction Log backup

✓ Simple recovery model

✓ Full recovery model

✓ Bulk-logged recovery model

✓ Point-in-time restoration

✓ Standby server

Techniques you'll need to master:

✓ Recognizing the differences among the three primary database backup types (full, differential, and transaction log) and using them in database restorations

✓ Planning database backup scheduling based on backup type and recovery model selection

✓ Determining when each of the three recovery model types (Simple, Full, and Bulk-logged) should be used

✓ Performing each of the three primary types of database backup

Perhaps the most crucial activities performed by a database administrator are backing up database information and restoring it when disaster strikes. Disaster may occur because of hardware failure (such as the loss of multiple disks in a RAID (Redundant Array of Independent Disks) configuration, data corruption (such as an accidental bulk update by users that replaces critical information), or catastrophic damage to the server environment (such as damage caused by natural disasters). It is not a matter of "whether" this will occur, but rather "when." Just as even the best-maintained vehicle eventually breaks down and requires repair, so will a database.

This chapter covers the processes used in backing up and restoring databases and database files within an instance of SQL Server 2000 using the SQL Server Enterprise Manager and the SQL Query Analyzer. An instance of SQL Server 2000 must already be installed (see Chapters 4 and 5) on a Windows 2000 server platform. This is not intended to be a complete listing of all possible backup and restoration scenarios, but rather an overview of the elements required for these operations, particularly those areas covered in the Microsoft Certification Exam. Additional references are listed at the end of this chapter.

Disaster Recovery Planning

The best guide for effective disaster recovery is "Plan for the worst, hope for the best." When the worst does occur (and it will, eventually), it is crucial that you have good backups, know the recovery plan, and have practiced this process. Some databases require more frequent backup than others, especially if their data changes often. Online transaction processing (OLTP) scenarios, such as Web-enabled shopping cart databases, may require transactional backup every 15 minutes, whereas read-only inventory pricing lists may require only daily backup to ensure full recoverability.

Considerations

A complete disaster recovery plan includes the following:

➤ Notification of the personnel responsible for recovery

➤ Acquisition of replacement hardware

➤ Complete documentation of information required for database reconstruction and recovery

➤ Access to regular offsite backups

Obviously, many other considerations must be included in a complete disaster recovery plan. There are as many possible backup scenarios as there are database server configurations. Additional issues, such as business model impact, add further complexity.

Following are some examples of the questions that you should consider before planning a disaster recovery strategy suitable to your particular scenario:

➤ What is the maximum acceptable downtime in the event of a hardware failure?

➤ How difficult will it be to recreate lost data?

➤ During what hours must the database be accessible for users?

➤ Are onsite database administrators available at all critical times?

➤ How often is information contained within the databases changed or updated?

➤ How large are the databases that must be backed up?

➤ Does your database server support other applications that may impair database functionality?

➤ How much storage (such as number of tapes or size of file storage) is available for backups? This limits the number of backups that may be maintained for point-in-time recovery actions.

➤ How often must media (such as tapes) be changed during backups of very large databases?

➤ When performing backup operations to remote storage locations, does high network utilization during certain times impair backup performance?

Planning a schedule for backing up your data is equally complex, but a few guidelines are readily identifiable for when backups should be performed:

➤ At regular intervals not exceeding the maximum-allowable loss as required by the company's business model

➤ When significant changes are made to the structure of a database (backing up the **master** database is essential to allow for the recovery of system changes)

➤ After any bulk updates or mass import operations

➤ Before applying service packs or system updates to the operating system or database application

➤ Before weekends and holidays

➤ Whenever you feel that it has been too long since the last backup (The worst experience for database administrators is when a failure occurs right after they felt they should have backed up the database but did not do so.)

Backup Types

There are three primary types of data backup used for databases. Individual files can also be backed up, which is especially useful when working with very large databases.

 Many exam scenarios will require a thorough understanding of the three primary backup types, so be sure to know these well.

The three backup types are as follows:

➤ *Full*—A complete backup of all database files:

  ➤ Requires a large amount of file storage.

  ➤ Takes longer than a differential backup.

  ➤ Does not back up transaction log data.

➤ *Differential*—A backup of database information that has changed since the last full backup:

  ➤ Requires a Full backup as well to perform restoration.

  ➤ Requires a variable amount of file storage.

  ➤ Does not back up transaction log data.

➤ *Transaction Log*—A backup of the transaction log files:

  ➤ Does not back up database files.

  ➤ Requires a Full backup and the most recent Differential backup to perform recovery.

  ➤ Allows for point-in-time recovery (rolls forward each transaction to a specified date and time), which is useful for recovering from corruption caused by a particular transaction because it allows recovery to the point just prior to the error.

Recovery strategies include scheduling the available types of backup to optimize data recoverability as well as system performance. Following is an example of a backup schedule that you may set up:

➤ A Full backup nightly during low use times

➤ A Differential backup every 4 hours through the day

➤ A Transaction Log backup every 15 minutes

Using this example, if a critical failure occurred, you could recover the database by reloading the Full backup, the most recent Differential backup, and all Transaction Log backups since the last differential backup. Only transactions that occurred after the last Transaction Log backup would have to be recreated.

 Always perform a Full backup prior to making significant changes to a database, and another of the **master** database after you have completed the changes.

Recovery Model Options

Microsoft provides three standard recovery models (the default model is Full). These differ in terms of availability, recoverability, and optimization of file space during operation. New databases have the same recovery model as the **modal** database by default.

 Some exam scenarios require an understanding of the recoverability of the three recovery models, so be sure to review these before taking the exam.

The three recovery models are as follows:

➤ *Simple*—A simple backup of database files:

  ➤ Uses Full and Differential (optional) backup types.

  ➤ Does not allow Transaction Log, File, and File Differential backups.

  ➤ Can only be recovered to the last database backup and cannot recover recent transactional changes.

  ➤ Can be scheduled to avoid affecting performance while minimizing the amount of data that could be lost.

  ➤ Is not considered adequate for production environments.

➤ *Full*—The most flexible database recovery model:

  ➤ Uses Full, Differential (optional), and Transaction Log backups.

  ➤ Can recover to a specified point in time.

  ➤ Logs every action including bulk transactions individually, thus creating a very high log storage overhead.

  ➤ Is the default for the **modal** database after installation.

➤ *Bulk-logged*—A complete recovery model with minimal bulk-transaction logging:

> ➤ Uses Full, Differential (optional), and Transaction Log backups.

> ➤ Allows recovery to the end of the last Transaction Log backup.

> ➤ Minimally logs bulk transactions (such as **SELECT INTO, BULK IN-SERT, CREATE INDEX**) to reduce log storage requirements during bulk operations.

Changing the Recovery Model

The recovery model can be changed during database operation, allowing such options as the Full recovery model except during periods of bulk transactions. To change the recovery model using the Enterprise Manager, take the following steps:

1. Open the SQL Server 2000 Enterprise Manager by selecting Start|Programs |Microsoft SQL Server|Enterprise Manager.

2. In the left panel, expand the desired server group by clicking the plus (+) sign.

3. Expand the configuration on the desired server by clicking the plus sign next to it, and enter authentication information if required.

4. Expand the Databases folder by clicking the plus sign next to it.

5. Select the database to be modified by right-clicking the mouse. Select Properties from the drop-down menu.

6. Select the Options tab, and select the desired recovery model from the pull-down list (see Figure 8.1).

7. Click OK to apply the change.

> ➤ The recovery model may be changed during bulk operations. Bulk-logging of the operation changes when the recovery model is changed.

Database Backups

Database and transaction log files can be backed up using either the Enterprise Manager or the Query Analyzer command-line interface. The required types of backup vary according to the recovery model chosen, because the Simple model does not support Transaction Log backups.

SQL Server 2000 allows information to be backed up to file, tape, or named pipe destinations. Files may be located on local or network shares, although network performance may be affected during backup in the latter case. Tapes and other forms of removable storage are easily moved to an offsite location, improving

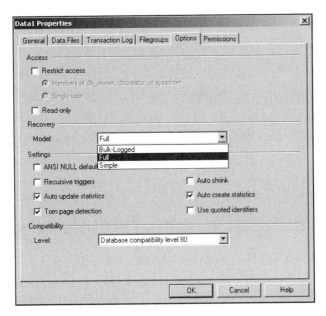

Figure 8.1   The Options tab of database Properties shows recovery model options.

recoverability in the event of catastrophic failure. Named pipe destinations allow backups to centralized solutions such as tape silos, which are useful in large enterprise backup scenarios.

Performing a Full Backup

A Full backup creates a copy of all database data. This is the most time-consuming and resource-intensive backup type. Adequate file storage must be available to store all data in the database. To back up a Full database using the Enterprise Manager, take the following steps:

1. Open the SQL Server 2000 Enterprise Manager by selecting Start|Programs |Microsoft SQL Server|Enterprise Manager.

2. In the left panel, expand the desired server group by clicking the plus sign.

3. Expand the configuration on the desired server by clicking the plus sign next to it, and enter authentication information if required.

4. Expand the Databases folder by clicking the plus sign next to it.

5. Select the database to be modified by right-clicking the mouse. Select All Tasks and then Backup Database from the drop-down menu to open the Backup Database screen (see Figure 8.2).

6. Give the backup a meaningful name and description, select Backup type (in this example, Full), and select the proper destination for the backup. Click Add to open the Backup Destination screen, where you can add a new destination to the list.

➤ You can select backup options from the Options tab, such as verification after the backup is complete. This assures you that the backup was successful, but it extends the time required to complete the backup.

7. Select a backup device from the pull-down list or specify a file destination for the backup in the appropriate box. Click OK to add the new destination and return to the Backup Database screen.

8. On the Backup Database screen, you can select a schedule for this backup specification by selecting the Schedule checkbox. Click Details to the right of the schedule text box to open the Edit Recurring Job Schedule screen (see Figure 8.3).

9. Click OK to apply the change and return to the Database Backup screen.

10. After all information is correct on the Database Backup screen, click OK to execute the backup or schedule it for execution.

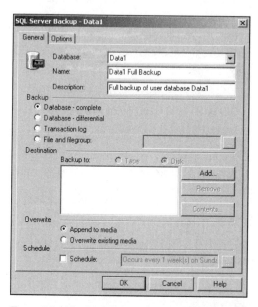

Figure 8.2 The Backup Database screen shows that no schedule or destination is specified.

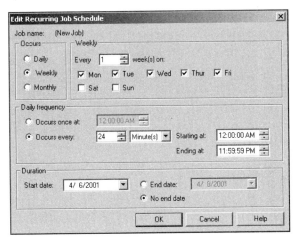

Figure 8.3   The Edit Recurring Job Schedule screen shows a Monday through Friday schedule every 24 minutes without a specified end date.

Performing a Differential Backup

A Differential backup creates a copy of all database data that has changed since the last Full backup. This backup type allows for a more rapid, smaller (in terms of space utilization) backup, but it does not provide all of the information necessary for a database restoration. A Full backup is required in addition to the most recent Differential backup to restore a database. To back up a Differential database using the Enterprise Manager, take the following steps:

1. Open the SQL Server 2000 Enterprise Manager by selecting Start|Programs |Microsoft SQL Server|Enterprise Manager.

2. In the left panel, expand the desired server group by clicking the plus sign.

3. Expand the configuration on the desired server by clicking the plus sign next to it, and enter authentication information if required.

4. Expand the Databases folder by clicking the plus sign next to it.

5. Select the database to be modified by right-clicking the mouse. Select All Tasks and then Backup Database from the drop-down menu to open the Backup Database screen.

6. Give the backup a meaningful name and description, select Backup type (in this example, Differential), and select the proper destination for the backup. Click Add to open the Backup Destination screen where you can add a new destination to the list.

➤ Because you will generally do multiple Differential backups between Full backups, choose names that identify the most recent for recovery purposes.

7. To create a schedule for this backup specification, select the Schedule checkbox, and click Details to the right of the schedule text box to open the Edit Recurring Job Schedule screen.

8. After all information is correct on the Backup Database screen, click OK to execute the backup or schedule it for execution.

Performing a Transaction Log Backup

To recover a very recent transaction, you must perform a Transaction Log backup under the Full and Bulk-logged recovery models. Transaction Log backups do not provide all of the information necessary for a database restoration. A Full backup and the most recent Differential backup are required to restore a database, in addition to any Transaction Log backups used in the recovery of the most recent transactions. To back up a Transaction Log using the Enterprise Manager, take the following steps:

1. Open the SQL Server 2000 Enterprise Manager by selecting Start|Programs|Microsoft SQL Server|Enterprise Manager.

2. In the left panel, expand the desired server group by clicking the plus sign.

3. Expand the configuration on the desired server by clicking the plus sign next to it, and enter authentication information if required.

4. Expand the Databases folder by clicking the plus sign next to it.

5. Select the database to be modified by right-clicking the mouse. Select All Tasks and then Backup Database from the drop-down menu to open the Backup Database screen.

6. Give the backup a meaningful name and description, select Backup type (in this example, Transaction Log), and select the proper destination for the backup. Click Add to open the Backup Destination screen where you can add a new destination to the list.

➤ Because you will generally do multiple Transaction Log backups between database backups, choose names that identify the most recent for recovery purposes.

➤ Selecting the Append to Existing Media option works well if the storage destination has sufficient capacity for multiple backups.

7. To create a schedule for this backup specification, select the Schedule checkbox, and click Details to the right of the schedule text box to open the Edit Recurring Job Schedule screen.

8. After all information is correct on the Backup Database screen, click OK to execute the backup or schedule it for execution.

Performing a File or Filegroup Backup

Backing up a very large database can place a heavy load on system resources. At times, it is better to back up a single file or filegroup. SQL Server 2000 has added this capability under both the Full and Bulk-logged recovery models. This backup type allows for a more rapid, smaller (in terms of space utilization) backup, but it does not provide all of the information necessary for a database restoration, only for the restoration of the specified file or filegroup. To back up a file or filegroup database using the Enterprise Manager, take the following steps:

1. Open the SQL Server 2000 Enterprise Manager by selecting Start|Programs |Microsoft SQL Server|Enterprise Manager.

2. In the left panel, expand the desired server group by clicking the plus sign.

3. Expand the configuration on the desired server by clicking the plus sign next to it, and enter authentication information if required.

4. Expand the Databases folder by clicking the plus sign next to it.

5. Select the database to be modified by right-clicking the mouse. Select All Tasks and then Backup Database from the drop-down menu to open the Backup Database screen.

6. Give the backup a meaningful name and description, select Backup type (in this example, File and Filegroup), and click Details to the right of the File and Filegroup text box to open the Filegroups and Files screen.

7. Select the desired filegroups or files, and click OK to return to the Backup Databases screen (see Figure 8.4).

8. Select the proper destination for the backup. Click Add to open the Backup Destination screen where you can add a new destination to the list.

9. To create a schedule for this backup specification, select the Schedule checkbox, and click Details to the right of the schedule text box to open the Edit Recurring Job Schedule screen.

10. After all information is correct on the Backup Database screen, click OK to execute the backup or schedule it for execution.

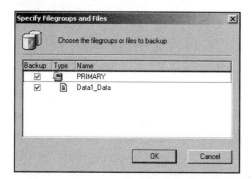

Figure 8.4 The Specify Filegroups And Files screen shows the PRIMARY filegroup and its subfile selected.

Database Restoration

The unthinkable has happened. All of your data was lost when a pipe burst and turned your server room into an aquarium. You have rebuilt the server and reinstalled SQL Server 2000. Now you are ready to restore the database files and transaction logs. Fortunately, the backups were moved offsite just before disaster struck, so very little information was lost. The restoration order varies according to the recovery model that you choose, but you generally follow these steps:

1. Restore the hardware to full operation.

2. Restore the software and all patches, service packs, and updates.

3. Perform the recovery of the **master, msdb, modal,** and **distribution** system databases.

   ➤ You may not have to restore a **distribution** system database because it is used for replication and synchronization events. It is not included in a single-server backup situation.

   ➤ You do not have to restore the **tempdb** database because it is recreated each time that an instance of SQL Server 2000 is restarted and is not backed up.

4. Restart the instance after recovering the **master** database.

5. Restore the most recent Full database backup.

6. Restore the most recent Differential backup (if used).

7. Apply all Transaction Log backups since the most recent database backup in order.

8. Repeat Steps 4 through 7 for each additional user database.

Network performance may be affected during restoration from a remote location, so try to schedule restorations during low-use times if possible.

Performing Database Restorations

The Simple recovery model involves only Full and Differential (optional) database backup types. Any data following the last backup is lost if a full restoration is required. Both the Full and Bulk-logged recovery models enable you to restore additional transactions present in the Transaction Log backups made since the last database backup.

 If one of the Transaction Log files is corrupted or lost, recovery may only be possible up to the last Transaction Log backup in sequence before the missing or damaged one. A restoration cannot skip to the next Transaction Log backup.

To restore a database using the most recent backups and the Enterprise Manager utility, take the following steps:

1. Open the SQL Server 2000 Enterprise Manager by selecting Start|Programs |Microsoft SQL Server|Enterprise Manager.

2. In the left panel, expand the desired server group by clicking the plus sign.

3. Expand the configuration on the desired server by clicking the plus sign next to it, and enter authentication information if required.

4. Expand the Databases folder by clicking the plus sign next to it.

5. Select the database to be recovered by right-clicking the mouse. Select All Tasks and then Restore Database from the drop-down menu to open the Restore Database screen.

6. Specify the restoration destination if an alternate destination is desired, the restoration type (in this example, Database) and select any applicable files if you do not want to use the default files already selected for the restoration (see Figure 8.5).

    ➤ If an alternative source device is to be used, select the From Device option and select the appropriate share and files.

    ➤ If you are performing a Full recovery mode restoration, you can select the Point in Time Restore option to recover that data up to a particular time.

7. After all information is correct on the Restore Database screen, click OK to execute the restoration.

Figure 8.5 The Restore Database screen shows the selection of the most recent Full, Differential, and Transaction Log backups of the **Data1** user database.

Filegroup and File Restoration

At times, you may want to restore only a single file or filegroup rather than to perform a full database recovery. To restore a file or filegroup from a previous file or filegroup backup using the Enterprise Manager utility, take the following steps:

1. Open the SQL Server 2000 Enterprise Manager by selecting Start|Programs |Microsoft SQL Server|Enterprise Manager.

2. In the left panel, expand the desired server group by clicking the plus sign.

3. Expand the configuration on the desired server by clicking the plus sign next to it, and enter authentication information if required.

4. Expand the Databases folder by clicking the plus sign next to it.

5. Select the database to be recovered by right-clicking the mouse. Select All Tasks and then Restore Database from the drop-down menu to open the Restore Database screen.

6. Specify the restoration destination if an alternate destination is desired, the restoration type (in this example, Filegroups Or Files), and the files or filegroups available from the backup (see Figure 8.6).

7. After all information is correct on the Restore Database screen, click OK to execute the restoration.

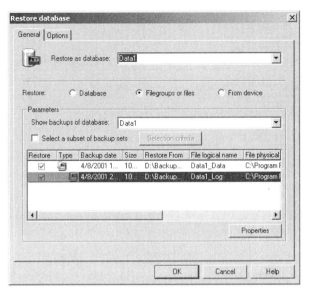

Figure 8.6 The Restore Database screen shows the Primary Filegroup backup of the **Data1** user database selected.

Creating a Standby Server

Using the backup and restore functions, you can create a standby server. Unlike the failover clustering solution discussed in Chapter 4, a standby server must be manually activated if the primary server fails. Standby servers are often configured as read-only access options during Full recovery on a failed primary server.

A cold standby server requires manual actions to maintain synchronization with the primary, whereas a warm standby server is maintained automatically. The use of Log Shipping to maintain a warm standby server is covered in Chapter 12.

Creating a Cold Standby Server

Creating a standby server requires the configuration and installation of an identical server. SQL Server 2000 must be installed using the same configuration as the primary server, including code page and collation settings. After this has been completed, you can create a cold standby server by taking the following steps:

1. Back up all of the databases on the primary server.

2. Restore the databases on the standby server by specifying a different restore location and directing the restore to the local (standby) server.

3. Perform regular synchronization by applying the Transaction Log backups from the primary server.

If the primary server fails, you can make the standby server available to users by taking the following steps:

1. Apply the most recent Transaction Log backups to the standby server.

2. Rename the primary server, and remove it from the network.

3. Rename the secondary server as the original primary server.

4. Restart the server to refresh all configuration information.

5. Check connections to the new primary server.

6. Begin repairing the original primary server.

After you have completed the repairs, use the same process in reverse to restore all functions to the original primary server.

Practice Questions

Question 1

> Which of the following are primary backup types within SQL Server 2000?
> [Check all correct answers]
>
> ❑ a. Differential
>
> ❑ b. Full
>
> ❑ c. **master**
>
> ❑ d. **msdb**
>
> ❑ e. System
>
> ❑ f. Restoration
>
> ❑ g. Transaction Log

Answers a, b, and g are correct. The three primary backup types within SQL Server 2000 are Full, Differential, and Transaction Log. Answers c and d are incorrect because **master** and **msdb** are system databases, not backup types. Answers e and f are incorrect because there are no system or restoration backup types.

Question 2

> Which of the following are recovery models used within SQL Server 2000?
> [Check all correct answers]
>
> ❑ a. Backup
>
> ❑ b. Bulk-logged
>
> ❑ c. Complex
>
> ❑ d. Full
>
> ❑ e. **modal**
>
> ❑ f. Recovery
>
> ❑ g. Simple

Answers b, d, and g are correct. The three recovery models within SQL Server 2000 are Simple, Full, and Bulk-logged. Answers a and f are incorrect because backup and recovery are operations performed relating to disaster recovery, not recovery model options. Answer c is incorrect because there is no Complex recovery model. Answer e is incorrect because **modal** is one of the system databases, not a recovery model.

Question 3

Several backup types are available within SQL Server 2000:

    Full backups

    Differential backups

    Transaction Log backups

Match the following characteristics with the appropriate backup type (some may be used more than once):

    Allows for point-in-time recovery

    Backup of changed data since the last complete backup

    Complete backup of database files

    Does not back up log files

    Optional backup type

    Requires other backup files to restore a backup

    Serial backup of transactions since the last database backup

---

The correct answers are:

Full backups

    Complete backup of database files

    Does not back up log files

Differential backups

    Backup of changed data since the last complete backup

    Does not back up log files

    Optional backup type

    Requires other backup files to restore a backup

Transaction Log backups

    Allows for point-in-time recovery

    Requires other backup files to restore a backup

    Serial backup of transactions since the last database backup

Question 4

> Which of the following backup types are available within the Simple recovery model? [Check all correct answers]
>
> ❑ a. Differential
>
> ❑ b. File
>
> ❑ c. Filegroup
>
> ❑ d. Full
>
> ❑ e. Transaction Log

Answers a and d are correct. Full and Differential backups may be created within the Simple recovery model. Answers b, c, and e are incorrect because the Simple recovery model does not provide backup of files, filegroups, or transaction logs.

Question 5

> Several recovery models are available within SQL Server 2000:
>
> Simple
>
> Full
>
> Bulk-logged
>
> Match the following characteristics with the appropriate backup type (some may be used more than once):
>
> Allows for file and filegroup backups
>
> Allows the recovery of recent transactions using Transaction Log backups
>
> Logs every action including bulk transactions individually and has very high log storage requirements
>
> Can only be recovered to the last database backup
>
> Can utilize the optional Differential backup type
>
> Not considered adequate for production environments
>
> Utilizes the Full backup type
>
> Utilizes the Transaction Log backup type

The correct answers are:

Simple

> Can only be recovered to the last database backup
>
> Can utilize the optional Differential backup type
>
> Not considered adequate for production environments
>
> Utilizes the Full backup type

Full

> Allows for file and filegroup backups
>
> Allows the recovery of recent transactions using Transaction Log backups
>
> Logs every action including bulk transactions individually and has very high log storage requirements.
>
> Can utilize the optional Differential backup type
>
> Utilizes the Full backup type
>
> Utilizes the Transaction Log backup type

Bulk-logged

> Allows for file and filegroup backups
>
> Allows the recovery of recent transactions using Transaction Log backups
>
> Can utilize the optional Differential backup type
>
> Utilizes the Full backup type
>
> Utilizes the Transaction Log backup type

Question 6

You have created a user database **SalesData** using the default recovery model assigned to the **modal** database during installation. The **SalesData** database is used for OLTP operations normally, except during a six-hour period each Sunday morning used for bulk updates to pricing field values. You must remember to pause the SQL Server 2000 instance during the change in recovery model before and after the bulk-update period.

○ a. True

○ b. False

Answer b is correct. The recovery model may be changed while the database is in operation.

Question 7

> Several steps are required to replace a failed primary server with a cold standby server. Arrange the following steps in the proper order:
>
>> Apply the most recent Transaction Log backups to the standby server.
>>
>> Begin the repair of the original primary server.
>>
>> Check connections to the new primary server.
>>
>> Rename the secondary server as the original primary server.
>>
>> Rename the primary server, and remove it from the network.
>>
>> Restart the server to refresh all configuration information.

The correct answer is:

Apply the most recent Transaction Log backups to the standby server.

Rename the primary server, and remove it from the network.

Rename the secondary server as the original primary server.

Restart the server to refresh all configuration information.

Check connections to the new primary server.

Begin the repair of the original primary server.

Question 8

> Several backups of the **Employees** database have been enacted within the
> Full recovery model. Which of these files should be used to perform a com-
> plete recovery of the database through 4:00 PM? [Check all correct answers]
>
> ❑ a. Full backup at 2:00 AM
>
> ❑ b. Differential backup at 4:00 AM
>
> ❑ c. Transaction Log backup at 6:00 AM
>
> ❑ d. Full backup at 8:00 AM
>
> ❑ e. Differential backup at 10:00 AM
>
> ❑ f. Differential backup at 12:00 PM
>
> ❑ g. Transaction Log backup at 2:00 PM
>
> ❑ h. Transaction Log backup at 4:00 PM

Answers d, f, g, and h are correct. The latest Full backup must be installed, followed by the latest Differential backup and all Transaction Logs since the last
database backup applied to perform a complete recovery. Answers a, b, and c are
incorrect because files before the last Full backup are unnecessary. Answer e is
incorrect because only the last Differential backup is required. A Differential
backup saves all changes since the last Full backup, which means that the differential backup at 12:00 PM includes all information contained within the earlier
differential backup at 10:00 AM.

Question 9

> Which of the following recovery options are available within the Full recov-
> ery model? [Check all correct answers]
>
> ❑ a. Differential
>
> ❑ b. File
>
> ❑ c. Filegroup
>
> ❑ d. Full
>
> ❑ e. Point-in-time
>
> ❑ f. Transaction Log

Answers a, b, c, d, e, and f are all correct. The Full recovery model provides for all three primary backup types (Full, Differential, and Transaction Log) as well as file and filegroup restorations and point-in-time recovery.

Question 10

> Several backups of the **Employees** database have been enacted within the Full recovery model.
>
> - Full backup at 2:00 AM
> - Differential backup at 4:00 AM
> - Transaction Log backup at 6:00 AM
> - Full backup at 8:00 AM
> - Differential backup at 10:00 AM
> - Differential backup at 12:00 PM
> - Transaction Log backup at 2:00 PM
> - Transaction Log backup at 4:00 PM
>
> Physical damage to the tapes used in the 2:00 PM backup has rendered them unusable. What is the most current state recoverable?
>
> ○ a. 6:00 AM
> ○ b 8:00 AM
> ○ c. 10:00 AM
> ○ d. 12:00 PM
> ○ e. 4:00 PM

Answer d is correct. The last Differential backup after the most recent Full backup is the most current recoverable state. Answer a is incorrect because all backups before the most recent Full backup are not the most recent recoverable options. Answers b and c are incorrect because a more recent Differential backup exists from 12:00 PM. Answer e is incorrect because transaction logs after the damaged Transaction Log backup cannot be used.

Need to Know More?

 Dalton, Patrick, and Paul Whitehead. *SQL Server 2000 Black Book.* The Coriolis Group: Scottsdale, Arizona, 2001. ISBN 1-57610-770-1. An excellent reference to keep close at hand during installation of SQL Server 2000. This is a necessary book in any DBA's library, as it has many solutions to commonly experienced issues.

 Delaney, Kalen. *Inside Microsoft SQL Server 2000.* Microsoft Press: Redmond, WA, 2000. ISBN 0-7356-0998-5. A good review of SQL Server 2000 components including white papers and articles on a broad range of topics.

 Iseminger, David. *Microsoft SQL Server 2000 Reference Library with CD-ROM.* Microsoft Press: Redmond, WA, 2000. ISBN 0-7356-1280-3. An exhaustive library covering detailed information on all aspects of SQL Server 2000 implementations. A necessary reference for IT departments supporting Microsoft SQL Server 2000 implementations.

 Shapiro, Jeffrey. *SQL Server 2000—The Complete Reference.* Osborne/McGraw-Hill: Berkeley, CA, 2001. ISBN 0-07-212588-8. A detailed, if somewhat lengthy, reference for SQL Server 2000 administration.

 http://msdn.microsoft.com/library/default.asp?URL=/library/psdk/sql/portal_7ap1.htm. *Microsoft SQL Server 2000 Books Online.* A complete online copy of the documentation for SQL Server 2000. This is an SQL Server 2000 database administrator's best friend because it is included on the installation CD-ROM.

Troubleshooting
and Integrity Checking

. . . .

Terms you'll need to understand:

✓ Data integrity

✓ Foreign key

✓ Primary key

✓ Constraints

✓ Table integrity

✓ Type integrity

✓ Referential integrity

✓ Entity integrity

✓ Transaction integrity

✓ Check constraints

✓ Table relationships

✓ Cascading

✓ Orphaned records

✓ UNIQUE constraints

✓ Deadlocking

✓ Deadlock victim

✓ SQL Profiler

✓ DBCC statements

Techniques you'll need to master:

✓ Identifying the types of integrity found in database implementations

✓ Enforcing data integrity by the use of constraints and relationships

✓ Using SQL Server 2000 and Windows 2000 tools to troubleshoot transactions and perform integrity checks

✓ Performing system monitoring using the SQL Profiler, Enterprise Manager, and Transact-SQL (T-SQL) command-line actions

✓ Understanding and using **sp_action** and Database Console Commands (DBCC) T-SQL statements

An instance of SQL Server 2000 shared by multiple users requires maintenance to avoid conflicts arising from changes and updates enacted by several users simultaneously. Data integrity is a significant concern in database implementations that are undergoing a large number of transactions. Online Transaction Processing (OLTP) applications have thousands of transactions occurring each hour, and the sheer volume makes conflict resolution extremely important for the application's database server to continue functioning.

This chapter covers troubleshooting transactions and options for checking data integrity using the SQL Server Enterprise Manager or the SQL Query Analyzer for command-line actions. An instance of SQL Server 2000 must already be installed (see Chapters 4 and 5) on a Windows 2000 server platform. Additional references are listed at the end of this chapter.

Data Integrity

A database without structure is simply a large agglomeration of information—about as useful as a pile of 3x5 cards that are occasionally shuffled. The structure within SQL Server 2000 is provided by indexes (which serve the same role as a book index), proper table design, foreign and primary key relationships, data constraints, and coded business rules within an application itself. Following are some of the data integrity categories that must be considered:

➤ *Table integrity*—As the saying goes, "Garbage-in-garbage-out." If "bad" data is entered in a table or business rules are not sufficiently enforced, disallowed actions or inappropriate data may be input. Table integrity is violated if a transaction violates a business rule or if bad data (such as accidental entry of a name in a date field) is input. Coded business rules must be written to prevent such illegal operations.

➤ *Type integrity*—Type constraints are rules defining allowable data types for each field in a table. These constraints may specify that only numeric data may be input into a field, may include a list of allowable values, or may state whether a NULL value is allowed. If NULL values are not allowed in a field, a default value must be provided for a transaction to create a new record in the table. Proper use of the appropriate data type during table design is one method of avoiding this type of integrity violation.

➤ *Referential integrity*—Tables within a relational database management system such as SQL Server 2000 are related to each other by a series of shared keys. A customer ID may be a *primary key* in a **customers** table. This same customer ID may be a *foreign key* in an **invoices** table, thus relating invoice transactions to the appropriate customer for each table. Referential integrity is violated if a record that is used in both tables (for example, the **invoices** table and the **customers** table) is deleted from one but not the other. This type of integrity violation can be avoided if database constraints are included that require all related records to be removed when a record is deleted.

➤ *Entity integrity*—Entity constraints ensure that no two records in a table are identical. UNIQUE identity values require that each record has some value that differentiates it from all others even if the same entry is somehow enacted multiple times. Accidental reentries of a customer invoice without a timestamp or otherwise UNIQUE identifier for each record are an example of this type of integrity violation. UNIQUE or IDENTITY constraints avoid such integrity violations.

➤ *Transaction integrity*—Often, multiple steps must be performed in distributed applications or n-tier server implementations before a transaction is completed. If all steps are not completed, the transaction fails and must be rolled back. Only when all steps are completed should the entire transaction be rolled forward and applied. SQL Server 2000 automatically rolls back incomplete transactions caused by loss of connectivity or server function, such as in the event of a power failure. Coded business rules should also be written to prevent incomplete transactions from being applied to the database.

Enforcing Integrity

Coded business rules, constraints, check constraints, and relationships are important factors to consider in database planning and configuration for proper data integrity enforcement.

 Coded business rules and application actions are not the focus of this exam, but the use of relationship keys and constraints are important topics.

Constraints and relationships may be configured within SQL Server 2000 using both the graphical Enterprise Manager and the command-line SQL Query Analyzer using the **ALTER DATABASE** command. To create and alter these elements of integrity enforcement using the Enterprise Manager, take the following steps:

1. Open the SQL Server 2000 Enterprise Manager by selecting Start|Programs |Microsoft SQL Server|Enterprise Manager.

2. In the left panel, expand the desired server group by clicking the plus (+) sign.

3. Expand the configuration on the desired server by clicking the plus sign next to it, and enter authentication information if required.

4. Expand the desired database by clicking the plus sign next to it.

5. Expand the Tables node by clicking the plus sign next to it.

6. Select the appropriate table by right-clicking the mouse and choosing Design Table to open the Design Table screen. Select any of the three icons on the right of the taskbar to open the Properties screen (see Figure 9.1).

7. After selecting the proper tab on the Properties screen, you can begin creating the appropriate element, as detailed in the following sections.

Creating Table Relationships

Existing relationships may be edited or deleted and new relationships created on the Relationships tab of the Properties screen (see Figure 9.2).

You can establish a new relationship by selecting the Primary key from the Primary key table and its related Foreign key in the Foreign key table. Several options are available, including the ability to *cascade* (or implement through all related files) all of the changes and deletions in related field values and records.

Cascaded updates cause all Foreign key related field values to change when the Primary key value is changed. Cascaded deletions cause all related records to be deleted when the Primary record is deleted, thus avoiding the creation of

Figure 9.1   The Design Table screen shows the taskbar icon used for relationship management.

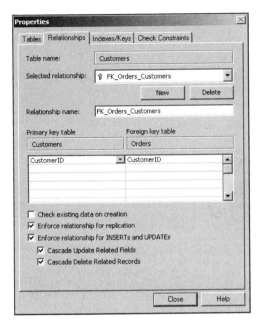

Figure 9.2   The Relationships tab on the Properties screen is used to create a relationship using the CustID key, in this example configured to cascade record deletion and update related field values.

orphaned records (records that reference deleted related records) in violation of referential integrity.

After changes have been completed, click Close to close the Properties editing screen.

Creating a UNIQUE Constraint

The UNIQUE constraint can be enacted on the Indexes/Keys tab of the Properties screen (see Figure 9.3). The Fill Factor option in the figure specifies the amount of space that will be taken up in the new index by information already present and is expressed as a percentage. The Create as Clustered option allows the table data to be reorganized according to the clustered index order (see Chapter 6 for more information about clustered indexes).

Selecting the appropriate field within the table and then selecting the Create UNIQUE and Constraint options establishes a new UNIQUE constraint.

After changes have been completed, click Close to close the Properties editing screen.

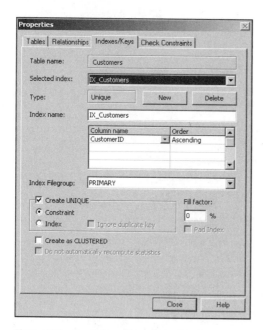

Figure 9.3 The Indexes/Keys tab on the Properties screen shows a new UNIQUE constraint on the CustomerID field.

Creating Check Constraint

Other constraints can be used to check input data before a record is created or updates are completed. Check constraints ensure that data values are allowable or properly formatted. Check constraints are established on the Check Constraints tab of the Properties screen (see Figure 9.4).

Construction of the constraint expression provides logical testing capability as well as format testing. This type of constraint is used to avoid the input of garbage data into a table and ensures uniformity of input for later data comparison and sorting.

After changes have been completed, click Close to close the Properties editing screen.

Deadlocking

When several users must access data, perform updates, and import data into tables, the data must be protected to avoid the possibility of conflicting updates to the same fields.

SQL Server 2000 prevents simultaneous updates by locking the record so that only one change action can occur at a time. When a record is locked, additional updates cannot be made until the lock is released. If other updates are pending the actions of the first update, they are queued until the first locking contention is resolved.

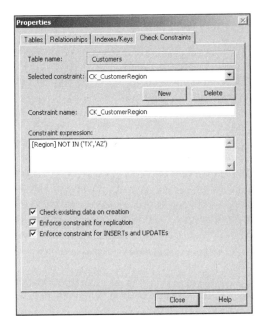

Figure 9.4   The Check Constraints tab on the Properties screen shows that the Customer Region values are not Arizona (AZ) or Texas (TX).

A *deadlock* occurs if two processes are pending the actions of each other at the same time. For example, process B may be awaiting the release of a lock imposed by process A, while process A is awaiting the release of a lock imposed by process B. Neither process can be resolved, which consumes resources and also block other transactions from being completed.

When circular locking of this type occurs, SQL Server 2000 creates a lock monitor process, called an *eager deadlock search*. This thread eventually traces the activity to the deadlock and selects one process as the *deadlock victim*, which is aborted with an error message returned to the calling application. This enables the other process to be completed. The error message (1205) displayed is:

```
Your transaction (process ID #100) was deadlocked on {lock |
    communication buffer | thread} resources with another
    process and has been chosen as the deadlock victim. Rerun
    your transaction.
```

SQL Server 2000 selects the deadlock victim by determining the least expensive process in terms of resource utilization.

Monitoring Transactions and Data Integrity

SQL Server 2000 and Windows 2000 provide a number of tools for monitoring transactions and data integrity. These include the following:

➤ *SQL Profiler*—A graphical tool that allows the monitoring and logging of events within an instance of SQL Server 2000. Each trace can quickly become very large, so you should monitor system resources carefully during SQL Profiler trace activity, just as with any type of constant logging. SQL Profiler provides filtering options to extract useful subsets of monitored data.

➤ *System Monitor*—A graphical tool that allows the monitoring and logging of system resources and process activities, accessed within the Windows 2000 Performance Console. As with SQL Profiler traces, System Monitor logs can rapidly grow in size.

➤ *Error logs*—Events within SQL Server 2000 generate items in the Windows 2000 application event log when errors occur. When you are attempting to determine the source and type of errors that have occurred, this is a good location for reference.

➤ *Enterprise Manager*—The Enterprise Manager graphical utility provides a great deal of information that is useful in monitoring and resolving conflicts. The Current Activity and Database Usage windows provide a wealth of information necessary for the proper maintenance of your database.

➤ *Transact-SQL (T-SQL)*—The command-line options in this utility provide similar information to that available via the Enterprise Manager. User activity, current locking actions, database space usage, and many other functions provide information on the current status of the database.

➤ *DBCC statements*—Database Console Commands (DBCC) are a subset of the command-line options. These statements provide access to a variety of maintenance, status, validation, and other tasks necessary for the proper maintenance of your SQL Server instance.

For the exam, you should be most familiar with these monitoring tools: SQL Profiler, Enterprise Manager, T-SQL command-line actions, and DBCC statements.

Monitoring with SQL Profiler

The SQL Profiler is a graphical tool accessed within the Enterprise Manager. Each trace may monitor events selected by the database administrator and saved to an external file or to a trace table within the database. To avoid overrunning all available space, the SQL Profiler will not execute if less than 10MB of drive space remains free or if the amount of available drive space drops below 10MB.

To open the SQL Profiler tool, take the following steps:

1. Open the SQL Server 2000 Enterprise Manager by selecting Start|Programs |Microsoft SQL Server|Enterprise Manager.

2. From the Tools pull-down menu, select SQL Profiler.

3. Open the Trace Properties screen by selecting New from the File pull-down menu.

4. On the General tab, give the trace a meaningful name, select the appropriate template file previously saved with the .tdf file extension, configure a trace destination for the file or table storage, and configure the time restrictions (see Figure 9.5).

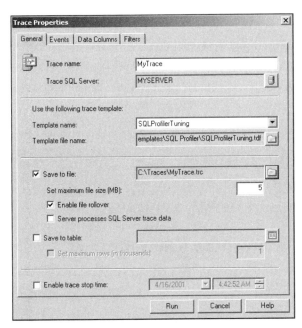

Figure 9.5   The General tab on the Trace Properties screen shows that trace information for MyTrace is to be stored in the file, C:\Traces\MyTrace.trc.

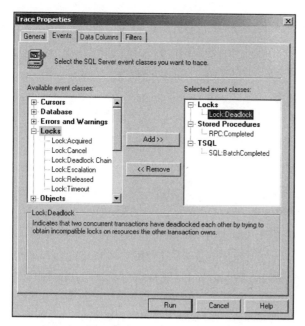

Figure 9.6   The Events tab on the Trace Properties screen for MyTrace shows that the Lock: Deadlock Event is added to those to be monitored by the trace.

5. On the Events tab, configure any additional events to be monitored by the trace (see Figure 9.6).

6. Configure the data columns to be included in the trace and any filters to be used on the appropriate tabs. Click Run to start the trace.

   The SQL Profiler trace displays a real-time series of event notifications, which provides additional information related to each action (see Figure 9.7). This trace file can be reopened later to view past trace data.

7. Configure the data columns to be included in the trace and any filters to be used on the appropriate tabs. Click Run to start the trace.

Monitoring with the Enterprise Manager

The Enterprise Manager graphical utility provides a great deal of information about database usage and current activity.

Database Usage

To examine database usage at a glance, take the following steps:

1. Open the SQL Server 2000 Enterprise Manager by selecting Start|Programs |Microsoft SQL Server|Enterprise Manager.

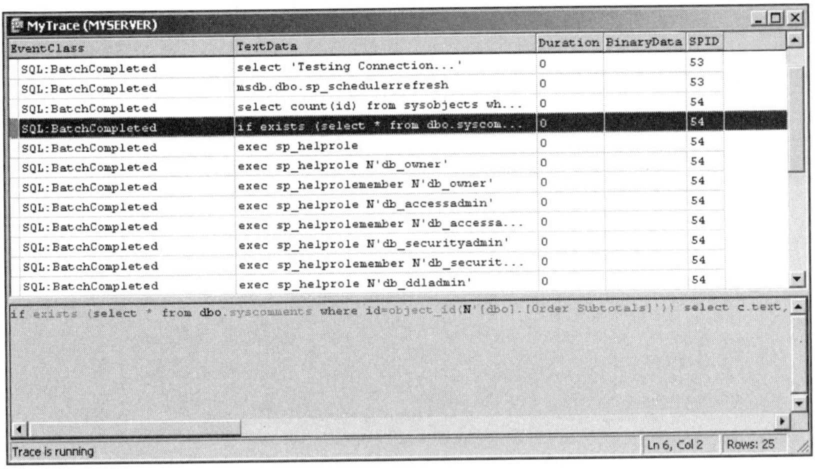

EventClass	TextData	Duration	BinaryData	SPID
SQL:BatchCompleted	select 'Testing Connection...'	0		53
SQL:BatchCompleted	msdb.dbo.sp_schedulerrefresh	0		53
SQL:BatchCompleted	select count(id) from sysobjects wh...	0		54
SQL:BatchCompleted	if exists (select * from dbo.syscom...	0		54
SQL:BatchCompleted	exec sp_helprole	0		54
SQL:BatchCompleted	exec sp_helprole N'db_owner'	0		54
SQL:BatchCompleted	exec sp_helprolemember N'db_owner'	0		54
SQL:BatchCompleted	exec sp_helprole N'db_accessadmin'	0		54
SQL:BatchCompleted	exec sp_helprolemember N'db_accessa...	0		54
SQL:BatchCompleted	exec sp_helprole N'db_securityadmin'	0		54
SQL:BatchCompleted	exec sp_helprolemember N'db_securit...	0		54
SQL:BatchCompleted	exec sp_helprole N'db_ddladmin'	0		54

`if exists (select * from dbo.syscomments where id=object_id(N'[dbo].[Order Subtotals]')) select c.text,`

Trace is running   Ln 6, Col 2   Rows: 25

Figure 9.7   The SQL Profiler MyTrace screen displays additional event information about a trace.

2. In the left panel, expand the desired server group by clicking the plus sign.

3. Expand the configuration on the desired server by clicking the plus sign next to it, and enter authentication information if required.

4. Expand the Databases folder by clicking the plus sign next to it.

5. Select the appropriate database, and select View|Taskpad to bring up the Taskpad view of database space usage (see Figure 9.8).

Current Activity

To observe current activity including ongoing processes, locks, and other transaction information, take the following steps:

1. Open the SQL Server 2000 Enterprise Manager by selecting Start|Programs |Microsoft SQL Server|Enterprise Manager.

2. In the left panel, expand the desired server group by clicking the plus sign.

3. Expand the configuration on the desired server by clicking the plus sign next to it, and enter authentication information if required.

4. Expand the Management folder by clicking the plus sign next to it.

5. Expand the Current Activity node by clicking the plus sign next to it, and select the subnode for the appropriate type of activity to monitor (see Figure 9.9).

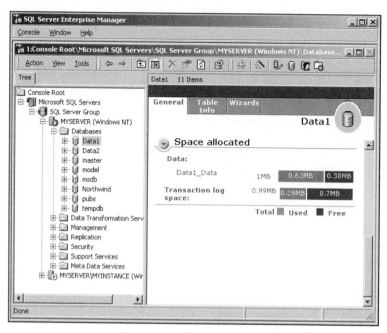

Figure 9.8   The General tab on the Taskpad screen for the **Data1** user database shows Space Allocated information.

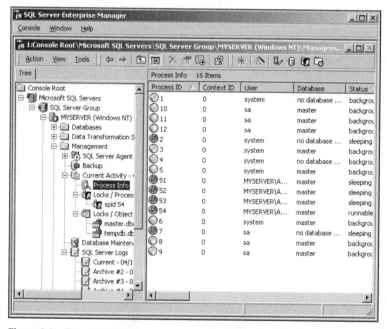

Figure 9.9   The subnode Process Info under the Current Activity node displays detailed information about ongoing processes, locks, and other transactions.

Monitoring with Transact-SQL (T-SQL)

A wide variety of T-SQL commands can be used to monitor and resolve transaction and integrity issues. To access the Query Analyzer within the Enterprise Manager, take the following steps:

1. Open the SQL Server 2000 Enterprise Manager by selecting Start|Programs |Microsoft SQL Server|Enterprise Manager.

2. In the left panel, expand the desired server group by clicking the plus sign.

3. Click on the desired server, and select View|Taskpad to see an overview of its characteristics, entering authentication information if required.

4. On the Wizards tab, under the General heading, select the Run SQL Query Analyzer option.

5. After the SQL Query Analyzer has opened, execute the appropriate command-line processes (see Figure 9.10).

sp_lock

The **sp_lock** statement reports information about current transaction locks. The syntax of the **sp_lock** statement is:

```
sp_lock [[@spid1 =] 'spid1'] [,[@spid2 =] 'spid2']
```

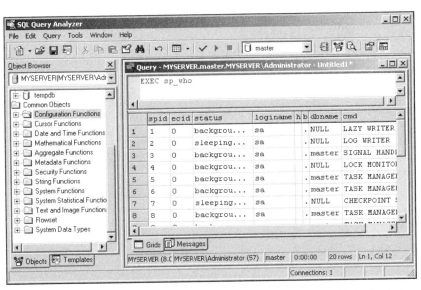

Figure 9.10   The SQL Query Analyzer screen shows the **sp_who** command being invoked.

Locking information is returned about the SQL Server process with ID number 'spid1' (obtained by an **sp_who**). If no process ID number is specified, SQL Server will display information about all locks.

sp_monitor

The **sp_monitor** statement displays statistics and activity since the last time **sp_monitor** was enacted. This includes CPU and I/O usage statistics as well as idle time and other information. The syntax of the **sp_monitor** statement is:

```
sp_monitor
```

sp_spaceused

The **sp_spaceused** statement reports the current disk space usage for a database or table. The syntax of the **sp_spaceused** statement is:

```
sp_spaceused [[@objname =] 'objname']
    [,[@updateusage =] 'updateusage']
```

sp_who

The **sp_who** statement reports information about current users and processes. The syntax of the **sp_who** statement is:

```
sp_who [[@login_name =] 'login']
```

DBCC Statements

Database Console Commands (DBCC) statements are a very important subset of command-line maintenance actions that allow verification of the physical and logical consistency of the database. To access the Query Analyzer from within the Enterprise Manager, take the following steps:

1. Open the SQL Server 2000 Enterprise Manager by selecting Start|Programs |Microsoft SQL Server|Enterprise Manager.

2. In the left panel, expand the desired server group by clicking the plus sign.

3 Click on the desired server, and select View|Taskpad to see an overview of its characteristics, entering authentication information if required.

4. On the Wizards tab, under the General heading, select the Run SQL Query Analyzer option.

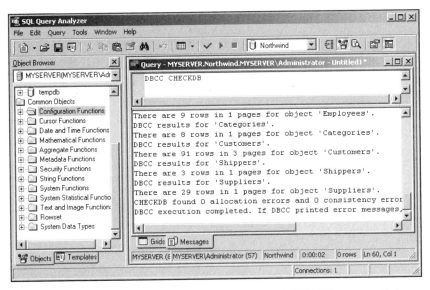

Figure 9.11 The SQL Query Analyzer screen shows the **DBCC CHECKDB** command being invoked.

5. After the SQL Query Analyzer has opened, execute the appropriate DBCC command-line processes (see Figure 9.11).

The DBCC commands are grouped into four categories: Maintenance, Status, Validation, and Miscellaneous (see Table 9.1).

 The Status and Validation DBCC statements are most often found on the exam.

Table 9.1	DBCC statement categories.
Category	**Use**
Maintenance	Maintenance tasks on tables, filegroups, or databases
Status	Status checks
Validation	Validation tasks on tables, indexes, catalogs, filegroups, or databases
Miscellaneous	Other maintenance tasks and backward-compatibility holdovers

Maintenance DBCC Statements

The Maintenance DBCC statements provide command-line access to basic database maintenance functions.

DBCC DBREINDEX

The **DBCC DBREINDEX** statement rebuilds indexes for a table in the specified database. The syntax of the **DBCC DBREINDEX** statement is:

```
DBCC DBREINDEX
    (    [ 'database.owner.table_name'
            [ , index_name
                [ , fillfactor ]
            ]
        ]
    )    [ WITH NO_INFOMSGS ]
```

DBCC DBREPAIR

The **DBCC DBREPAIR** statement is included for backward compatibility. **DROP DATABASE** should be used instead of this command in order to remove an existing database.

DBCC INDEXDEFRAG

This **DBCC INDEXDEFRAG** statement defragments indexes of the specified table or view. The syntax of the **DBCC INDEXDEFRAG** statement is:

```
DBCC INDEXDEFRAG
    ( { database_name | database_id | 0 }
        , { table_name | table_id | 'view_name' | view_id }
        , { index_name | index_id }
    )    [ WITH NO_INFOMSGS ]
```

DBCC SHRINKDATABASE

The **DBCC SHRINKDATABASE** statement shrinks the size of the data files in a database. The syntax of the **DBCC SHRINKDATABASE** statement is:

```
DBCC SHRINKDATABASE
    ( database_name [ , target_percent ]
        [ , { NOTRUNCATE | TRUNCATEONLY } ]
    )
```

DBCC SHRINKFILE

The **DBCC SHRINKFILE** statement is similar to **DBCC SHRINKDATABASE**, but it operates at the file level to shrink the size of the specified data file or log file for a database. The syntax of the **DBCC SHRINKFILE** statement is:

```
DBCC SHRINKFILE
    ( { file_name | file_id }
        { [ , target_size ]
            | [ , { EMPTYFILE | NOTRUNCATE | TRUNCATEONLY } ]
        }
    )
```

DBCC UPDATEUSAGE

The **DBCC UPDATEUSAGE** statement reports and corrects errors in the **sysindexes** table, which could cause incorrect reporting of space usage by the **sp_spaceused** stored procedure. The syntax of the **DBCC UPDATEUSAGE** statement is:

```
DBCC UPDATEUSAGE
    (    { 'database_name' | 0 }
        [ , { 'table_name' | 'view_name' }
        [ , { index_id | 'index_name' } ] ]
    )
    [ WITH    [ COUNT_ROWS ] [ , NO_INFOMSGS ]
        ]
```

Status DBCC Statements

The Status DBCC statements provide access to information necessary for the continued maintenance of a database.

DBCC INPUTBUFFER

The **DBCC INPUTBUFFER** statement displays the last statement sent from a client application. The syntax of the **DBCC INPUTBUFFER** statement is:

```
DBCC INPUTBUFFER (spid)
```

DBCC OPENTRAN

The **DBCC OPENTRAN** statement displays information about the oldest active transaction within a database. The syntax of the **DBCC OPENTRAN** statement is:

```
DBCC OPENTRAN
    (    { 'database_name' | database_id} )
        [ WITH TABLERESULTS
            [ , NO_INFOMSGS ]
        ]
```

DBCC OUTPUTBUFFER

The **DBCC OUTPUTBUFFER** statement returns the current output buffer for a system process ID (SPID). The syntax of the **DBCC OUTPUTBUFFER** statement is:

```
DBCC OUTPUTBUFFER ( spid )
```

DBCC PROCCACHE

The **DBCC PROCCACHE** statement displays information about the procedure cache. The syntax of the **DBCC PROCCACHE** statement is:

```
DBCC PROCCACHE
```

DBCC SHOWCONTIG

The **DBCC SHOWCONTIG** statement displays fragmentation information for a table. The syntax of the **DBCC SHOWCONTIG** statement is:

```
DBCC SHOWCONTIG
    [    ( { table_name | table_id | view_name | view_id }
          [ , index_name | index_id ]
       )
    ]
    [ WITH { ALL_INDEXES
             | FAST [ , ALL_INDEXES ]
             | TABLERESULTS [ , { ALL_INDEXES } ]
             [ , { FAST | ALL_LEVELS } ]
           }
    ]
```

DBCC SHOW_STATISTICS

The **DBCC SHOW_STATISTICS** statement displays the current distribution statistics for a table. The syntax of the **DBCC SHOW_STATISTICS** statement is:

```
DBCC SHOW_STATISTICS ( table , target )
```

DBCC SQLPERF

The **DBCC SQLPERF** statement provides transaction log space statistics. The syntax of the **DBCC SQLPREF** statement is:

```
DBCC SQLPERF ( LOGSPACE )
```

DBCC TRACESTATUS

The **DBCC TRACESTATUS** statement displays trace flag status. The syntax of the **DBCC TRACESTATUS** statement is:

```
DBCC TRACESTATUS ( trace# [ ,...n ] )
```

DBCC USEROPTIONS

The **DBCC USEROPTIONS** statement returns the active SET options for the current connection. The syntax of the **DBCC USEROPTIONS** statement is:

```
DBCC USEROPTIONS
```

Validation DBCC Statements

The Validation DBCC statements perform operations on databases and database objects to validate data and data integrity.

DBCC CHECKALLOC

The **DBCC CHECKALLOC** statement verifies the consistency of disk space allocation for a database. The syntax of the **DBCC CHECKALLOC** statement is:

```
DBCC CHECKALLOC
    ( 'database_name'
          [ , NOINDEX
            |
            { REPAIR_ALLOW_DATA_LOSS
              | REPAIR_FAST
              | REPAIR_REBUILD
            } ]
    )   [ WITH { [ ALL_ERRORMSGS | NO_INFOMSGS ]
                 [ , [ TABLOCK ] ]
                 [ , [ ESTIMATEONLY ] ]
               }
        ]
```

DBCC CHECKCATALOG

The DBCC CHECKCATALOG statement checks for system table consistency in a database. The syntax of the **DBCC CHECKCATALOG** statement is:

```
DBCC CHECKCATALOG
    ( 'database_name'
    )    [ WITH NO_INFOMSGS ]
```

DBCC CHECKCONSTRAINTS

The **DBCC CHECKCONSTRAINTS** statement checks constraint integrity on a specified table. The syntax of the **DBCC CHECKCONSTRAINTS** statement is:

```
DBCC CHECKCONSTRAINTS
    [( 'table_name' | 'constraint_name'
    )]
    [ WITH { ALL_ERRORMSGS | ALL_CONSTRAINTS } ]
```

DBCC CHECKDB

The **DBCC CHECKDB** statement verifies the allocation and integrity of database objects in a database. The syntax of the **DBCC CHECKDB** statement is:

```
DBCC CHECKDB
    ( 'database_name'
            [ , NOINDEX
                | { REPAIR_ALLOW_DATA_LOSS
                    | REPAIR_FAST
                    | REPAIR_REBUILD
                    } ]
    )    [ WITH { [ ALL_ERRORMSGS ]
                    [ , [ NO_INFOMSGS ] ]
                    [ , [ TABLOCK ] ]
                    [ , [ ESTIMATEONLY ] ]
                    [ , [ PHYSICAL_ONLY ] ]
                    }
        ]
```

DBCC CHECKFILEGROUP

The **DBCC CHECKFILEGROUP** statement verifies the allocation and integrity of all tables in a filegroup in the current database. The syntax of the **DBCC CHECKFILEGROUP** statement is:

```
DBCC CHECKFILEGROUP
    ( [ { 'filegroup' | filegroup_id } ]
        [ , NOINDEX ]
    )    [ WITH { [ ALL_ERRORMSGS | NO_INFOMSGS ]
                    [ , [ TABLOCK ] ]
                    [ , [ ESTIMATEONLY ] ]
                    }
        ]
```

DBCC CHECKIDENT

The **DBCC CHECKIDENT** statement checks and corrects the current identity value for a table. The syntax of the **DBCC CHECKIDENT** statement is:

```
DBCC CHECKIDENT
    ( 'table_name'
        [ , { NORESEED
                | { RESEED [ , new_reseed_value ] }
            }
        ]
    )
```

DBCC CHECKTABLE

The **DBCC CHECKTABLE** statement verifies the integrity of the data, index, text, n-text, and image pages for a table or indexed view. The syntax of the **DBCC CHECKTABLE** statement is:

```
DBCC CHECKTABLE
    ( 'table_name' | 'view_name'
        [ , NOINDEX
            | index_id
            | { REPAIR_ALLOW_DATA_LOSS
                | REPAIR_FAST
                | REPAIR_REBUILD }
        ]
    )   [ WITH { [ ALL_ERRORMSGS | NO_INFOMSGS ]
                [ , [ TABLOCK ] ]
                [ , [ ESTIMATEONLY ] ]
                [ , [ PHYSICAL_ONLY ] ]
            }
        ]
```

DBCC NEWALLOC

The **DBCC NEWALLOC** statement is included for backward compatibility. The **DBCC CHECKALLOC** statement should be used instead in order to verify the consistency of disk space allocation.

Miscellaneous DBCC Statements

Several additional DBCC statements are grouped in the Miscellaneous category.

DBCC dllname (FREE)

The **DBCC dllname (FREE)** statement unloads the specified dynamic link library (DLL) from memory. The syntax of the **DBCC dllname** statement is:

```
DBCC dllname ( FREE )
```

DBCC HELP

The **DBCC HELP** statement returns syntax help for the specified DBCC statement. The syntax of the **DBCC HELP** statement is:

```
DBCC HELP ( 'dbcc_statement' | @dbcc_statement_var | '?' )
```

DBCC PINTABLE

The **DBCC PINTABLE** statement marks a table to be pinned, which prevents pages from being deleted from cached memory. The syntax of the **DBCC PINTABLE** statement is:

```
DBCC PINTABLE ( database_id , table_id )
```

DBCC ROWLOCK

The **DBCC ROWLOCK** statement is no longer required. Row-level locking is enabled by default. It is included for backward compatibility to SQL Server Version 6.5.

DBCC TRACEOFF

The **DBCC TRACEOFF** statement disables a trace flag. The syntax of the **DBCC TRACEOFF** statement is:

```
DBCC TRACEOFF ( trace# [ ,...n ] )
```

DBCC TRACEON

The **DBCC TRACEON** statement enables a trace flag. The syntax of the **DBCC TRACEON** statement is:

```
DBCC TRACEON ( trace# [ ,...n ] )
```

DBCC UNPINTABLE

The **DBCC UNPINTABLE** statement marks a table as unpinned. After a table is unpinned, table pages in the buffer cache may be flushed. The syntax of the **DBCC UNPINTABLE** statement is:

```
DBCC UNPINTABLE ( database_id , table_id )
```

Practice Questions

Question 1

You are a new database administrator responsible for maintaining an instance of SQL Server 2000. During the planning for improved data integrity, there are a number of issues that you must consider. Which of the following items are types of integrity that you should consider? [Check all correct answers]

❑ a. Entity integrity

❑ b. Referential integrity

❑ c. Table integrity

❑ d. Transaction integrity

❑ e. Type integrity

Answers a, b, c, d, and e are all correct. When planning for improved data integrity within a database, the types of integrity that must be considered are Entity, Referential, Table, Transaction, and Type.

Question 2

Which of the following items can be used to enforce data integrity? [Check all correct answers]

❑ a. Business rules

❑ b. Check constraints

❑ c. Constraints

❑ d. Foreign keys

❑ e. Primary keys

❑ f. Table relationships

❑ g. UNIQUE constraints

Answers a, b, c, d, e, f, and g are all correct. Table relationships are created using Primary and Foreign keys. Constraints, including Check and UNIQUE constraints, limit possible entry of "bad" data, as will properly coded Business Rules.

Question 3

> You are the database administrator responsible for an instance of SQL Server 2000. While monitoring the **Sales** database, you notice that two users have processes that are deadlocked. You do not have enough time to correct this right now and still make a critical budget meeting. Should you skip the meeting with the boss or attend the meeting and correct the single deadlock later?
>
> You decide that the budget is more important than the deadlock. Can the database recover from the deadlock without you?
>
> ○ a. Yes
>
> ○ b. No

Answer a is correct. SQL Server 2000 will spawn an eager deadlock search, which will identify the deadlock and select the least expensive process to be aborted. When you return, you should check the Event Log to verify which process was terminated without completion. However, the database resolved the lock in your absence and continued processing normally.

Question 4

> Several tools are provided for troubleshooting transactions and integrity checks:
>
> DBCC statements
>
> Enterprise Manager
>
> Error logs
>
> SQL Profiler
>
> System Monitor
>
> Transact-SQL statements
>
> Match the following characteristics with the appropriate tool (some may be used more than once):
>
> Can be accessed within the Windows 2000 application log
>
> Can be accessed within the Windows 2000 Performance Console
>
> Enact command-line statements within the SQL Query Analyzer
>
> Creates real-time monitoring traces
>
> Uses Database Console Commands (DBCC)
>
> Provides command-line current activity monitoring
>
> Provides graphical current activity monitoring

The correct answers are:

DBCC statements

> Can enact command-line statements within the SQL Query Analyzer

> Use Database Console Commands (DBCC)

> Provide command-line current activity monitoring

Enterprise Manager

> Provides graphical current activity monitoring

Error logs

> Can be accessed within the Windows 2000 application log

SQL Profiler

> Creates real time monitoring traces

System Monitor

> Can be accessed within the Windows 2000 Performance Console

Transact-SQL statements

> Enact command-line statements within the SQL Query Analyzer

> Provide command-line current activity monitoring

Question 5

Several Transact-SQL (T-SQL) command-line statements are available for troubleshooting transactions and integrity checks:

sp_lock

sp_monitor

sp_spaceused

sp_who

Match the following characteristics with the appropriate tool:

Reports current disk space usage

Reports information about current processes and users

Reports information about current transaction locks

Reports statistics and activity since the last time this command was run

The correct answers are:

sp_lock

> Reports information about current transaction locks

sp_monitor

> Reports statistics and activity since the last time this command was run

sp_spaceused

> Reports current disk space usage

sp_who

> Reports information about current processes and users

Question 6

Several categories of DBCC Transact-SQL (T-SQL) command-line statements are available for troubleshooting transactions and integrity checks:

> Maintenance
>
> Miscellaneous
>
> Status
>
> Validation

Match the following DBCC statements with the appropriate category:

> **DBCC CHECKCONSTRAINTS**
>
> **DBCC CHECKDB**
>
> **DBCC CHECKTABLE**
>
> **DBCC DBREINDEX**
>
> **DBCC HELP**
>
> **DBCC SHOW_STATISTICS**
>
> **DBCC SHRINKFILE**

The correct answers are:

Maintenance

> **DBCC DBREINDEX**
>
> **DBCC SHRINKFILE**

Miscellaneous

DBCC HELP

Status

DBCC SHOW_STATISTICS

Validation

DBCC CHECKCONSTRAINTS

DBCC CHECKDB

DBCC CHECKTABLE

Question 7

You are the database administrator responsible for a very overloaded server running an instance of SQL Server 2000. You have created several SQL Profiler traces, but none of them seem to collect any data.

Your configuration is as follows:

- System RAM: 512MB (less than 35 percent capacity free)
- CPU: One 500MHz Pentium III (less than 50 percent capacity used)
- Drive Capacity: 10GB (less than 8MB free)
- Network connectivity: Two 1GB Ethernet cards

You plan to resolve this problem by adding an additional 512MB for a total of 1GB of RAM and add a second CPU to boost processing power. Will this resolve your problem?

○ a. Yes

○ b. No

Answer b is correct. SQL Profiler requires at least 10MB of file space available in order to operate. You must either free up space on the drive by clearing unneeded files, packages, and logs, or add additional drive capacity to your server.

Question 8

Which of the following DBCC statements are Validation commands? [Check all correct answers]

❏ a. **DBCC CHECKCATALOG**

❏ b. **DBCC CHECKFILEGROUP**

❏ c. **DBCC SHOWCONTIG**

❏ d. **DBCC SHRINKDATABASE**

❏ e. **DBCC TRACEON**

❏ f. **DBCC TRACESTATUS**

Answers a and b are correct. Both the **DBCC CHECKCATALOG** and **DBCC CHECKFILEGROUP** statements are Validation category commands. Answers c and f are incorrect because **DBCC SHOWCONTIG** and **DBCC TRACESTATUS** are Status category commands. Answer d is incorrect because **DBCC SHRINKDATABASE** is a Maintenance category command. Answer e is incorrect because **DBCC TRACEON** is a Miscellaneous category command.

Question 9

By default, the deadlock victim is the most expensive process involved in the deadlock.

○ a. True

○ b. False

Answer b is correct. By default, SQL Server 2000 resolves deadlocks by terminating the least expensive process in contention.

Question 10

Which of the following can you use for a quick graphical overview of a database's statistics?

○ a. Enterprise Manager Taskpad

○ b. Query Analyzer

○ c. SQL Profiler

Answer a is correct. The Taskpad view within the Enterprise Manager provides an overview of a database's statistics. Answer b is incorrect because the Query Analyzer is used to build and enact command-line SQL language actions, not for graphical presentation of data. Answer c is incorrect because the SQL Profiler is used to trace real-time transaction events.

Need to Know More?

 Dalton, Patrick, and Paul Whitehead. *SQL Server 2000 Black Book*. The Coriolis Group: Scottsdale, Arizona, 2001. ISBN 1-57610-770-1. An excellent reference to keep close at hand during installation of SQL Server 2000. This is a necessary book in any DBA's library, as it has many solutions to commonly experienced issues.

 Iseminger, David. *Microsoft SQL Server 2000 Reference Library with CD-ROM*. Microsoft Press: Redmond, WA, 2000. ISBN 0-7356-1280-3. An exhaustive library covering detailed information on all aspects of SQL Server 2000 implementations. A necessary reference for IT departments supporting Microsoft SQL Server 2000 implementations.

 Shapiro, Jeffrey. *SQL Server 2000—The Complete Reference*. Osborne/McGraw-Hill: Berkeley, CA, 2001. ISBN 0-07-212588-8. A detailed, if somewhat lengthy, reference for SQL Server 2000 administration.

 Stanek, William. *Microsoft SQL Server 2000 Administrator's Pocket Consultant*. Microsoft Press: Redmond, WA, 2000. ISBN 0-7356-1129-7. A condensed reference for SQL Server 2000 that provides ready access to important tips for database administrators.

 http://msdn.microsoft.com/library/default.asp?URL=/library/psdk/sql/portal_7ap1.htm. *Microsoft SQL Server 2000 Books Online*. A complete online copy of the documentation for SQL Server 2000. This is an SQL Server 2000 database administrator's best friend because it is included on the installation CD-ROM.

Extracting and Transforming Data

Terms you'll need to understand:

✓ **INSERT** and **BULK INSERT** commands

✓ **SELECT INTO** command

✓ bcp utility

✓ Data Transformation Services (DTS)

✓ Heterogeneous data sources

✓ Snapshot replication

✓ Merge replication

✓ Transactional replication

✓ Publisher

✓ Distributor

✓ Subscriber

✓ Linked server

Techniques you'll need to master:

✓ Importing data into a database using the **INSERT** and **BULK INSERT** commands

✓ Creating new tables using data derived from other tables using the **SELECT INTO** command

✓ Performing bulk imports, exports, and updates using the bcp utility

✓ Creating and scheduling DTS packages

As a database administrator, you will often be asked to extract a subset of the available data for various purposes. You will also be asked to load bulk data input, for example, to populate tables of sales prospects, inventory price listings, and other large input or update actions. Many times, this data must also be converted to the format used in your database during the process, which can further complicate matters.

This chapter covers the use of bulk insertion and update tools including both command-line and graphical user interface tools, such as the Data Transformation Services (DTS) utility. An instance of SQL Server 2000 must already be installed (see Chapters 4 and 5) on a Windows 2000 server platform. Additional references may be found at the end of this chapter.

Bulk update actions may affect a large number of records within your database. It is often useful to change your security model to Bulk-logged (discussed in Chapter 8) before performing these actions to reduce the resources necessary to log every transaction separately.

Command-Line Statements

A number of command-line statements are available to perform bulk import or update actions. These include the **INSERT, BULK INSERT,** and **SELECT INTO** Transact-SQL (T-SQL) commands, which may be enacted within the SQL Query Analyzer. To open the Query Analyzer, take the following steps:

1. Open the SQL Server 2000 Enterprise Manager.

2. In the left panel, expand the desired server group by clicking the plus (+) sign.

3. From the Tools pull-down menu, select the SQL Query Analyzer option.

INSERT Statement

The command-line **INSERT** statement is the simplest form of data insertion, which is used in Transact-SQL (T-SQL) statements to add a new record to an existing table or view.

Views created using multiple *joined* tables will not accept **INSERT** statements creating new rows. Insertions into views that do not include table columns that require values are not possible unless default or appropriate values for the missing required fields are provided. Values are automatically provided if the column:

➤ Has an **IDENTITY** property

➤ Has a **DEFAULT** value

➤ Is of the **timestamp** data type

➤ Is Nullable

The syntax of the **INSERT** command is:

```
INSERT [INTO]
    { table_name WITH ( < table_hint_limited > [ ...n ] )
        | view_name
        | rowset_function_limited
    }
    {    [ ( column_list ) ]
        { VALUES
            ( { DEFAULT | NULL | expression } [ ,...n] )
            | derived_table
            | execute_statement
        }
    }
    | DEFAULT VALUES

< table_hint_limited > =
    { FASTFIRSTROW
        | HOLDLOCK
        | PAGLOCK
        | READCOMMITTED
        | REPEATABLEREAD
        | ROWLOCK
        | SERIALIZABLE
        | TABLOCK
        | TABLOCKX
        | UPDLOCK
    }
```

Following are the arguments for the **INSERT** command:

➤ **INTO**—An optional keyword separating the **INSERT** command and table name.

➤ *table_name*—The name of the table into which the data will be inserted.

➤ **WITH** (<table_hint_limited> [...*n*])—Used to specify indexes to be used by the query optimizer or locking methods to be used to aid in optimization.

➤ *view_name*—The alias of the view into which the data will be inserted.

➤ *rowset_function_limited*—Used for **OPENROWSET** and **OPENQUERY** functions.

➤ *(column_list)*—A comma-delimited list of columns into which data will be inserted. This must be used whenever an **INSERT** statement attempts to insert data that is not organized in the same order as the columns in the table or to insert fewer columns than the entire table or view requires.

➤ **VALUES**—A comma-delimited list of data values to be inserted. If *column_list* is specified, a **VALUE** must exist for each item in the *column_list*.

➤ **DEFAULT**—Forces the load of the specified column's default value. Null and timestamp values may also be filled using this setting if no default value is specified.

➤ *Expression*—An expression using constant or variable identifiers but not derived T-SQL statements, such as **SELECT**.

➤ *derived_table*—A **SELECT** T-SQL statement returning data to be inserted into the table or view.

➤ *execute_statement*—An **EXECUTE** T-SQL statement returning data to be inserted into the table or view. Used with the **SELECT** and **READTEXT** statements to execute stored procedures.

➤ **DEFAULT VALUES**—Forces the new record to contain default values for each column. This is often used to create a new record that will later be edited or updated with valid data.

BULK INSERT Statement

A more complex form of data insertion may be accomplished using the command-line **BULK INSERT** statement, which is used in Transact-SQL (T-SQL) statements to add new records from data files into an existing table or view.

The syntax of the **BULK INSERT** command is

```
BULK INSERT [ [ 'database_name'.] [ 'owner' ].] { 'table_name'
      FROM 'data_file' }
   [ WITH
      (
            [ BATCHSIZE [ = batch_size ] ]
            [ [ , ] CHECK_CONSTRAINTS ]
            [ [ , ] CODEPAGE [ = 'ACP' | 'OEM' | 'RAW' |
               'code_page'] ]
            [ [ , ] DATAFILETYPE [ =
               {'char'|'native'|'widechar'|'widenative'}]]
            [ [ , ] FIELDTERMINATOR [ = 'field_terminator' ] ]
            [ [ , ] FIRSTROW [ = first_row ] ]
            [ [ , ] FIRE_TRIGGERS ]
            [ [ , ] FORMATFILE = 'format_file_path' ]
            [ [ , ] KEEPIDENTITY ]
            [ [ , ] KEEPNULLS ]
            [ [ , ] KILOBYTES_PER_BATCH [= kilobytes_per_batch] ]
            [ [ , ] LASTROW [ = last_row ] ]
            [ [ , ] MAXERRORS [ = max_errors ] ]
            [ [ , ] ORDER ({ column [ ASC | DESC ] } [ ,...n ]) ]
            [ [ , ] ROWS_PER_BATCH [ = rows_per_batch ] ]
            [ [ , ] ROWTERMINATOR [ = 'row_terminator' ] ]
            [ [ , ] TABLOCK ]
      )
   ]
```

Following are the arguments for the **BULK INSERT** command:

➤ **INTO**—An optional keyword separating the **INSERT** command and table name.

➤ '*database_name*'—The name of the database where the table or view is located. If not listed, the current database is assumed.

➤ '*owner*'—Specifies the owner of the table or view. This is optional if the user performing the operation is the owner.

➤ '*table_name*'—The name of the table or view into which the data is to be inserted.

➤ '*data_file*'—The full path and file name of the source data file to be used. This may be a remote Universal Naming Convention (UNC) path or a file on a local drive.

➤ BATCHSIZE [= *batch_size*]—Limits the number of records to be inserted in a batch. Each batch is processed as one transaction. If not specified, all rows are inserted as a single batch.

➤ CHECK_CONSTRAINTS—Specifies whether input data will be checked against table constraints during the operation. If not specified, constraints are not checked.

➤ CODEPAGE [= 'ACP' | 'OEM' | 'RAW' | '*code_page*']—Specifies the code page to be used for **char, varchar,** and **text** data columns.

➤ DATAFILETYPE [= {'char' | 'native' | 'widechar' | 'widenative' }]—Specifies the default type of copy operation.

➤ FIELDTERMINATOR [= '*field_terminator*']—Specifies a field terminator for **char** and **wildchar** data types. This specifies the separator between field values. If not specified, the tab (\t) character is used by default.

➤ FIRSTROW [= *first_row*]—Allows the specification of a specific row where copying is to start. This allows the input to begin after header file information or after a specific number of rows. If not specified, the default is the first row of the table.

➤ FIRE_TRIGGERS—Specifies whether triggers on the destination table will occur during the operation. If not specified, no insert triggers will fire.

➤ FORMATFILE [= '*format_file_path*']—Specifies a format file if available. Format files are created by the bcp utility, covered later in this chapter.

➤ KEEPIDENTITY—Specifies whether identity values are kept from the import data. If not specified, new identity values are assigned during the operation.

➤ KEEPNULLS—Specifies whether columns in the destination table that do not receive data during the insertion operation should be filled with Null values or should use the default values specified for each column.

➤ KILOBYTES_PER_BATCH [= *kilobytes_per_batch*]—Limits batch size to a specified size (in KB).

➤ LASTROW [= *last_row*]—Allows the specification of a specific row where the copying is to end. This allows the input to stop prior to aggregated footer information or after a specific number of rows. If not specified, the default is the final row of the table.

➤ MAXERRORS [= *max_errors*]—Limits the maximum number of allowable errors before the bulk operation is terminated. If not specified, the default is 10 errors.

➤ ORDER ({ *column* [ASC | DESC] } [,...*n*])—Specifies the sort order for the import data. This is used to optimize data importation into tables with clustered indexes. If not specified, the data is assumed to be in no particular order.

➤ ROWS_PER_BATCH [= *rows_per_batch*]—Used when **BATCHSIZE** is not specified to restrict the size of each input batch to the specified number of rows.

➤ ROWTERMINATOR [= '*row_terminator*']—Specifies a row terminator for **char** and **wildchar** data types. This specifies the separator between records. If not specified, the newline (\n) character is used by default.

➤ TABLOCK—Specifies whether the table is locked during the bulk operation. Locking the table during this operation improves import performance and prevents other updates to the table during the import operation.

SELECT...INTO Statement

The Transact-SQL **SELECT** statement may be used with the optional **INTO** option to select data from existing tables and views into a new table specified in the statement.

Because of the possible complexity of the **SELECT** statement, the full details are not presented here. Just be aware that the **SELECT** statement using the **INTO** option allows the creation of a new table using data extracted from other tables. Details of SQL statement design using the **SELECT** statement are covered more extensively in the Microsoft Certification Exam 70-229: Designing and Implementing Databases with Microsoft SQL Server 2000 Enterprise Edition.

bcp Utility

Another command-line option is the bcp utility located in the \MSSQL\BINN directory. This command-line program is often used in batch files and scripted processes for such actions as extracting database data into an external data file. This is similar to the **BULK INSERT** statement used in Transact-SQL (T-SQL) statements.

The syntax of the bcp utility is

```
bcp {[[database_name.][owner].]{table_name | view_name} |
      "query"}
   {in | out | queryout | format} data_file
   [-m max_errors] [-f format_file] [-e err_file]
   [-F first_row] [-L last_row] [-b batch_size]
   [-n] [-c] [-w] [-N] [-V (60 | 65 | 70)] [-6]
   [-q] [-C code_page] [-t field_term] [-r row_term]
   [-i input_file] [-o output_file] [-a packet_size]
   [-S server_name[\instance_name]] [-U login_id] [-P password]
   [-T] [-v] [-R] [-k] [-E] [-h "hint [,...n]"]
```

Following are the arguments for the bcp utility:

➤ *database_name*—The name of the database in which the table or view may be found. If not listed, the default database for the specified user is assumed.

➤ *owner*—Specifies the owner of the table or view. This is optional if the specified user is the owner.

➤ *table_name*—The name of the table where the data is to be inserted (**in**) or copied from (**out**).

➤ *view_name*—The name of the view where the data is to be inserted (**in**) or copied from (**out**).

➤ "query"—A Transact-SQL (T-SQL) statement that returns the result set to be used.

➤ **in | out | queryout | format**—Specifies the type of bulk operation.

  ➤ **in**—Imports data into the table or view from a data file.

  ➤ **out**—Exports data from the database to the destination file.

  ➤ **queryout**—Required when using a Transact-SQL query as the source.

  ➤ **format**—Produces a format file based on the bulk copy specifications. If this is used, the **-f** option must also be specified.

➤ *data_file*—The full path and file name of the data file to be used. This may be a remote Universal Naming Convention (UNC) path or a file on a local drive.

 The data file path may not exceed 255 characters in length.

➤ **-m** *max_errors*—Limits the maximum number of allowable errors before the bulk operation is terminated. If not specified, the default is 10 errors.

Options are case-sensitive. The **-f** option is not the same as the **-F** option. Be careful when reading any questions that involve bcp options.

➤ **-f** *format_file*—Specifies a previously created format file for use in the operation. If not specified and the **-c**, **-n**, **-N**, **-w**, or **-6** options are not used, the user is prompted for format information.

➤ **-e** *err_file*—The full path and file name of the error file containing stored rows that bcp was unable to import.

➤ **-F** *first_row*—Allows the specification of a specific row where copying is to begin. This allows the input to begin after header file information or after a specific number of rows. If not specified, the default is the first row of the table.

➤ **-L** *last_row*—Allows the specification of a specific row as the last row to be copied. This allows the input to stop prior to aggregated footer information or after a specific number of rows. If not specified, the default is the final row of the table.

➤ **-b** *batch_size*—Limits the number of records to be inserted in a batch. Each batch is processed as one transaction. If not specified, all rows are inserted as a single batch.

➤ **-n**—Specifies the native data types (specified in the database) for transferred data.

➤ **-c**—Specifies the character data type for transferred data.

➤ **-w**—Specifies Unicode characters for transferred data. This may not be used with SQL Server version 6.5 or earlier.

➤ **-N**—Specifies the native data types for noncharacter data and Unicode characters for character data. Like **-w**, this option may not be used for SQL Server version 6.5 or earlier. This option should be used when transferring data containing ANSI extended characters.

➤ **-V (60 | 65 | 70)**—Used together with the **-c** or **-n** options, this option performs operations using the data types from earlier versions of SQL Server. This is useful when transferring data from earlier versions of SQL Server to SQL Server 2000.

➤ **-6**—Provided for backward compatibility. Specifies the use of SQL Server 6.0 or 6.5 data types for operations. The **-V** option should be used instead of this command.

➤ **-q**—Specifies the use of a database, table, view, or owner name that contains spaces or single quotation marks ('). The name must be enclosed using double quotation marks (" ").

➤ **-C** *code_page*—Provided for backward compatibility. Specifies the code page to be used for **char**, **varchar**, and **text** data columns.

➤ **-t** *field_term*—Specifies a field terminator for **char** and **wildchar** data types. This specifies the separator between field values. If not specified, the tab (\t) character is used by default.

➤ **-r** *row_term*—Specifies a row terminator for **char** and **wildchar** data types. This specifies the separator between records. If not specified, the newline (\n) character is used by default.

➤ **-i** *input_file*—The full path and file name of a response file to be used to respond automatically to command prompt questions when formatting is not predefined.

➤ **-o** *output_file*—The full path and file name of an output file to be used when redirecting command prompt output.

➤ **-a** *packet_size*—Specifies the packet size (in bytes) used in transferring data to and from the server. This may be a value between 4096 and 65535 bytes. If not specified, the default value is 4096.

➤ **-S** *server_name*[*instance_name*]—Specifies the instance on which the operation is to be performed. If not specified, the default instance of SQL Server on the local server is used.

➤ **-U** *login_id*—Specifies the SQL Server logon ID to use for the operation.

➤ **-P** *password*—Specifies the password for the logon ID used. If not specified, the bcp utility prompts for a password.

➤ **-T**—Specifies the use of a trusted connection using the security of the network user performing the operation. This is used instead of **-U** and **-P**.

➤ **-v**—Displays the bcp version number and copyright information.

➤ **-R**—Specifies the use of regional settings for currency, date, and time data for the operation. If not specified, regional settings are ignored.

➤ -k—Specifies whether columns in the destination table that do not receive data during the insertion operation should be filled with Null values or should use the default values specified for each column.

➤ -E—Specifies whether identity values are kept from the import data. If not specified, new identity values are assigned during the operation.

➤ -h "hint [,...n]"—Used to specify options to be used by the query optimizer or locking methods to be used to aid in optimization.

> ➤ ORDER (column [ASC | DESC] [,...n])—Specifies the sort order for the imported data. This is used to optimize data importation into tables with clustered indexes. If not specified, the data is assumed to be in no particular order.

> ➤ ROWS_PER_BATCH = bb—Used when -b is not specified to restrict the size of each input batch to the specified number of rows.

> ➤ KILOBYTES_PER_BATCH = cc—Limits batch size to a specified size (in KB).

> ➤ TABLOCK—Specifies whether the table is locked during the bulk operation. Locking the table during this operation improves import performance and prevents other updates to the table during the import operation.

> ➤ CHECK_CONSTRAINTS—Specifies whether input data is checked against table constraints during the operation. If not specified, constraints are not checked.

> ➤ FIRE_TRIGGERS—Specifies whether insert triggers on the destination table occur during the operation. If not specified, no insert triggers will fire during the bulk import operation.

Data Transformation Services (DTS)

Data Transformation Services (DTS) packages provide a graphical bulk operations utility within the SQL Server 2000 Enterprise Manager. DTS packages may be created and saved for reuse or scheduled for later or recurring operations. DTS packages are often used to transfer data from *heterogeneous* data sources (deriving data from non-SQL databases) by configuring the appropriate OLE DB connection type as required for each source.

To create a new export DTS package using the DTS Designer from within the Enterprise Manager, take the following steps:

1. Open the SQL Server 2000 Enterprise Manager by selecting Start|Programs |Microsoft SQL Server|Enterprise Manager.

2. In the left panel, expand the desired server group by clicking the plus sign.

3. Expand the configuration on the desired server by clicking the plus sign next to it, and enter authentication information if required.

4. Expand the Data Transformation Services node by clicking the plus sign next to it. Select Local Packages to edit an existing package, or right-click and select New Package from the drop-down menu to open the DTS Designer.

5. Select Source from the icons at the left, and drag it into the Designer pane. Right-click and select Properties to edit the Connection Properties for the source (see Figure 10.1).

6. Select Destination from the icons at the left, and drag it into the Designer pane. Right-click and select Properties to edit the Connection Properties for the destination (see Figure 10.2).

7. Right-click on the Designer pane, and select New Task. Select the type of action to perform (in this case, a Transform Data task). When prompted, click on the Source and Destination connections for the task to be performed, creating a graphical task link (see Figure 10.3).

8. On the Source tab, specify the appropriate source table or view, or input an SQL query for the source data (see Figure 10.4).

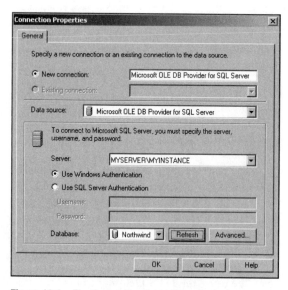

Figure 10.1 The Connection Properties screen shows a new connection selected for an OLE DB Provider for SQL Server.

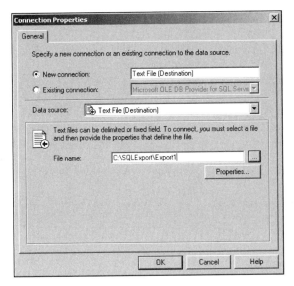

Figure 10.2   The Connection Properties screen shows a new connection selected for a Text File destination.

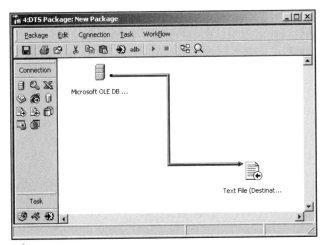

Figure 10.3   The DTS Designer screen shows Source, Destination, and Task connections.

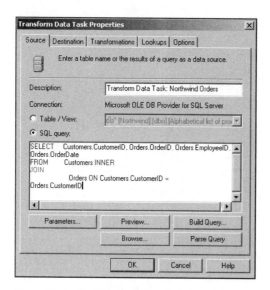

Figure 10.4 The Transform Data Task Properties screen shows the Source tab and an SQL query selected.

9. Click Build Query to open the graphical query designer interface (see Figure 10.5). Click OK to return to the Transform Data Task Properties screen.

10. Configure the requirements on the Destination, Transformations, Lookups, and Options tabs (see Figure 10.6). Click OK to return to the DTS Designer interface.

11. Select Package|Save As and enter the package name, location, and server in the appropriate boxes. Click OK to save the package and return to the Local Packages portion of the Data Transformation Services node.

12. To schedule the package for later or recurring operation, right-click on the package, and select Schedule Package to open the Edit Recurring Job Schedule interface (see Figure 10.7). Click OK when done.

Distributed Solutions

SQL Server 2000 provides a number of other options for distributed data operations including server replication and the use of linked server configurations.

Replication

Replication involves the copying of data and database objects from one database to another and the synchronization of data between servers. Table 10.1 details the three main types of replication.

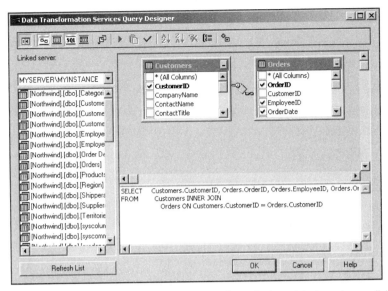

Figure 10.5 The Data Transformation Services Query Designer interface shows a link set up between Customers and Orders.

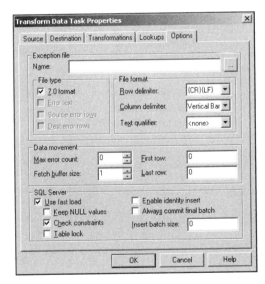

Figure 10.6 The Transform Data Task Properties screen shows the choices available on the Options tab.

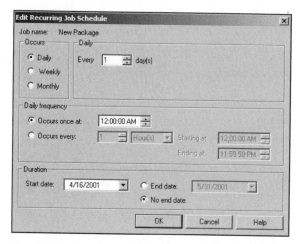

Figure 10.7 The Edit Recurring Job Schedule screen gives the options for setting the frequency and start and end dates for recurring jobs.

Table 10.1	Replication types.
Type	**Use**
Snapshot	The Publisher replaces data periodically on the Subscriber with a new snapshot.
Merge	Data updates occur in both Publisher and Subscriber and are synchronized routinely at the Publisher. This is often used for disconnected or mobile users.
Transactional	Data updates occur mainly at the Publisher and are transmitted to the Subscriber. Subscriber transaction updates preserve consistency.

 Know the three elements and their roles in replication.

Replication involves three elements:

➤ Publishers

➤ Distributors

➤ Subscribers

Publishers provide data to distributors, which in turn distribute data to subscribers. A Publisher may also be a distributor for its own data.

To configure replication within the Enterprise Manager, expand the Replication node for a selected server and select the appropriate type of replication role or action. A Publisher and a Distributor must be established before a Subscriber can be created.

A server can play multiple roles, serving as the Publisher and Distributor for one set of database objects while also serving as the Subscriber for another set of database objects. Proper planning of replication topologies can significantly improve performance in distributed scenarios utilizing slower WAN links.

The Replication Monitor provides information on replication processes, subscribers, and other types of information.

Linked Server

Linked servers allow SQL Server 2000 to process distributed transactions against heterogeneous OLE DB data sources located on different servers throughout an enterprise environment.

To configure a linked server within the Enterprise Manager, expand the Security node for a selected server and then select the Linked Servers subnode to create a new Linked Server. Specifying the appropriate connection type and credentials is similar to establishing other heterogeneous data access connections for DTS packages, detailed earlier in this chapter.

Practice Questions

Question 1

Which of the following are Transact-SQL commands used for update operations? [Check all correct answers]

❏ a. **bcp**

❏ b. **BULK INSERT**

❏ c. **EXPORT**

❏ d. **IMPORT**

❏ e. **INSERT**

❏ f. **SELECT INTO**

Answers b, e, and f are correct. **BULK INSERT, INSERT,** and **SELECT INTO** are Transact-SQL (T-SQL) statements used for update operations in SQL Server 2000. Answer a is incorrect because the bcp command-line utility is a separate utility, not a Transact-SQL operation. Answers c and d are incorrect because they are not valid T-SQL commands.

Question 2

Several T-SQL commands are provided to perform update operations:

> **BULK INSERT**
>
> **INSERT**
>
> **SELECT INTO**

Match the following characteristics with the appropriate operation (some may be used more than once):

> Creates a new table
>
> Inserts a single record
>
> Can create many new records in one operation
>
> Performs data insertion into an existing table or view

The correct answers are:

BULK INSERT

Can create many new records in one operation

Performs data insertion into an existing table or view

INSERT

Inserts a single record

Performs data insertion into an existing table or view

SELECT INTO

Creates a new table

Can create many new records in one operation

Question 3

> If the **BATCHSIZE** is not specified, SQL Server 2000 processes a **BULK INSERT** operation row by row.
>
> ○ a. True
>
> ○ b. False

Answer b is correct. If **BATCHSIZE** is not specified, SQL Server 2000 processes the entire operation as a single batch by default.

Question 4

The bcp utility has a number of formatting options:

    -c

    -n

    -N

    -w

    -V

Match the following characteristics with the appropriate bcp option (some may be used more than once):

    Specifies the data types from previous SQL Server versions

    Specifies the character data type

    Specifies the use of native data types

    Specifies the use of Unicode characters

The correct answers are:

-c

    Specifies the character data type

-n

    Specifies the use of native data types

-N

    Specifies the use of native data types

    Specifies the use of Unicode characters

-w

    Specifies the use of Unicode characters

-V

    Specifies the data types from previous SQL Server versions

Question 5

You are the database administrator responsible for administration of an SQL Server 2000 instance. You have created a script that uses the bcp utility to perform routine data updates in one of your supported databases. No format file is available, but you have set up your script using the **-i** and **-o** options.

Assuming that all files are properly created, will these options allow the script to be called without user interaction, or will you need to respond to command prompts?

○ a. Yes

○ b. No

Answer a is correct. The **-i** (input file) option provides responses for command prompt formatting questions, and the **-o** (output file) option provides an output file for the redirection of command prompt output. Together, these handle response requirements and allow the script to be called without user interaction.

Question 6

If the **-m** option is not specified in a bcp call, SQL Server 2000 halts when it reaches the first translation error.

○ a. True

○ b. False

Answer b is correct. If the **-m** (max errors) option is not specified, SQL Server 2000 uses 10 as the default number of errors that can occur before an operation is terminated.

Question 7

You have several DTS packages created and saved. You need to schedule them for future repeated operation. You have decided to set up a Windows AT command that calls a script to execute the DTS package. Your boss has specified that the update frequency may occasionally need to be changed and the DTS schedule should be configured to make it easy to modify and support.

Is your solution the best way to set up the scheduling of DTS packages to make it easy to change and support?

○ a. Yes

○ b. No

Answer b is correct. Configuring the DTS package for recurring scheduling using the Enterprise Manager is a better choice for updates that are simple to perform using the GUI interface. It also avoids the need to use any processes outside of the SQL Server 2000 instance, reducing support overhead.

Question 8

There are three main types of replication:

Snapshot

Merge

Transactional

Match the following characteristics with the appropriate replication type (some may be used more than once):

Used when Subscriber data is routinely replaced

Used when updates can occur at the Subscriber

Used when updates occur at the Publisher

Used for disconnected or mobile users

The correct answers are:

Snapshot

Used when Subscriber data is routinely replaced

Used when updates occur at the Publisher

Merge

Used when updates can occur at the Subscriber

Used when updates occur at the Publisher

Used for disconnected or mobile users

Transactional

Used when updates occur at the Publisher

Question 9

Which of the following statements regarding replication are true? [Check all correct answers]

❑ a. A server may be both a Publisher and a Distributor.

❑ b. A server may be both a Publisher and a Subscriber.

❑ c. Distributors distribute data to Subscribers.

❑ d. Publishers provide data to Distributors.

Answers a, b, c, and d are all correct. Publishers provide data to Distributors who distribute data to Subscribers. A Publisher can also be configured as its own Distributor. A Publisher for one set of data can also be a Subscriber for another set of data.

Question 10

Linked servers allow distributed transactions to be run against only other SQL servers in the enterprise.

○ a. True

○ b. False

Answer b is correct. Linked servers can allow distributed transactions to be run against many different database types (heterogeneous data sources). This allows for queries to be run using table and view information from SQL, Oracle, Sybase, and other sources in a single action.

Need to Know More?

 Dalton, Patrick, and Paul Whitehead. *SQL Server 2000 Black Book.* The Coriolis Group: Scottsdale, Arizona, 2001. ISBN 1-57610-770-1. An excellent reference to keep close at hand during installation of SQL Server 2000. This is a necessary book in any DBA's library, as it has many solutions to commonly experienced issues.

 Delaney, Kalen. *Inside Microsoft SQL Server 2000.* Microsoft Press: Redmond, WA, 2000. ISBN 0-7356-0998-5. A good review of SQL Server 2000 components including white papers and articles on a broad range of topics.

 Stanek, William. *Microsoft SQL Server 2000 Administrator's Pocket Consultant.* Microsoft Press: Redmond, WA, 2000. ISBN 0-7356-1129-7. A condensed reference for SQL Server 2000 that provides ready access to important tips for database administrators.

 http://msdn.microsoft.com/library/default.asp?URL=/library/psdk/sql/portal_7ap1.htm/. *Microsoft SQL Server 2000 Books Online.* A complete online copy of the documentation for SQL Server 2000. This is an SQL Server 2000 database administrator's best friend because it is included on the installation CD-ROM.

SQL Server 2000 Security

Terms you'll need to understand:

- ✓ Authentication
- ✓ Granting connection rights
- ✓ Revoking connection rights
- ✓ Denying connection rights
- ✓ Windows Authentication Mode
- ✓ Windows user
- ✓ Windows group
- ✓ Inherited permissions
- ✓ Login setup
- ✓ SQL Server Mode (Mixed-Mode)
- ✓ SQL User
- ✓ **sa** Account
- ✓ Authorization
- ✓ Object permissions
- ✓ Statement permissions
- ✓ Implied permissions
- ✓ Server roles
- ✓ Database roles
- ✓ User-defined database roles
- ✓ Application roles
- ✓ Auditing security
- ✓ C2 security requirements

Techniques you'll need to master:

- ✓ Creating logins under Windows and SQL Server (Mixed-Mode) Authentication
- ✓ Granting, revoking, and denying connection rights to users and groups
- ✓ Creating and removing user-defined database roles
- ✓ Granting, revoking, and denying access permissions to users and groups using fixed and user-defined roles

Previous chapters have covered the creation of databases, bulk data operations, and data recovery methods. A critical missing element involves granting users access to the data and, often more importantly, restricting access to data. SQL Server 2000 integrates with Windows NT 4.0 and Windows 2000 integrated security, while also providing SQL Server based security for backward compatibility and access by users utilizing other operating systems. Any operating system that supports one or more of the network libraries listed in Chapter 3 can connect to SQL Server 2000.

This chapter covers SQL Server 2000 security modes, connection authentication, access authorization, and the assignment and revocation of permissions on a user and role basis. This chapter focuses on methods employing the SQL Server Enterprise Manager, as well as command-line options for use within the SQL Query Analyzer. An instance of SQL Server 2000 must already be installed (see Chapters 4 and 5) on a Windows 2000 server platform. The network administrator must have created both Windows users and groups. Additional references are listed at the end of this chapter.

Overview

It has often been said that any system can be made perfect—until a user is allowed to touch it. The unfortunate fact of any database administrator's life is that users want to access data within his or her pristine databases, often expecting to extract and modify that data as well. Imagine the shock you will feel when such audacious requests are made.

When dealing with modern Web-deployed database access, such as those found in many e-commerce deployment scenarios, the network administrator will attempt to provide network security, but you, as database administrator, will be the ultimate keeper of the keys—securing the gates of your databases to keep miscreants and fools from causing harm to the precious data kept safe within. A helpful hint: Stay on good terms with your network administrator because he or she provides the security involving the creation of domain and local users and groups. Your responsibility starts where the network administrator's ends.

Two layers of security are provided within SQL Server 2000. Users attempting to access data must first connect to the database through a process called *login authentication*. After a connection has been established, a user may access database objects according to permissions verified through a process called *authorization*. Users may be granted, not granted (revoked), or denied access at either of these levels. Permissions may be specified to whatever level you desire using both user and role assignment.

This is a complex yet elegant topic that factors into a large number of questions you may encounter on the exam. Be certain to know this topic very well before attempting the exam.

Authentication

The first requirement for any database access is the establishment of a database connection. SQL Server 2000 provides two modes for this that restrict the available forms of login authentication. Table 11.1 details the two authentication modes.

Chapters 3 and 4 detailed the configuration of the initial authentication mode used by an instance of SQL Server 2000. To change the authentication mode after the initial setup using the Enterprise Manager interface, take the following steps:

1. Open the SQL Server 2000 Enterprise Manager by selecting Start|Programs| Microsoft SQL Server|Enterprise Manager.

2. In the left panel, expand the desired server group by clicking the plus (+) sign.

3. Right-click on the desired server, and enter authentication information if required. Select the Properties option from the drop-down menu.

4. Select the Security tab to reveal the current security settings (see Figure 11.1).

5. Change the security mode by clicking the appropriate button. Click OK to apply the change.

Windows Authentication

The Windows Authentication Mode integrates with native Windows security principles within a homogenous Windows NT 4.0 and Windows 2000 enterprise environment. This means, for example, that the Windows Authentication mode uses security principles such as users and groups to manage server logins. As database administrator, you can grant or deny login access to an instance of SQL Server 2000 by local and domain users and groups.

Table 11.1	SQL Server 2000 authentication modes.
Mode	**Authorization Principles**
Windows	Windows User and Windows Group
SQL Server	Windows User, Windows Group, and SQL User

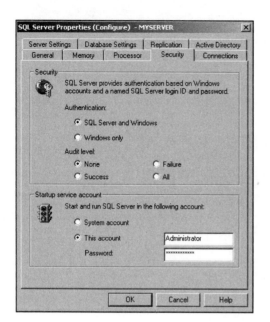

Figure 11.1 The Server Properties screen shows the Security tab selected.

Group permissions allow access rights to be granted or revoked for large numbers of users at once by applying authentication restrictions to the group as a whole. These rights are then inherited by the members of that group. In a large enterprise environment, user-level assignment of access would become problematic if groups were not used to aggregate users into functional groupings. For example, if the Sales team needs access to the database, it is easier to grant access permissions to the Sales group and then simply move users in and out of the group as needed.

An important consideration when planning access security is that a user may belong to many groups. If a user or any of the groups to which they belong are specifically denied access to a server, that user will be unable to log in even if he or she has the inherited ability to log in as a member of another group. A denial always takes precedence.

Creating a New Login Using Enterprise Manager

To configure a Windows login using the Enterprise Manager, take the following steps:

1. Open the SQL Server 2000 Enterprise Manager by selecting Start|Programs| Microsoft SQL Server|Enterprise Manager.

2. In the left panel, expand the desired server group by clicking the plus sign.

3. Expand the configuration on the desired server by clicking the plus sign next to it, and enter authentication information if required.

4. Expand the Security node by clicking the plus sign next to it. Select Logins|View Existing Logins, or right-click and select New Login from the drop-down menu to open the Server Login Properties interface (see Figure 11.2).

5. Select the appropriate Windows user or group name, select the type of authentication (in this case, Windows), and select either Grant or Deny access. Specify the default database for the login on this screen as well.

6. Configure Database access permissions and Server Role membership on the appropriate tabs, if desired. These settings are discussed in greater detail later in this chapter.

7. After all settings are as desired, click OK to create the new Windows login for the selected user or group.

Creating a New Login Using SQL Query Analyzer

To configure a Windows login using the command-line SQL Query Analyzer interface, use the **sp_grantlogin, sp_revokelogin,** or the **sp_denylogin** commands.

The syntax of the **sp_grantlogin** command is:

```
sp_grantlogin [@loginame =] 'login'
```

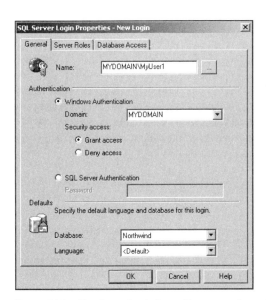

Figure 11.2   The Server Login Properties screen shows the General tab selected.

Following are the arguments for the **sp_grantlogin** command:

➤ **[@loginame =]** '*login*'—The name of the Windows user or group being granted access in the form: DOMAIN\Name (for example, MYDOMAIN\MyGroup1).

The syntax of the **sp_revokelogin** command is:

```
sp_revokelogin [@loginame =] 'login'
```

Following are the arguments for the **sp_revokelogin** command:

➤ **[@loginame =]** '*login*'—The name of the Windows user or group whose access is being revoked, in the form: DOMAIN\Name (for example, MYDOMAIN\MyGroup1).

The syntax of the **sp_denylogin** command is:

```
sp_denylogin [@loginame =] 'login'
```

Following are the arguments for the **sp_denylogin** command:

➤ **[@loginame =]** '*login*'—The name of the Windows user or group being denied access in the form of DOMAIN\Name (for example, MYDOMAIN\MyUser1).

SQL Server Authentication (Mixed-Mode)

SQL Server authentication is provided for backward compatibility with earlier versions of SQL Server. Mixed Mode authentication includes both Windows and SQL Server authentication. It also provides an access method for remote users who do not have a Windows user account, for example, those attempting to access the SQL Server 2000 instance from a non-NT 4.0 or Windows 2000 domain.

 SQL Server (Mixed Mode) Authentication is required for instances of SQL Server 2000 loaded on Windows 98 or Windows ME systems. These systems do not support Windows Authentication even in Mixed Mode.

When a user attempts a connection using a nontrusted connection, SQL Server 2000 attempts to authenticate the connection using a SQL Server login account.

Creating a New SQL Login Using Enterprise Manager

To configure a SQL login using the Enterprise Manager, take the following steps:

1. Open the SQL Server 2000 Enterprise Manager by selecting Start|Programs| Microsoft SQL Server|Enterprise Manager.

2. In the left panel, expand the desired server group by clicking the plus sign.

3. Expand the configuration on the desired server by clicking the plus sign next to it, and enter authentication information if required.

4. Expand the Security node by clicking the plus sign next to it. Select Logins|View Existing Logins, or right-click and select New Login from the drop-down menu to open the Server Login Properties interface.

5. Select the type of authentication (in this case, SQL Server), and enter a name for the SQL login. Select either Grant or Deny access. Specify the default database for the login on this screen as well.

6. Configure Database access permissions and Server Role membership on the appropriate tabs if desired.

7. After all settings are correct, click OK to create the new Windows login for the selected user or group.

Creating a New SQL Login Using SQL Query Analyzer

To configure a SQL login using the command-line SQL Query Analyzer interface, use the **sp_addlogin** command.

The syntax of the **sp_addlogin** command is:

```
sp_addlogin [ @loginame = ] 'login'
    [ , [ @passwd = ] 'password' ]
    [ , [ @defdb = ] 'database' ]
    [ , [ @deflanguage = ] 'language' ]
    [ , [ @sid = ] sid ]
    [ , [ @encryptopt = ] 'encryption_option' ]
```

Following are the arguments for the **sp_addlogin** command:

➤ [@loginame =] 'login'—The name of the SQL login being granted access.

➤ [@passwd =] 'password'—The password for the login. If not specified, a null password is assigned.

➤ [@defdb =] 'database'—Specifies the default database to be used for the login. If not specified, the **master** database is selected.

➤ [@deflanguage =] 'language'—Specifies the default language to be used for the login. If not specified, the server's default language is used.

➤ [@sid =] sid—Allows the specification of a unique 16-digit security identification number (SID) for the new login. If not specified, a null value is assigned.

➤ [@encryptopt =] 'encryption_option'—Specifies how the password is encrypted and stored in the system tables. If not specified, NULL is assumed.

➤ NULL—The password is encrypted.

➤ Skip_encryption—The password should be stored without reencryption.

➤ skip_encryption_old—The password was encrypted by a previous version of SQL Server and should be stored without reencryption. Used for upgrade purposes.

 The related **sp_password** command is used to reset a password using the SQL Query Analyzer.

Removing (Revoking) a Login Entry Using SQL Query Analyzer

A login entry is removed (revoked) using the Enterprise Manager to select and delete the entry. To remove (revoke) a Windows login using the command-line SQL Query Analyzer interface, use the **sp_revokelogin** command.

The syntax of the **sp_revokelogin** command is:

```
sp_revokelogin [@loginame =] 'login'
```

Following are the arguments for the **sp_revokelogin** command:

➤ [@loginame =] '*login*'—The name of the Windows user or group being revoked access in the form: DOMAIN\Name (for example, MYDOMAIN\MyGroup1).

 Login revocation does not prevent access to the database if the user or group is granted access through another login; it merely removes a particular login entry. For access by a user or group to be blocked, it must explicitly be denied.

Special Logins

A number of special logins exist including the local Windows Administrator user and Administrators group, which are both created as logins for each database. The guest SQL user may also be granted access permissions in cases where an access login is not otherwise available.

To provide backward compatibility with older versions of SQL Server, the **sa** account is also configured as a built-in Administrator login. It is best to change the password for this account or remove it when no longer needed to secure your database against unwanted access.

Authorization

After a connection has been completed, a user still has not been granted access permission to databases or database objects. Authorization is the process by which a user's access rights and permissions are determined. A login may be granted, not granted (revoked), or denied permissions either directly or through roles.

Permissions

Permissions include the rights granting or denying access to certain functions or database objects. Permissions may be granted at the server, database, or database object level. Just as users are assigned to groups and groups are granted login rights, permissions can be assigned to roles and logins are assigned to those roles. This simplifies complex permission assignments to large groups of logins in an enterprise deployment.

Table 11.2 details the three types of permissions.

Object Permissions

Object permissions involve the manipulation of data and the execution of procedures within a database. Object permissions apply to the **DELETE, EXECUTE, INSERT, SELECT,** and **UPDATE** commands and are granted on the object to be affected.

➤ **DELETE** and **INSERT** permissions can only be applied to entire tables or views because they affect entire rows.

➤ **EXECUTE** permissions affect stored procedures and functions.

➤ **SELECT** and **UPDATE** permissions can be applied to full tables and views or to specific columns. **SELECT** permissions can also affect access to user-defined functions.

Table 11.2	SQL Server 2000 permission types.
Type	**Scope**
Object	Manipulation of data and execution of procedures
Statement	Manipulation of databases and database objects
Implied	Permissions granted through membership in one of the fixed server roles or inherited by ownership* of the database object

*Ownership defaults to the user creating a database or database object if not otherwise specified, except when created by members of the sysadmin server role. The automatically created dbo (database owner) user owns objects created by members of this role. A table (for example, Table1) created by a member of the sysadmin role would be qualified as dbo.Table1 or simply Table1. If this table were created by a nonmember of this role named MyUser1, the table would be qualified as MyUSer1.Table1. Users accessing database objects owned by other users to which they have been granted permissions must specify the full qualifier if the object was not created by a member of the sysadmin server role or not configured to use the dbo user as its owner.

Statement Permissions

Statement permissions involve the manipulation of databases and database objects. These permissions are applied at the statement level, not to any particular object within a database. Statement permissions include the following:

➤ BACKUP—DATABASE and LOG (for example, **BACKUP DATABASE**)

➤ CREATE—DATABASE, DEFAULT, FUNCTION, PROCEDURE, RULE, TABLE, and VIEW

Implied Permissions

Implied permissions involve permissions granted through membership in one of the system roles or inherited by ownership of a database object. A number of roles are configured by default (see Figure 11.3), each of which has a large number of assigned permissions (see Figure 11.4).

Newly created logins are only granted the rights available to the **public** role and must be assigned any access permissions on databases and database objects directly or through role assignment inheritance.

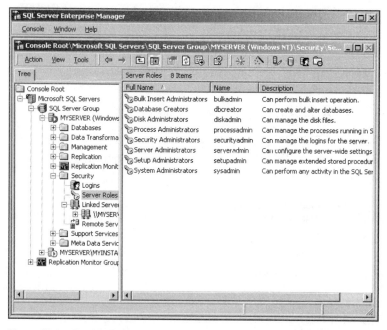

Figure 11.3 The SQL Server 2000 Security Roles screen lists the fixed server roles and a description of each.

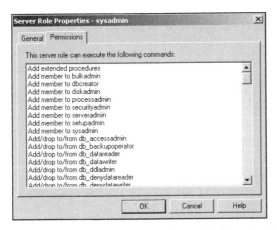

Figure 11.4 The SQL Server 2000 Server Role Properties Permissions tab lists the permissions for the **sysadmin** fixed server role.

Roles

Roles are groupings of permissions that may be assigned to logins. SQL Server includes eight fixed server roles (see Table 11.3) and nine fixed database roles (see Table 11.4) in addition to the **public** role, which is a special database role assigned to all database users.

User-defined roles can also be created and assigned, allowing for customized access configurations.

Table 11.3 SQL Server 2000 fixed server roles.	
Role	**Scope**
bulkadmin	Execution of the BULK INSERT statement
dbcreator	Creation and alteration of databases and database objects
diskadmin	Management of disk files
processadmin	Management of processes running in an instance of SQL Server
securityadmin	Management of login entries and permission to execute the **sp_password** stored procedure for all roles except **sysadmin**
serveradmin	Management of server-wide settings
setupadmin	Management of linked servers and execution of some system stored procedures
sysadmin	The overall administrative role, including the permissions of all other fixed server roles

Table 11.4 SQL Server 2000 fixed database roles.	
Role	Scope
db_accessadmin	Management of login access within the database
db_backupoperator	Backup of the database
db_datareader	Selection of data from any user table in the database
db_datawriter	Addition, modification, or deletion of data from any user table in the database
db_denydatareader	Denial of permission to select data from the database
db_denydatawriter	Denial of permission to add, change, or delete data within the database
db_ddladmin	Execution of all dynamic link libraries (DLLs) including the addition, modification, and deletion of database objects
db_owner	Overall maintenance and configuration of the database, including the permissions of all other fixed database roles
db_securityadmin	Management of database statement and object permissions, as well as roles and role membership within the database

Creating a User-Defined SQL Server Database Role Using Enterprise Manager

To create a user-defined database role using Enterprise Manager, take these steps:

1. Open the SQL Server 2000 Enterprise Manager by selecting Start|Programs| Microsoft SQL Server|Enterprise Manager.

2. In the left panel, expand the desired server group by clicking the plus sign.

3. Expand the configuration on the desired server by clicking the plus sign next to it, and enter authentication information if required.

4. Expand the Databases node by clicking the plus sign.

5. Expand the appropriate Database by clicking the plus sign.

6. Expand the Security node by clicking the plus sign. Select Roles to view existing database roles, or right-click and select New Database Role from the drop-down menu to open the Database Role Properties interface (see Figure 11.5).

7. Select the type of role (in this case, Standard), and select any logins to be assigned this role.

8. Click OK to create the new role and assign it to the specified users.

9. Right-click the new role and select Properties from the drop-down menu to open the Database Role Properties interface. Click Permissions to open the Permissions screen (see Figure 11.6).

Figure 11.5   The Database Role Properties screen for the user-defined database role **Data1Role1** shows the users included in this role.

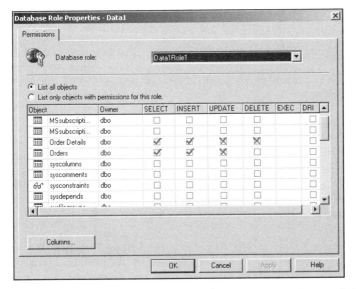

Figure 11.6   The Database Role Properties Permissions screen lists permissions granted for objects in the user-defined database role **Data1Role1**.

10. Set permissions for each database object desired by clicking on the checkbox. Clicking once generates a green checkmark (grant), twice generates a red "X" (deny), and three times removes the permission assignment (revoke).

11. After configuring all permissions for the role, click OK to apply the changes.

Creating a User-Defined SQL Server Database Role Using SQL Query Analyzer

To create a user-defined role using the command-line SQL Query Analyzer interface, use the **sp_addrole** command.

The syntax of the **sp_addrole** command is:

```
sp_addrole [ @rolename = ] 'role'
    [ , [ @ownername = ] 'owner' ]
```

Following are the arguments for the **sp_addrole** command:

➤ [@rolename =] '*role*'—The name of the new role, which must be unique within the database.

➤ [@ownername =] '*owner*'—Specifies an owner of the new role. If not specified, the owner of the role is the dbo user.

Adding Members to a SQL Server Database Role Using SQL Query Analyzer

To add a member to a user-defined role using the command-line SQL Query Analyzer interface, use the **sp_addrolemember** command.

The syntax of the **sp_addrolemember** command is:

```
sp_addrolemember [ @rolename = ] 'role' ,
    [ @membername = ] 'security_account']
```

Following are the arguments for the **sp_addrolemember** command:

➤ [@rolename =] '*role*'—The name of the user-defined role in the current database.

➤ [@membername =] '*security_account*'—Specifies the security account being added. A security account may be any valid Windows or SQL Server User login, Windows Group login, or SQL Server role.

Removing a Member from a SQL Server Database Role Using SQL Query Analyzer

To remove a member entry using the Enterprise Manager, select the properties of the desired role and remove the member from the list. To remove a member using the command-line SQL Query Analyzer interface, use the **sp_droprolemember** command.

The syntax of the **sp_droprolemember** command is:

```
sp_droprolemember [ @rolename = ] 'role' ,
    [ @membername = ] 'security_account'
```

Following are the arguments for the **sp_droprolemember** command:

➤ **[@rolename =]** '*role*'—The name of the user-defined role in the current database.

➤ **[@membername =]** '*security_account*'—Specifies the security account being removed.

Removing a User-Defined SQL Server Database Role Using SQL Query Analyzer

To remove a member entry using the Enterprise Manager, select the desired role and delete it. To remove a user-defined database role using the command-line SQL Query Analyzer interface, use the **sp_droprole** command.

The syntax of the **sp_droprole** command is:

```
sp_droprole  [ @rolename = ] 'role'
```

Following are the arguments for the **sp_droprole** command:

➤ **[@rolename =]** '*role*'—The name of the user-defined role in the current database being dropped.

Fixed server and database roles cannot be dropped.

Adding Members to a SQL Server Fixed Server Role Using SQL Query Analyzer

To add a member to a fixed server role using the command-line SQL Query Analyzer interface, use the **sp_addsrvrolemember** command.

The syntax of the **sp_addsrvrolemember** command is:

```
sp_addsrvrolemember [ @loginame = ] 'login' ,
    [ @rolename = ] 'role']
```

Following are the arguments for the **sp_addsrvrolemember** command:

➤ **[@loginame =]** 'login'—The login or Windows account being added. If the Windows account does not already have a login, this command will create it.

➤ **[@rolename =]** '*role*'—Specifies the fixed server role for the member addition. This must be one of the fixed server roles.

Removing a Member from a SQL Server Fixed Server Role Using SQL Query Analyzer

To remove a member entry using the Enterprise Manager, select the properties of the desired role and remove the member from the list. To remove a member from a fixed server role using the command-line SQL Query Analyzer interface, use the **sp_dropsrvrolemember** command.

The syntax of the **sp_dropsrvrolemember** command is:

```
sp_dropsrvrolemember [ @loginame = ] 'login' ,
    [ @rolename = ] 'role']
```

Following are the arguments for the **sp_dropsrvrolemember** command:

➤ [@loginame =] 'login'—The login being dropped from the role.

➤ [@rolename =] 'role'—Specifies the fixed server role for the removal.

Application Roles

At times, you may want to assign a role to an application rather than to a particular user login so that you can restrict database access. Application roles are user-defined database roles that are not associated with a particular login. When creating a new user-defined database role, select the application role option and specify a password. The password is used in establishing the application connection, which uses the permissions specified for the role.

Auditing SQL Server Security

After you have properly configured database security, you need to trace and record security-related activity, such as failed and successful logins.

Auditing of security is performed using the SQL Profiler utility detailed in Chapter 9. The Security Audit event classes cover most security monitoring needs. By default, the Audit Login and Audit Logoff classes are selected in the default trace template.

Computers used in governmental work may be required to conform to C2 security requirements. A C2 certified server must be configured according to published C2 requirements.

Practice Questions

Question 1

> Which of the following are valid authentication modes for SQL Server 2000?
> [Check all correct answers]
>
> ❏ a. C2
>
> ❏ b. NT Security
>
> ❏ c. Roles
>
> ❏ d. SQL Server (Mixed-Mode)
>
> ❏ e. Windows

Answers d and e are correct. The valid authentication modes available within SQL Server 2000 are SQL Server (also called Mixed-Mode) and Windows Authentication. Answer a is incorrect because C2 security requirements are governmentally specified requirements for securing a server, not an authentication mode. Answer b is incorrect because there is no NT Security Authentication Mode; the Windows Authentication Mode uses Windows NT 4.0 and Windows 2000 security principles. Answer c is incorrect because roles are used for assigning aggregated permissions, not as a connection authentication mode.

Question 2

> Three actions are possible when assigning login access and permissions:
>
> Deny
>
> Grant
>
> Revoke
>
> Match the following characteristics with the appropriate action:
>
> Explicitly prevents the action
>
> Overrides all other actions if present
>
> Removes the action
>
> Specifically allows the action

The correct answers are:

Deny

> Explicitly prevents the action

> Overrides all other actions if present

Grant

> Specifically allows the action

Revoke

> Removes the action specification

Question 3

> Which of the following are valid Transact-SQL (T-SQL) commands used in configuring login access? [Check all correct answers]
>
> ❏ a. sp_addlogin
>
> ❏ b sp_alterlogin
>
> ❏ c. sp_denylogin
>
> ❏ d. sp_grantlogin
>
> ❏ e. sp_revokelogin

Answers a, c, d, and e are correct. All four are valid T-SQL commands for manipulating login access. Answer b is incorrect because there is no **sp_alterlogin** T-SQL command.

Question 4

> Windows user User1 is a member of the Windows group Group1 within the domain MYDOMAIN. MYDOMAIN\User1 and MYDOMAIN\Group1 have been granted login rights to your server. Later, the login for MYDOMAIN\Group1 was revoked.
>
> Will MYDOMAIN\User1 be able to connect to the server?
>
> ○ a. Yes
>
> ○ b. No

Answer a is correct. Revoking access simply removes the login. MYDOMAIN\ User1 can still log in because it has its own rights, even though the group to which it belongs has lost its login access. Had MYDOMAIN\Group1 been denied access, MYDOMAIN\User1 would not have been able to log in, because a denial of access overrides any other options.

Question 5

> By default, newly created logins have access to all databases until permissions are denied to them.
>
> ❍ a. True
>
> ❍ b. False

Answer b is correct. Newly created logins only have access to permissions inherited from the **public** role and must be granted access permissions on databases and database objects before they can manipulate the data contained therein.

Question 6

> There are three types of permissions within SQL Server 2000:
>
> Implied
>
> Object
>
> Statement
>
> Match the following characteristics with the appropriate permission type:
>
> Allows procedure execution
>
> Is granted permission because of membership in one of the fixed server roles
>
> Inherits permission because of database or database object ownership
>
> Manipulates databases and database objects
>
> Is used in manipulations of data

The correct answers are:

Implied

Is granted permission because of membership in one of the fixed server roles

Inherits permission because of database or database object ownership

Object

Allows procedure execution

Is used in data manipulations

Statement

Manipulates databases and database objects

Question 7

Which of the following object permissions can only be applied to entire tables or views? [Check all correct answers]

❑ a. **DELETE**

❑ b. **EXECUTE**

❑ c. **INSERT**

❑ d. **SELECT**

❑ e. **UPDATE**

Answers a and c are correct. The **DELETE** and **INSERT** actions affect entire rows and can only be applied to entire tables or views. Answer b is incorrect because the **EXECUTE** command is used with stored procedures and functions and does not apply to tables and views. Answers d and e are incorrect because both **SELECT** and **UPDATE** actions can be applied to entire tables and views or to individual data columns.

Question 8

Which of the fixed server roles encompasses the permissions of all of the others?

- ○ a. **bulkadmin**
- ○ b. **dbcreator**
- ○ c. **diskadmin**
- ○ d. **processadmin**
- ○ e. **securityadmin**
- ○ f. **serveradmin**
- ○ g. **setupadmin**
- ○ h. **sysadmin**

Answer h is correct. The **sysadmin** fixed server role encompasses the permissions of all of the other fixed server roles. Answers a, b, c, d, e, f, and g are all incorrect because each has its own unique set of access permissions.

Question 9

Which of the following fixed database roles encompasses the permissions of all of the others?

- ○ a. **db_accessadmin**
- ○ b. **db_backupoperator**
- ○ c. **db_datareader**
- ○ d. **db_datawriter**
- ○ e. **db_denydatareader**
- ○ f. **db_denydatawriter**
- ○ g. **db_ddladmin**
- ○ h. **db_owner**
- ○ i. **db_securityadmin**

Answer h is correct. The **db_owner** fixed database role encompasses the permissions of all of the other fixed database roles. Answers a, b, c, d, e, f, g, and i are all incorrect because each has its own unique set of access permissions.

Question 10

Application roles use only SQL Server user logins for authentication.

○ a. True

○ b. False

Answer b is correct. Application roles do not use a user login for authentication. They have their own password, restricting access permissions for application access.

Need to Know More?

 Dalton, Patrick, and Paul Whitehead. *SQL Server 2000 Black Book.* The Coriolis Group: Scottsdale, Arizona, 2001. ISBN 1-57610-770-1. An excellent reference to keep close at hand during installation of SQL Server 2000. This is a necessary book in any DBA's library, as it has many solutions to commonly experienced issues.

 Iseminger, David. *Microsoft SQL Server 2000 Reference Library with CD-ROM.* Microsoft Press: Redmond, WA, 2000. ISBN 0-7356-1280-3. An exhaustive library covering detailed information on all aspects of SQL Server 2000 implementations. A necessary reference for IT departments supporting Microsoft SQL Server 2000 implementations.

 http://msdn.microsoft.com/library/default.asp?URL=/library/psdk/sql/portal_7ap1.htm. *Microsoft SQL Server 2000 Books Online.* A complete online copy of the documentation for SQL Server 2000. This is an SQL Server 2000 database administrator's best friend because it is included on the installation CD-ROM.

Automation
and Server Agents

. . . .

Terms you'll need to understand:

✓ SQL Server Agent

✓ Jobs

✓ Alerts

✓ Operators

✓ Fail-safe operator

✓ Master server

✓ Target server

✓ SQLAgentMail

✓ SQL Mail

✓ Database Maintenance Planning Wizard

✓ Log Shipping

Techniques you'll need to master:

✓ Managing a multiserver administration configuration

✓ Configuring the SQL Server Agent

✓ Creating automated Jobs, Alerts, and Operators

✓ Assigning alerts to notify operators when events occur during jobs

Maintaining a single server on a personal system is a daunting task. Expand this to an enterprise deployment involving a high-availability online transaction-processing (OLTP) multiserver configuration, and the requirements for routine checks and maintenance can rapidly drive even the most skilled database administrator to consider a job change to a lower stress environment. Simply remembering to perform each of the seemingly minor actions required for day-to-day performance maintenance is difficult, especially with servers that must be maintained around the clock. Automation is obviously necessary, but choosing from among the myriad options for automating routine tasks can be daunting.

This chapter covers the capabilities included in SQL Server 2000 for automating routine tasks, allowing the database administrator to concentrate on development and tasks too complex for automation. Command-line options are available for most automation capabilities, but the graphical user interface (GUI) management tools access in the SQL Server 2000 Enterprise Manager provides the most robust and rapidly deployed automation options. This chapter focuses on the tasks covered on the exam and is not intended to be an exhaustive rendering of all possible automation options. An instance of SQL Server 2000 must already be installed (see Chapters 4 and 5) on a Windows 2000 server platform. Additional references are listed at the end of this chapter.

Automating Administration Tasks

Automation comprises the programmed scheduling, processing, and success or failure notification of tasks performed by the SQL Server Agent without direct interaction by the database administrator. Good task candidates for automation include jobs that are:

➤ One time, prescheduled (running at a time other than immediate)

➤ Recurring

➤ In response to a predefined condition generating an alert

➤ Based on unpredictable conditions, such as CPU idle time

Automated jobs may also be manually run at other times as required. They are intended to simplify the administrative overhead required to support SQL Server databases.

Administration Components

The SQL Server Agent service is required to schedule tasks for automated independent action. Configuration of this service during installation was discussed in Chapters 6 and 7. Additionally, several other components are required to perform task automation.

Table 12.1	SQL Server 2000 automation components.
Component	**Description**
Jobs	A series of operations to be performed by the SQL Server Agent. Jobs are scheduled for execution or are triggered by an alert and may generate operator notifications based on the events occurring on each execution.
Alerts	An automated response to an event, which may be used to signal an operator that the event has occurred or to trigger a job in response to conditions on the server.
Operators	Individuals responsible for the maintenance of some aspect of a SQL Server instance. One or more operators can be notified of events that meet defined criteria using electronic mail (email), pager notification (using email), or the net send utility available in Windows NT and Windows 2000.

Table 12.1 details the three main automation components.

Multiserver Administration

Centralized management of automated tasks may be required in an enterprise environment. The SQL Server Agent is required for multiserver administration functions. Multiserver administration requires a master server that stores a copy of all automation tasks and one or more target servers that connect to the master server periodically to update the list of jobs they are to perform.

 Target servers can only be enlisted by one master server at a time. A target server must be defected (disconnected) from its master server before a different master server can enlist it.

Members of the **sysadmin** role manage multiserver administrative features on the master server but cannot make changes to the jobs scheduled on the target servers, ensuring security and centralized control of automation tasks in a large distributed environment.

 The master server Operator (MSXOperator), configured on the master server, is the only operator able to receive multiserver job notifications.

All target servers must be defected from the master server before a multiserver configuration can be dismantled, and a target server must be defected from the master server before renaming the target server.

Creating a Master Server

To create a master server using the Enterprise Manager, take the following steps:

1. Open the SQL Server 2000 Enterprise Manager by selecting Start|Programs| Microsoft SQL Server|Enterprise Manager.

2. Expand the desired server group by clicking the plus (+) sign.

3. Expand the configuration on the desired server by clicking the plus sign next to it, and enter authentication information if required.

4. Expand the Management node, and right-click the SQL Server Agent folder. Select Multiserver Administration and the Make This a Master option to open the Make MSX Wizard screen.

5. Follow the steps through the Wizard, setting up the MSXOperator account and configuring multiserver notification options (see Figure 12.1).

6. Select target servers and click OK to complete the server Make MSX operation.

After configuring the initial master and target servers, you can enlist additional target servers or delete existing target servers by right-clicking the SQL Server Agent folder. Select Multiserver Administration for the Add Target Servers and Manage Target Servers Now options.

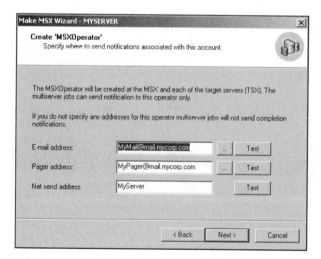

Figure 12.1   The Master Server Operator (MSXOperator) screen shows the notifications configuration setup.

Administration Agents

Task automation requires the functioning of several system agents, or services, that must be run on Windows NT or Windows 2000. The SQL Server (MSSQLServer) service must be started for any database functionality to be available. In addition, you must consider the following components when planning for system automation:

➤ *SQLServerAgent*—The service responsible for administering and enacting automation tasks. Without this service, SQL Server cannot perform automated jobs or generate alerts.

➤ *SQLAgentMail*—The mail component used by SQLServerAgent. It may use its own domain account and mail profile, different from that used by SQL Mail. SQLAgentMail can be used to send email notifications when an event is triggered or a scheduled task succeeds or fails.

➤ *SQL Mail*—The mail component accessed by MSSQLServer that must access email services provided by a host, such as Microsoft Exchange Server. To function, it must have its own domain account and mail profile on the host server. This component can return result sets and other forms of process-derived information generated from within the MSSQLServer session.

SQL Mail establishes a connection with a mail host, whereas SQLAgentMail establishes the connection on its own. Both may function with Microsoft Exchange Server. Use the Windows Event Viewer and Task Manager to verify proper functioning of these services, as detailed in Chapters 9 and 13.

Configuring the SQL Server Agent

Although you can accomplish basic configuration of the SQL Server Agent during installation (as covered in Chapters 6 and 7), you must configure the more advanced features in a separate operation before you can implement an automation plan.

To configure the options available within SQL Server Agent using the Enterprise Manager, take the following steps:

1. Open the SQL Server 2000 Enterprise Manager by selecting Start|Programs| Microsoft SQL Server|Enterprise Manager.

2. Expand the desired server group by clicking the plus sign.

3. Expand the configuration on the desired server by clicking the plus sign next to it, and enter authentication information if required.

4. Expand the Management node, and right-click the SQL Server Agent folder. Select Properties.

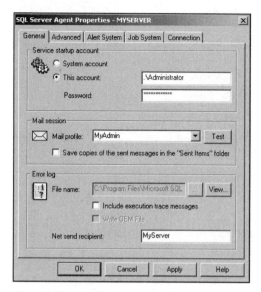

Figure 12.2 The SQL Server Agent Properties screen showing the General tab where auto mated mail options can be selected.

5. Configure the appropriate startup account, mail profile, and net send options on the General tab (see Figure 12.2).

6. On the Advanced tab, you can configure auto restart options, SQL event forwarding to a different server based on a defined severity level, and the conditions under which the CPU is considered to be idle (see Figure 12.3).

7. Configure Alert System details on the appropriate tab, including the specification for the fail-safe operator (see Figure 12.4).

 The fail-safe operator is contacted if all other pager notifications for an event alert have failed.

8. Set any limitations on log size and authentication details on the remaining tabs. Click OK to apply the changes.

Creating Jobs

A Job is a sequence of actions to be performed by the SQL Server Agent service at a scheduled time or on a recurring schedule. It can include notifying operators of job status via alerts. Jobs can be composed of Transact-SQL (T-SQL) commands, command-line application calls, and Microsoft ActiveX scripts.

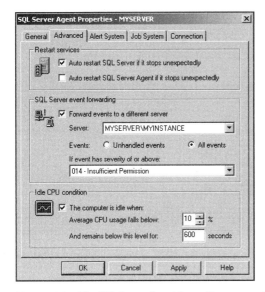

Figure 12.3   The SQL Server Agent Properties screen showing the Advanced tab where auto restart, event forwarding, and CPU idle conditions are set.

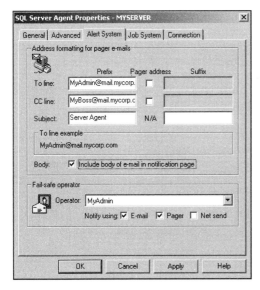

Figure 12.4   The SQL Server Agent Properties screen showing the Alert System tab where pager notifications and the fail-safe operator can be entered.

Jobs can be organized into categories to ease filtering and grouping according to logical or functional collections. Multiserver categories are only available on a master server (by default, [Uncategorized (Multi-Server)]). When copied to the target server, the multiserver category is changed to Jobs from MSX.

If replication is configured, a number of jobs are automatically created in the Local Server Jobs subfolder. This is why SQL Server Agent must be running for replication tasks to function properly.

To create a new job using the Enterprise Manager, take the following steps:

1. Open the SQL Server 2000 Enterprise Manager by selecting Start|Programs |Microsoft SQL Server|Enterprise Manager.

2. Expand the desired server group by clicking the plus sign.

3. Expand the configuration on the desired server by clicking the plus sign next to it, and enter authentication information if required.

4. Expand the Management node, and expand the SQL Server Agent folder. Right-click the Jobs subfolder, and select New Job.

   ➤ Categories may be edited by selecting All Tasks and Manage Job Categories here.

   ➤ To edit an existing job, expand the Jobs folder, and expand the Local and Multi Server Jobs subfolders. Right-click an individual job, and select Properties to open it for editing.

5. On the General tab, give the job a meaningful name that is unique within the database. Configure the category, target, owner, and description (see Figure 12.5).

6. On the Steps tab, create new steps to be taken by the job, or edit existing steps as required (see Figure 12.6).

   ➤ The command used to enact operating system commands or execute executable files (.exe, .com, .cmd, and .bat) is **CmdExec**.

7. On the Schedules tab, create new schedules and alerts, or edit existing items as required (see Figure 12.7).

   ➤ To run a job manually, right-click the job in the appropriate Jobs subfolder, and select Start Job.

8. Configure event notifications on the Notifications tab (see Figure 12.8), and click Apply when done.

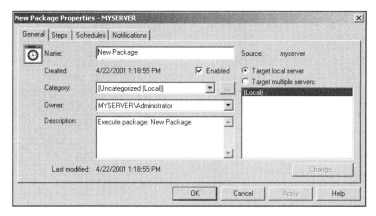

Figure 12.5 The New Package Properties screen showing the General tab with information about a job.

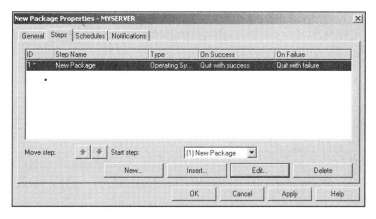

Figure 12.6 The New Package Properties screen showing the Steps tab containing the steps specified for the New Package job.

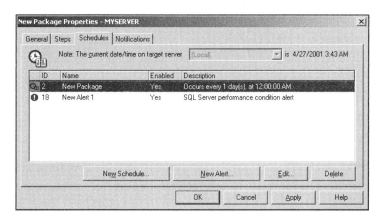

Figure 12.7 The New Package Properties screen showing the Schedules tab where schedules and alerts can be set up.

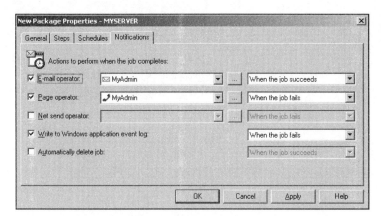

Figure 12.8   The New Package Properties screen showing the Notifications tab where actions to be performed when a job completes are set.

Creating Operators

Operators are those users responsible for the maintenance of a SQL Server instance. Events cause alerts to notify operators according to their configured methods of notification: email, pager (via email), and net send.

To create a new operator using the Enterprise Manager, take the following steps:

1. Open the SQL Server 2000 Enterprise Manager by selecting Start|Programs| Microsoft SQL Server|Enterprise Manager.

2. Expand the desired server group by clicking the plus sign.

3. Expand the configuration on the desired server by clicking the plus sign next to it, and enter authentication information if required.

4. Expand the Management node, and expand the SQL Server Agent folder. Right-click on the Operators subfolder, and select New Operator.

    ➤ To edit an existing operator, you must expand the Operators folder to view the operators. To open an operator for editing, right-click on it, and select Properties.

5. On the General tab, give the operator a unique name. Configure the appropriate notification details and pager availability (see Figure 12.9).

    ➤ The Test buttons allow you to verify each notification configuration.

6. On the Notifications tab, configure the appropriate notification for any events as desired. Click OK to create the new operator.

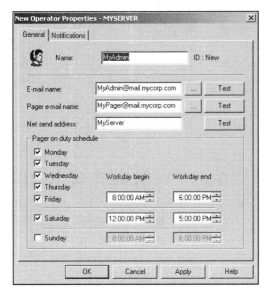

Figure 12.9   The New Operator Properties screen showing the General tab where you can enter information about an operator.

Creating Alerts

Alerts allow SQL Server 2000 to generate notifications, run jobs, or forward events to the Windows Application Log on another server. Before you create alerts for generating notifications, you must create operators who will receive the notifications.

To create a new alert using the Enterprise Manager, take the following steps:

1. Open the SQL Server 2000 Enterprise Manager by selecting Start|Programs| Microsoft SQL Server|Enterprise Manager.

2. Expand the desired server group by clicking the plus sign.

3. Expand the configuration on the desired server by clicking the plus sign next to it, and enter authentication information if required.

4. Expand the Management node and expand the SQL Server Agent folder. Right-click on the Alerts subfolder, and select New Alert.

   ➤ To edit an existing alert, you must expand the Alerts folder to view the individual alerts available. To open an alert for editing, right-click on it, and select Properties.

5. On the General tab, give the alert a meaningful name that is unique within the database. Configure the alert type and conditional boundaries (see Figure 12.10).

6. On the Response tab, configure the notification type for the appropriate operator (see Figure 12.11).

➤ Several operators may be notified by a single alert, each in its own manner as appropriate.

Database Maintenance Planning Wizard

Standard maintenance tasks are easily scheduled using the Database Maintenance Planning Wizard tool accessed within the Enterprise Manager utility. The Database Maintenance Planning Wizard provides scheduling of several types of tasks:

➤ Backing up databases and transaction log files

➤ Performing consistency checks

➤ Performing Log Shipping to maintain a "warm" standby server

➤ Rebuilding indexes using a new Fill Factor

➤ Removing empty database pages

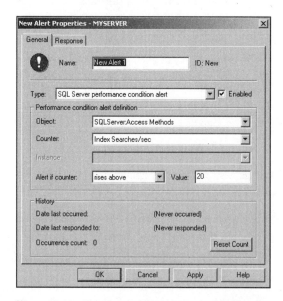

Figure 12.10 The New Alert Properties screen showing the General tab selected where a name and type can be assigned for an alert.

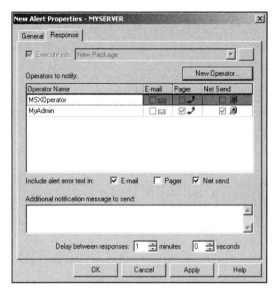

Figure 12.11 The New Alert Properties screen showing the Response tab where notification information is set.

 The Fill Factor is a number representing the percentage of the new index that will be populated by the existing data. A low Fill Factor (for example, 10) can be used in tables for such tasks as online transaction processing (OLTP) applications, whereas a higher Fill Factor can be used for more static tabular information to reduce the space allocated for the index.

Configuring the Log Shipping

To maintain a "warm" standby server (one that can be rapidly brought online in the event of a critical failure of the primary database server), Log Shipping can be configured by members of the **sysadmin** role, using the Database Maintenance Plan Wizard. Log Shipping involves the transfer of transaction log files to a standby server, maintaining the standby as a duplicate of the primary server. The process for bringing a standby server online was discussed in Chapter 8.

To configure the Log Shipping using the Database Maintenance Plan Wizard within the Enterprise Manager, take the following steps:

1. Open the SQL Server 2000 Enterprise Manager by selecting Start|Programs| Microsoft SQL Server|Enterprise Manager.

2. Expand the Tools menu, and select the Database Maintenance Plan Wizard.

3. Select the database that is to be synchronized with the standby server when prompted (see Figure 12.12).

Database Maintenance Plan Wizard - MYSERVER

Select Databases
Select the databases for which to create the maintenance plan.

   ○ All databases

   ○ All system databases (master, model, and msdb)

   ○ All user databases (all databases other than master, model, and msdb)

   ● These databases: Database

☑	Data1
☐	Data2
☐	distribution
☐	master

   ☑ Ship the transaction logs to other SQL Servers (log shipping)

      < Back   Next >   Cancel   Help

Figure 12.12   The Database Maintenance Plan Wizard screen showing Log Shipping selected for user database **Data1**.

Only one database can be selected for Log Shipping in a single Maintenance Plan package. If more than one database is selected, the Log Shipping option will be unavailable.

4. Continue through the Wizard, and add the appropriate destination database when prompted.

The destination must be a disk. Tape backup options are disabled for the Log Shipping process.

5. Configure the schedules, file retention periods, alerts, and any monitoring information required. Click OK to save the Log Shipping selections.

Practice Questions

Question 1

> You are the database administrator responsible for administration of a SQL Server 2000 instance. Your boss has given you a list of 17 unique, one-time tasks that must be performed when you have the time. You have decided to create scheduled jobs using the Enterprise Manager for these tasks.
>
> If this the most efficient use of the available tools?
>
> ○ a. Yes
>
> ○ b. No

Answer b is correct. Although it is possible to create jobs for each of the 17 tasks, automation should be used for recurring or scheduled tasks. Because none of these tasks will be repeated, and all may be completed whenever is convenient, it is generally simpler to perform the tasks manually than to create jobs for each.

Question 2

> Three administration components are involved in SQL Server automation:
>
> Alerts
>
> Jobs
>
> Operators
>
> Match the following characteristics with the appropriate component:
>
> A series of operations to be performed
>
> An automated response to an event
>
> Individuals responsible for SQL Server maintenance
>
> Scheduled for execution or triggered by an alert
>
> Used to trigger an event or generate a notification

The correct answers are:

Alerts

An automated response to an event

Used to trigger an event or generate a notification

Jobs

A series of operations to be performed

Scheduled for execution or triggered by an alert

Operators

Individuals responsible for SQL Server maintenance

Question 3

Which of the following are methods for Operator notification from within SQL Server 2000? [Check all correct answers]

❏ a. Email

❏ b. Net send

❏ c. Pager (email)

❏ d. Pager (tone dial)

❏ e. Printout

❏ f. Recurring

Answers a, b, and c are correct. The methods available for operator notification from within SQL Server 2000 are email, pager (via email), and the net send Windows utility. Answers d and e are incorrect because SQL Server does not have a native utility that allows for the generation of tone dialing or direct printout, although an alert could trigger an additional package, which could then create a printout. Answer f is incorrect—any of the three types of notification may repeat, but there is no Recurring notification type.

Question 4

> Target servers may be moved from one master server to another by simply enlisting the target server on the new master server.
>
> ○ a. True
> ○ b. False

Answer b is correct. A target server must first be defected from its original master server before being enlisted by another master server.

Question 5

> Two types of mail support are available within SQL Server 2000:
>
> SQL Mail
>
> SQLAgentMail
>
> Match the following characteristics with the appropriate mail support option (some may be used more than once):
>
> Establishes its own mail connection
>
> Can function with Microsoft Exchange Server
>
> Can only be used for event trigger and task completion notifications
>
> Must have a mail profile on the host
>
> Used by the MSSQLServer service
>
> Used by the SQLServerAgent service

The correct answers are:

SQL Mail

Can function with Microsoft Exchange Server

Must have a mail profile on the host

Used by the MSSQLServer service

SQLAgentMail

Establishes its own mail connection

Can function with Microsoft Exchange Server

Used by the SQLServerAgent service

Question 6

> The fail-safe operator is notified if the standby server must be synchronized.
>
> ○ a. True
> ○ b. False

Answer b is correct. The fail-safe operator is notified after an event has been unsuccessful in attempting to contact all available pager notifications. Synchronization with a standby server is configured using the Log Shipping automated task.

Question 7

> A new database administrator reports that he cannot change any of the jobs on one of the servers. He mentions that the Jobs from MSX are all locked and require your password to unlock them. Is this correct?
>
> ○ a. Yes
> ○ b. No

Answer b is correct. The category Jobs from MSX is created on a target server in a multiserver administration configuration. A user with the **sysadmin** role can change jobs, but only on the master server.

Question 8

> You are the database administrator responsible for a large number of servers running instances of SQL Server 2000. These servers are located in the main offices in Austin, Dallas, and Seattle. Because you are in meetings most of the day, you would like to have an easy way to log the completion of the automated index rebuilding on all of your servers. Can you configure alerts to create this central log?
>
> ○ a. Yes
> ○ b. No

Answer a is correct. Alerts can generate notifications, run jobs, or forward events to the Windows Application Log on another server. Because the servers are in such widely separated locations, you should consider using email notifications, however. In fact, email notifications are preferred in situations where network connectivity is sometimes intermittent because the email can retry via differing routes. Long distances are always good candidates for network troubles.

Question 9

> You are the database administrator responsible for a server used in the occasional reporting of archived sales data from past years. When you configured a Database Maintenance Plan to rebuild the clustered indexes on these tables, you configured the Fill Factor at 25 and the schedule to run nightly at 2:00 A.M.
>
> Is this an appropriate Maintenance Plan setup?
>
> ○ a. Yes
>
> ○ b. No

Answer b is correct. Because the database is rarely used, a nightly rebuild of indexes is probably not necessary. Yearly sales data does not need such regular rebuilding of clustered indexes, which reorders the data each time they are rebuilt, because data from past years changes only when a new year's data is added. Static data such as this also does not need a low Fill Factor. System resources may be better allocated using a high Fill Factor, leaving a small amount of empty space.

Question 10

> You are the database administrator responsible for an instance of SQL Server containing the **Sales**, **Customers**, and **Employees** databases. Because this server's availability is crucial to all operations within your business, rapid recovery from hardware failure is your highest priority. After buying a duplicate server, you plan to create a "warm" backup using a Database Management Planning package configured for Log Shipping of the three databases. Is this solution going to fulfill your needs in the event of a failure?
>
> ○ a. Yes
>
> ○ b. No

Answer b is correct. Although a "warm" standby server is an excellent backup solution in a high-availability or rapid-recovery scenario, Log Shipping cannot be configured for more than one database in a single package. You must create Log Shipping plans for the **Sales**, **Customers**, and **Employees** databases individually.

Need to Know More?

 Dalton, Patrick, and Paul Whitehead. *SQL Server 2000 Black Book.* The Coriolis Group: Scottsdale, Arizona, 2001. ISBN 1-57610-770-1. An excellent reference to keep close at hand during installation of SQL Server 2000. This is a necessary book in any DBA' library, as it has many solutions to commonly experienced issues.

 Delaney, Kalen. *Inside Microsoft SQL Server 2000.* Microsoft Press: Redmond, WA, 2000. ISBN 0-7356-0998-5. A good review of SQL Server 2000 components including white papers and articles on a broad range of topics.

 Iseminger, David. *Microsoft SQL Server 2000 Reference Library with CD-ROM.* Microsoft Press: Redmond, WA, 2000. ISBN 0-7356-1280-3. An exhaustive library covering detailed information on all aspects of SQL Server 2000 implementations. A necessary reference for IT departments supporting Microsoft SQL Server 2000 implementations.

 Shapiro, Jeffrey. *SQL Server 2000—The Complete Reference.* Osborne/McGraw-Hill: Berkeley, CA, 2001. ISBN 0-07-212588-8. A detailed, if somewhat lengthy, reference for SQL Server 2000 administration.

 http://msdn.microsoft.com/library/default.asp?URL=/library/psdk/sql/portal_7ap1.htm. *Microsoft SQL Server 2000 Books Online.* A complete online copy of the documentation for SQL Server 2000. This is an SQL Server 2000 database administrator's best friend because it is included on the installation CD-ROM.

Optimizing Performance

. . . .

Terms you'll need to understand:

✓ Baseline

✓ Resource bottlenecks

✓ Locking contention

✓ Index fragmentation

✓ **DBCC SHOWCONTIG** statement

✓ **DBCC REINDEX** statement

Techniques you'll need to master:

✓ Monitoring system performance using the available tools

✓ Creating and using a performance baseline to identify performance variance

✓ Defragmenting indexes on tables and indexed views

✓ Optimizing bulk copy process performance

After an instance of SQL Server 2000 has been in production for awhile, it does not always perform as well as it did when first installed. Normal use causes changes within the data and the indexes that reduce performance if not monitored and repaired. Bulk data operations using the **bcp** and **BULK INSERT** actions have a significant effect on performance and require special considerations. Hardware failure, process conflict with other applications running on the server, and insufficient resources can also contribute to a reduction in operational efficiency.

This chapter is an overview of the tools and techniques for monitoring SQL Server 2000 operations and discusses some of the common SQL Server performance optimization considerations that are included in the exam. There are as many specific configurations for performance optimization as there are installations of SQL Server 2000. As a database administrator, you should learn about the options that these tools have and determine which are useful for you. An instance of SQL Server 2000 must already be installed (see Chapters 4 and 5) on a Windows 2000 server platform. Additional references are listed at the end of this chapter.

Performance Monitoring

A detailed listing of troubleshooting tools and their uses was provided in Chapter 9. Familiarity with the following monitoring tools is essential in monitoring database and system operation:

➤ *SQL Profiler*—A graphical tool that allows the monitoring and logging of events within an instance of SQL Server 2000 using processes referred to as *traces*. Traces may be saved and later replayed on test servers configured identically to the production server from which they were obtained. This tool can monitor multiple instances including those on remote servers, but a separate trace must be established for each monitored instance.

➤ *System Monitor*—A graphical tool accessed within the Windows 2000 Performance Console (also called the *Performance Monitor* in Windows NT 4.0) that allows monitoring and logging of system resources and process activities. The system monitor can be used to monitor multiple servers at once, allowing easy graphical comparison of data. The System Monitor can be opened by way of the path Start|Programs|Administrative Tools|Performance.

 SQL Profiler and Windows System Monitor can both be configured to generate monitoring logs and respond to changing situations. SQL Profiler is used to monitor SQL Server processes and operational details, whereas the Windows System Monitor tracks system process and resource utilization.

➤ *Error Logs*—SQL Server generates events in the Windows 2000 and Windows NT 4.0 application event logs when errors occur (see Figure 13.1).

➤ *Enterprise Manager*—This graphical utility provides information on current activity and other ad hoc monitoring information. The Enterprise Manager can be used to view current information on any registered server.

➤ *Transact-SQL (T-SQL)*—Provides a wide variety of command-line statements helpful in performance monitoring, particularly the **sp_who, sp_lock,** and **sp_monitor** stored procedures.

➤ *DBCC statements*—The Database Console Commands (DBCC) also provide a number of command-line optimization tools, including the **DBCC SHOWCONTIG, DBCC REINDEX,** and **DBCC INDEXDEFRAG** statements.

➤ *Additional utilities*—Other command-line executables, such as the **sqldiag** utility and various third-party utilities, provide additional information useful for optimizing SQL Server 2000 instances.

Most command-line statements and utilities affect only the local server. Some are restricted to the default instance only because they were brought forward from earlier versions of SQL Server.

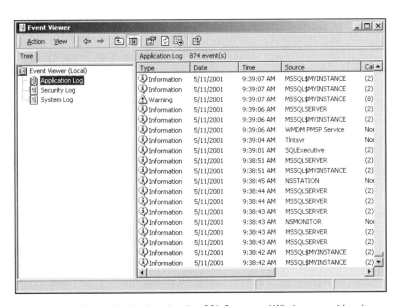

Figure 13.1   The Application log showing SQL Server and Windows event logging.

Establishing a Baseline

You must know what normal operational levels are before you can know if performance is being degraded. This is known as *establishing a baseline*—that is, what the "normal" level of operation is. You should monitor performance statistics for a period of time to spot high utilization periods of time, days of the week, or when routine operations are executed.

 Both unusually high and unusually low periods of operation are important—even exceptionally efficient periods of operation can be helpful in identifying areas for later performance optimization.

Compare new monitoring statistics to this baseline, and take a new baseline on a recurring basis to better understand the impact that changes in data, hardware, and utilization have on server performance. When establishing a baseline, watch for anything out of the ordinary, including the following:

➤ Peak and off-peak utilization periods on both an hourly and daily basis

➤ Query and command response time

➤ Routine maintenance response time including backup and restore job processing

➤ Any other odd or unusual recurring patterns or unique variations that coincide with other process occurrences

Identifying Problem Areas

A tremendous number of problem areas can affect the performance of a server. A clean and secure environment, well-maintained network and power connections, and continued maintenance on the server hardware form the first line of defense against failure. You should avoid running unnecessary processes on your database server to maximize available resources, but there are several other areas of difficulty that you may encounter during normal operations.

Resource Bottlenecks

System bottlenecks occur whenever the demand for resources exceeds their availability. Adding additional processors, memory, and disk storage can all improve performance when bottlenecks occur in these areas. Use the System Monitor to watch for resource bottlenecks with particular attention to disk read/write actions, processor utilization, and memory access including paging read/write actions. Check all drives and CPUs if multiples are available to watch for unbalanced access that can be resolved by such actions as reconfiguring file and filegroup locations.

The **sp_monitor** and **sp_spaceused** stored procedures are also helpful for viewing utilization statistics and may be enacted from within the SQL Query Analyzer or triggered by events within SQL Server, whereas the **sqldiag** executable command-line utility can be used to generate query history trace diagnostics on the local server from the command-line.

 All processes require system resources, including monitoring processes. Take care to avoid affecting performance by the very processes used to check for problems.

Record Locking

Record locking and deadlocks can significantly impair overall performance. Bulk updates and other types of user access can create locking issues during normal operating hours in a production environment. As more users access the database simultaneously, delays caused by locking contention increase. The Enterprise Manager provides an easy way to view current locks (see Figure 13.2). Viewing a lock's Properties and selecting Kill Process from the available options (see Figure 13.3) manually terminates a lock or deadlock.

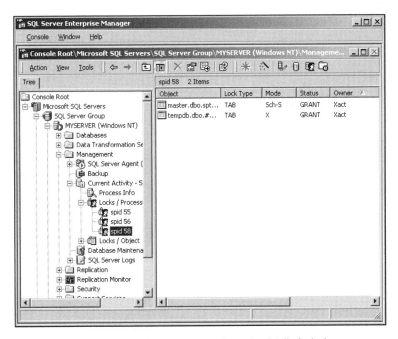

Figure 13.2   The Enterprise Manager screen shows the detail of a lock.

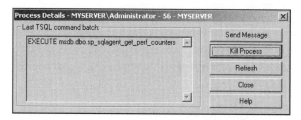

Figure 13.3 The Lock Properties screen shows the details of a Kill Process selection.

A SQL Profiler trace may be configured to monitor locking operations to identify trends and users who generate locking conditions more often than others do. Reconstructing views or access permissions can often help avoid this type of difficulty. The **sp_lock** stored procedure reports snapshots of current locking information similar to those provided by the Enterprise Manager.

User Activity

Monitoring user activity is also important to watch for unnecessary database access, inefficient ad hoc querying methods, and resource-intensive routine operations that should be conducted during off-peak hours, such as the BCP utility, which can impair performance. SQL Profiler and Windows System Monitor can be used to collect usage statistics, and the Enterprise Manager can be used for ad hoc monitoring of current usage. The **sp_who** stored procedure is also helpful in checking for current SQL Server users and process information including currently executing and blocked statements.

Optimizing Performance

After baselines have been established and monitoring has revealed problem areas, it is time for action. Resolving resource bottlenecks can be as simple as adding another processor or memory or as complex as redistributing often-accessed tables into files and filegroups spanning multiple drives to balance read/write performance better. Lock contention can be handled by moving conflicting bulk procedures to off-peak hours or redesigning application access and the stored procedures that are generating the locks.

Resolving user activity issues can require anything from resource upgrades, application redesign, or permissions reconfigurations. These issues tend to be fluid as well as intermittent because they are dependent on client access, which can vary widely in such environments as a large enterprise deployment or globally accessible e-commerce portal.

Index Defragmentation

Indexes, both clustered and nonclustered, on the tables and indexed views are also particularly important to the overall performance of a database. Whenever users report a slowing of database access, you should check the relevant indexes for fragmentation. Fragmentation occurs when large transactions require the reorganization of index information in a less efficient manner, creating an unequal distribution and unused space. The process of defragmentation involves the regeneration of indexes in a contiguous layout with only the additional space remaining as defined by the fill factor settings.

The **DBCC SHOWCONTIG** statement is used to display data and index fragmentation statistics for a specified table from within the SQL Query Analyzer. The syntax of the **DBCC SHOWCONTIG** statement is:

```
DBCC SHOWCONTIG
    [    ( { table_name | table_id | view_name | view_id }
            [ , index_name | index_id ]
        )
    ]
    [ WITH { ALL_INDEXES
                | FAST [ , ALL_INDEXES ]
                | TABLERESULTS [ , { ALL_INDEXES } ]
                [ , { FAST | ALL_LEVELS } ]
            }
    ]
```

Following are the arguments for the **DBCC SHOWCONTIG** command:

➤ *table_name* | *table_id* | *view_name* | *view_id*—The table or indexed view to be checked for fragmentation.

➤ *index_name* | *index_id*—The index to be checked for fragmentation.

➤ **WITH**—Specifies the types of fragmentation information to be returned by the command.

➤ **FAST**—Specifies whether a minimal scan should be performed and reported.

➤ **TABLERESULTS**—Specifies that the results should be returned as a rowset, for use in order commands (when the **ORDER BY** clause is used in a SELECT statement, or the **ORDER** hint is used during a bulk transaction).

➤ **ALL_INDEXES**—Specifies that results should be returned for all indexes on the specified table or view. This overrides the *index_name* specification, if present.

➤ **ALL_LEVELS**—Specifies that results should contain information for all levels of each index processed. Cannot be used with the **FAST** option, but can be used with the **TABLERESULTS** specification.

If fragmentation is discovered, you can defragment by using the **DBCC INDEXDEFRAG** command or by rebuilding the index. To rebuild an index, you first drop the index and then recreate it using the **DROP INDEX** and **CREATE INDEX** commands, by using the **ALTER TABLE** command detailed in Chapter 7. You can also use the **DBCC REINDEX** command, which performs the same actions as the **DROP INDEX** and **CREATE INDEX** commands and which can be applied to multiple indexes using a single statement. The syntax of the **DBCC REINDEX** statement is

```
DBCC DBREINDEX
    (    [ 'database.owner.table_name'
            [ , index_name
                [ , fillfactor ]
            ]
        ]
    )    [ WITH NO_INFOMSGS ]
```

Following are the arguments for the **DBCC REINDEX** command:

➤ *'database.owner.table_name'*—Specifies the name of table to be reindexed. If only *table_name* is provided, the single quotation marks (') are not needed.

➤ *index_name*—The name of a specific index to be rebuilt. If not specified, all indexes will be rebuilt.

➤ *fillfactor*—The percentage of index page space to be used for storing data when the index is created. A value of 0 specifies the use of the current fill factor value for each index.

➤ **WITH NO_INFOMSGS**—Suppresses all messages up to a severity level of 10.

Bulk Copy Optimization

Rebuilding clustered indexes reorganizes data within the specified table, consuming a large portion of the available resources and creating locking contention issues during the rebuild process. However, when performing bulk update procedures (detailed in Chapter 10), it is often best to drop clustered indexes first before performing the **bcp** or **BULK INSERT** action and then rebuild them. This is recommended because clustered indexes reorganize data within tables as each row is inserted, creating a tremendous performance bottleneck.

Following are a number of other actions that can improve bulk operation performance:

➤ Use the **BULK INSERT** statement rather than the bcp utility when possible, as it is faster.

➤ Use the **TABLOCK** hint to force the use of table-level locking rather than record-level locking during the update procedure.

➤ Use the largest batch size possible. Each batch is processed as a single action and will rollback entirely if a failure occurs. The larger the batch size, the fewer separate processes are required to complete the data update.

➤ Use the Bulk-logged recovery model during bulk updates, and return to Full recovery after completed.

➤ Load data in parallel from multiple clients. If a large bulk copy process must be performed and several servers are available, split the target data into smaller input files, and copy them into the target database in parallel.

 All indexes must be dropped and later recreated for this action. Clustered indexes must be recreated from a single process, but nonclustered indexes can be recreated in parallel.

➤ Use the **ORDER** hint matching the columns in the same order as the index to improve bulk copy performance. Organizing data in the same order as the index is more efficient than using bulk transactions that require data translation and reorganization before inserting or updating each row.

➤ Bypass the need for default value insertion in null fields using the **KEEPNULLS** or -k switch. This avoids the need to check each null value for the appropriate default value to insert in its place. The column must be configured to allow null values to use this option.

Practice Questions

Question 1

Several tools are available to monitor performance, including the following:

DBCC statements

Enterprise Manager

SQL Profiler

System Monitor

Match the following characteristics with the appropriate tool. (Note: some may be used more than once.):

Creates trace processes

Includes command-line options for index defragmentation

Can be used to log data to establish trends

Used for ad hoc monitoring of current activity

The correct answers are:

DBCC statements

    Includes command-line options for index defragmentation

Enterprise Manager

    Used for ad hoc monitoring of current activity

SQL Profiler

    Creates trace processes

    Can be used to log data to establish trends

System Monitor

    Can be used to log data to establish trends

Question 2

Splitting a bulk update into smaller input files and performing the bulk update actions from multiple clients simultaneously can improve bulk copy performance.

○ a. True

○ b. False

Answer a is correct. Parallel bulk copy operations can improve performance.

Question 3

Which of the following terms is used for the "normal" level of database operation against which later levels are measured for changes?

○ a. Baseline

○ b. Bottleneck

○ c. Defragmentation

○ d. Event log

○ e. Trace

Answer a is correct. A baseline is a measure of normal operational levels used to check for alter changes. Answer b is incorrect because a bottleneck occurs when resource demand exceeds availability. Answer c is incorrect because defragmentation involves the reorganization of fragmented data into a more compressed contiguous order. Answers d and e are incorrect because the Windows event logs and SQL Profiler traces are tools used to monitor operational performance.

Question 4

The Enterprise Manager should be used to create a system usage baseline.

○ a. True

○ b. False

Answer b is correct. To create a baseline, you should log system performance over a period of hours, days, and weeks to determine peak and off-peak times and other performance qualities. The Enterprise Manager is used to view current activity, whereas the SQL Profiler and Windows System Monitor provide logging capability useful in capturing trend data to establish a baseline.

Question 5

> Which of the following are actions that can improve bulk copy performance? [Check all correct answers]
>
> ❏ a. Drop indexes first and then rebuild them.
>
> ❏ b. Load data in parallel.
>
> ❏ c. Use the Full recovery model.
>
> ❏ d. Use the largest batch size possible.
>
> ❏ e. Use the **TABLOCK** hint.

Answers a, b, d, and e are correct. Answer c is incorrect because the Full recovery model logs each update action. The Bulk-logged recovery mode performs minimal bulk update logging.

Question 6

> The action of monitoring performance can cause a reduction in performance.
>
> ○ a. True
>
> ○ b. False

Answer a is correct. All processes require resources, and even the monitoring processes can reduce overall performance by utilizing needed resources.

Question 7

> Several steps are required to identify and resolve slowed table access due to index fragmentation. Arrange the following steps in the proper order:
>
> Check for index fragmentation on the table.
>
> Defragment or rebuild the appropriate indexes.
>
> Establish a performance baseline.
>
> Identify slowed tabular access.
>
> Monitor operational performance.
>
> Recheck operational performance for changes.

The correct answer is:

Establish a performance baseline.

Monitor operational performance.

Identify slowed tabular access.

Check for index fragmentation on the table.

Defragment or rebuild the appropriate indexes.

Recheck operational performance for changes.

Question 8

> Which of the following are statements that can be used to resolve index fragmentation? [Check all correct answers]
>
> ❏ a. **ALTER TABLE**
>
> ❏ b. **CREATE INDEX**
>
> ❏ c. **DBCC INDEXDEFRAG**
>
> ❏ d. **DBCC REINDEX**
>
> ❏ e. **DEFRAG INDEX**
>
> ❏ f. **DROP INDEX**

Answers a, b, c, d, and f are correct. The commands **ALTER TABLE, CREATE INDEX, DBCC REINDEX,** and **DROP INDEX** can be used to rebuild indexes. The **DBCC INDEXDEFRAG** command can be used to defragment an index. Answer e is incorrect because there is no **DEFRAG INDEX** command.

Question 9

> The **DBCC SHOWCONTIG** command identifies and corrects index fragmentation on a specified table or indexed view.
>
> ○ a. True
>
> ○ b. False

Answer b is correct. The **DBCC SHOWCONTIG** statement is used to check for index fragmentation but does not perform defragmentation actions.

Question 10

> Which of the following statements can be used to defragment all of the indexes on a table at once?
>
> ○ a. **ALTER TABLE**
>
> ○ b. **CREATE INDEX**
>
> ○ c. **DBCC REINDEX**
>
> ○ d. **DROP INDEX**

Answer c is correct. The **DBCC REINDEX** statement can be used to rebuild all of the indexes on a specified table. Answers a, b, and d are incorrect because the **ALTER TABLE, CREATE INDEX,** and **DROP INDEX** commands are used in combination to drop and recreate a specified index.

Need to Know More?

 Dalton, Patrick, and Paul Whitehead. *SQL Server 2000 Black Book.* The Coriolis Group: Scottsdale, Arizona, 2001. ISBN 1-57610-770-1. An excellent reference to keep close at hand during installation of SQL Server 2000. This is a necessary book in any DBA's library, as it has many solutions to commonly experienced issues.

 Iseminger, David. *Microsoft SQL Server 2000 Reference Library with CD-ROM.* Microsoft Press: Redmond, WA, 2000. ISBN 0-7356-1280-3. An exhaustive library covering detailed information on all aspects of SQL Server 2000 implementations. A necessary reference for IT departments supporting Microsoft SQL Server 2000 implementations.

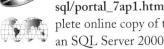 http://msdn.microsoft.com/library/default.asp?URL=/library/psdk/ sql/portal_7ap1.htm. *Microsoft SQL Server 2000 Books Online.* A complete online copy of the documentation for SQL Server 2000. This is an SQL Server 2000 database administrator's best friend because it is included on the installation CD-ROM.

Sample Test

Question 1

You are the database administrator responsible for administration of a SQL Server 2000 instance used by a regional furniture store chain. Any of the local store managers can mark an item in the **INVENTORY** table with a true value for the **ON_SALE** column, using a distributed Visual Basic application provided to them. You need to make sure that the Inventory Manager is notified via email when any items are listed as on sale, without changing the already deployed application.

Which of the following solutions would be the most efficient method to accomplish this?

○ a. Create a stored procedure to be used for changing the **ON_SALE** column and sending the notification.

○ b. Create a special login, and grant Update permission for the **ON_SALE** column only to that login.

○ c. Add an Update trigger to the **ON_SALE** column that will send the notification.

○ d. Schedule a recurring job that will run on a regular basis, checking for any changes to the **INVENTORY** table and raising an alert that will notify the proper operator if any changes have occurred.

Question 2

You are the database administrator responsible for the administration of three SQL Server 2000 instances used to track sales and employee data for a corporation with headquarters in New York, San Antonio, and Dallas. Both instances are using Windows Authentication Mode, and login rights are restricted to members of the domain-level Sales group. It becomes necessary to restrict login rights for the instance supporting the sales data to only the sales members located in the Texas offices using the simplest method available. Which of the following solutions is the most efficient?

○ a. Remove the Sales group's login rights from both instances, create a TexasSales domain group for the sales members in the Texas offices, and create logins for this group.

○ b. Deny login rights to the Sales group's login on both instances, create a TexasSales domain group for the sales members in the Texas offices, and create logins for this group.

○ c. Create a SQL user login called TexasSales, and grant login access to this login only on both instances.

○ d. Create a NewYorkSales domain group for the sales members in New York, create a login for this group on the instance supporting the sales data, and deny login rights for this login.

○ e. Remove the New York sales members from the Windows domain Sales group.

Question 3

You are the database administrator for a SQL Server 2000 instance used for tracking employee data for a large corporation. The server is using Windows Authentication Mode and is configured to allow access by the HumanResources and Managers domain groups. A new web portal has been created for reporting public data from the **Employees** database that displays the winners of the Employee of the Month award to anyone accessing the Web site. A Guest login to the database has been configured in the Web page code for accessing the necessary information, and the Web page has been granted Anonymous access. Users have reported that they do not see the Employee of the Month data when they access the Web page. What two steps must you take to allow anyone to access the data via the Web site? [Check all correct answers]

❏ a. Create a login for the Anonymous domain account.

❏ b. Create a login for the Guest domain account.

❏ c. Grant access permissions for the **Employees** database to the Guest login.

❏ d. Set a blank **sa** password.

❏ e. Configure the server for Mixed-Mode Authentication.

Question 4

The Managers domain group has been given login and access permission to the **Employees**, **Sales**, and **Inventory** databases in an instance of SQL Server 2000. Your company has recently acquired another company and has integrated both company's managers into the Managers group. The board has decided that the new members of the Managers group should not be allowed to modify data in the **Employees** database records until Human Resources has completed all reviews of the new employees.

You have been directed to remove data modification rights to tables in the **Employees** database for new managers. After creating a NewManagers domain group and adding all of the new managers to this group, you created a login for the NewManagers group. You now need to restrict update access for this group. Which of the following roles will restrict only the update permissions to the database?

○ a. **db_datareader**

○ b. **db_datawriter**

○ c. **db_dataupdate**

○ d. **db_denydatareader**

○ e. **db_denydatawriter**

○ f. **db_denydataupdate**

Question 5

A new sales manager's position has been created in your company. The new sales manager was promoted from within the sales force. You are the administrator for a SQL Server 2000 instance, which contains the **Employees**, **Sales**, and **Inventory** databases for your company. After you add the new manager, Arial Jones, to the Managers domain group, she reports that she can view but cannot change any information in the **HumanResources** table.

The roles assigned to the Sales and Managers groups are as follows:

- *Sales*—Employees (**db_denydatawriter**), Sales (**db_owner**), Inventory (**db_datareader** and **db_datawriter**)
- *Managers*—Employees (**db_datareader**, **db_datawriter**), Sales (**db_owner**), Inventory (**db_owner**)

You have decided that to grant Arial full access to the **Employees** database, you will add Arial to the **db_accessadmin** role.

Will this correct the problem?

- ○ a. Yes
- ○ b. No

Question 6

Three of the roles created by default within SQL Server 2000 are:

dbcreator

serveradmin

sysadmin

Match the following permissions with the appropriate role (some may be used more than once):

Creation and alteration of databases and database objects

Management of server-wide settings

Overall administration

Question 7

You are the database administrator for a SQL Server 2000 instance used for sensitive employee data for the Human Resources department of your company. You must make sure that all access to this database, both successful and failed, must be logged.

The auditing level on the Security tab of the server properties is now set to Failure. You decide to set the auditing level to All to start logging all access attempts to the Windows Application log immediately.

Is this all that you have to do to start access logging?

○ a. Yes

○ b. No

Question 8

Roles are available at two levels within SQL Server 2000:

Server

Database

Match the following roles with the appropriate operation level:

bulkadmin

processadmin

setupadmin

User-defined

Question 9

The login Martin has been created for a domain user account by the same name. Martin is also a member of the Managers domain group. Managers has been granted login rights to the **Inventory** database. Martin's login has been granted login rights as well. You have been directed to prevent Martin from accessing the database.

You decide that denying access rights for the user login Martin but leaving him as a member of the Managers group is the best solution available.

Will this prevent Martin's access to the database?

○ a. Yes

○ b. No

Question 10

You are the database administrator responsible for installing and administering a SQL Server 2000 instance that will be used by over 1,000 users within a Windows 2000 domain as well as Anonymous Web users.

You have decided to set up the instance using Windows Authentication Mode and the TCP/IP and Named Pipes network libraries and to grant database access to the Guest login and the Domain Users group.

Will this allow access as required?

- ○ a. Yes
- ○ b. No

Question 11

You are the database administrator responsible for administration of a SQL Server 2000 instance. You need to automate an update process affecting multiple tables in the **Sales** database each night.

Which of the following tools will you use to accomplish this?

- ○ a. Query Analyzer
- ○ b. Enterprise Manager
- ○ c. Data Transformation Services
- ○ d. SQL Profiler

Question 12

You are the database administrator responsible for an instance of SQL Server 2000 used as a centralized data repository to populate the **DailySales** table with data from instances of SQL Server 2000 located in 20 cities around the country. You have decided to use a distributed SELECT transaction, configuring all 20 remote instances as linked servers.

Will this solution perform the desired action?

- ○ a. Yes
- ○ b. No

Question 13

Several versions of SQL Server 2000 are available:

Desktop Engine

Developer

Enterprise

Evaluation

Personal

Standard

Windows CE

Match the following characteristics with the appropriate version (some may be used more than once):

A component that can be distributed with applications

Designed for replication of data on Windows CE devices

Designed for small workgroup environments

Licensed for development only

Limited to five concurrent batch processes

Expires after 120 days

Fully featured version

Standalone version for mobile users

Question 14

You are the database administrator responsible for several Windows 2000 servers running instances of SQL Server 2000. To better balance the usage load, you need to move the **Orders** database from one server to another. What is the easiest method to do this?

- ○ a. Backup the database and all transaction logs on the original server, restore the database and transaction logs on the destination server, and remove the database from the original server.

- ○ b. Create a Data Transformation Service (DTS) package that will export all of the data on the original server and remove the database, create a DTS package that will import the data into a new database on the new server, and schedule the automated tasks to run during a low-utilization time.

- ○ c. Detach the database from its original server, copy the database and transaction log files to the new server, attach the database to the new server, and remove the old copy of the files.

- ○ d. Configure Log Shipping to send all of the transaction logs to a "warm" standby server, synchronize the database and transaction log files, remove the old server from the network, rename the new server and restart it, and then remove the database from the old server.

Question 15

You are the database administrator for a SQL Server 2000 instance used for tracking employee data for a large corporation. The server is using Windows Authentication Mode and is configured to allow access by the HumanResources and Managers domain groups. A large data file has been provided, containing all data for employees terminated before the year 2000. You need to import this file, create a clustered index based on the **EmpID** field, and minimize the impact of the records on database backups. What two steps must you take to perform these tasks? [Check all correct answers]

- ❑ a. Build the clustered index with a high Fill Factor.
- ❑ b. Build the clustered index with a low Fill Factor.
- ❑ c. Configure the server for Mixed-Model recovery.
- ❑ d. Place the data in an OldTerm.ldf file.
- ❑ e. Place the data in an OldTerm.ndf file.

Question 16

You are the database administrator responsible for administration of a SQL Server 2000 instance used by a small grocery store. Whenever quantities are added to the **BACKORDER** column of the **Orders** table, you need to update the value stored in the **PENDING** column for that item in the **InvSummary** table. When you receive items from your vendor into the **Receiving** table, you must update the **PENDING** column in the **InvSummary** table to reflect values in the **ITEMS_REC** column of the **Receiving** table.

Which of the following solutions is the most efficient method to accomplish this?

○ a. Create a stored procedure UPDATE_PENDING that updates the value in the **PENDING** column of the **InvSummary** table and that is called by the inventory management application each time an invoice or receipt is posted.

○ b. Configure a recurring job that updates all of the fields in the **InvSummary** table based on aggregate queries of data in the **Orders**, **Receiving**, and **InvSummary** tables.

○ c. Add Update triggers to the **BACKORDER** column of the **Orders** table and the **ITEMS_REC** column of the **Receiving** table that update the related value stored in the **PENDING** column of the **InvSummary** table.

○ d. Configure a distributed transaction that will update the **PENDING** column of the **InvSummary** table based on aggregate queries of data in the **Orders**, **Receiving**, and **InvSummary** tables.

Question 17

Which of the following file types must be present to attach a detached database? [Check all correct answers]

❑ a. .ldf

❑ b. .mdb

❑ c. .mdf

❑ d. .ndf

❑ e. .rdf

Question 18

If you have a table associated with a filegroup that has been marked as read-only, will assigning users to the **db_datawriter** role allow them to view data stored in this table?

○ a. Yes

○ b. No

Question 19

You are the database administrator for a SQL Server 2000 instance used for tracking employee data for a small corporation with a high volume of data updates. The server is using Windows Authentication Mode, and the instance currently resides on the C: drive, the only drive available on the server. You have determined that available drive space is causing reduced performance for the instance and preventing expansion of the indexes on several tables associated with the PRIMARY filegroup. To improve performance, management has finally approved the purchase of two additional drives, which will be configured as D: and E: drives. To achieve the best performance, which of the following configurations should you use?

○ a. Place the primary data (.mdf) and transaction log (.ldf) files on the D: drive and the secondary data files (.ndf) on the E: drive.

○ b. Place the primary data (.mdf) files on the D: drive and secondary data (.ndf) and transaction log (.ldf) files on the E: drive.

○ c. Place the primary (.mdf) and secondary (.ndf) data files on the D: drive and the transaction log (.ldf) files on the E: drive.

○ d. Keep the primary (.mdf) data files on the C: drive, and place the secondary (.ndf) data files on the D: drive and the transaction log (.ldf) files on the E: drive.

Question 20

Three elements are required for successful snapshot replication:

Distributors

Publishers

Subscribers

Arrange these three in the order that data will traverse them during database replication.

Question 21

You are the database administrator for a SQL Server 2000 instance used as a central repository of data extracted from 11 independent SQL Server and 3 Oracle databases configured as OLE DB sources. Data values are stored in varying formats on the source servers. You want to compile all of the data into a standard format without losing any of the records during importation to the central data warehouse server.

Which of the following solutions will produce the desired results?

○ a. Create a single Data Transformation Service (DTS) package that copies the source columns directly to the destination columns.

○ b. Create a DTS package for each remote server configuration that uses a transformation script to transform information as it is copied to the destination.

○ c. Schedule a job that performs a bcp utility call using the Out option to create an export file from each source server and another job that performs a bcp utility call using the **-i *input_file*** argument to import the data on the destination server.

○ d. Perform distributed transactions to query data from each source server, transforming data formats within the query statements.

Question 22

Several options are available on the Select Components screen, including:

Client Connectivity Components

Development Tools

Management Tools

Server Components

Match the following components with the appropriate option:

Debug Viewer

Enterprise Manager

Query Analyzer

Replication

SQL Profiler

SQL Server

Question 23

Which of the following installation types will install the necessary components to access SQL Server instances on other machines? [Check all correct answers]

❏ a. Client Tools Only

❏ b. Connectivity Only

❏ c. Custom

❏ d. Minimum

❏ e. Typical

Question 24

You are the database administrator for a SQL Server 2000 instance used as a central repository of data extracted from several remote linked servers. Data is updated each night using scheduled DTS packages that cannot succeed if network connectivity is interrupted during the scheduled time for the jobs that execute the packages. Only POP3 mail access is available to the central repository server. You need to be notified when a scheduled job fails and generates an alert.

Which of the following types of notification can be used?

- ○ a. Email (SQLMail)
- ○ b. Email (SQLAgentMail)
- ○ c. Pager (email)
- ○ d. Pager (tone dial)
- ○ e. net send

Question 25

You are the database administrator for two SQL Server 2000 instances. One is used by a Web-enabled Online Transaction Processing (OLTP) application that experiences a large number of transactions each day. The second database is used for generating reports from weekly aggregated data. You have decided to set up replication between the source (publisher and distributor) and destination (subscriber) databases.

Which of the following replication types will produce the desired results most efficiently?

- ○ a. Merge replication
- ○ b. Push replication
- ○ c. Snapshot replication
- ○ d. Transactional replication

Question 26

You are the database administrator for several SQL Server 2000 instances. You have been asked to restore a backup of the user database **EUSales**, which was configured using a different collation than the default on the destination instance. After restoring the database into your new instance of SQL Server 2000, will its collation remain the same as it was at the time of its backup?

○ a. Yes

○ b. No

Question 27

Several DBCC statements can be used with the **REPAIR_REBUILD** option to correct consistency errors detected by a **DBCC CHECKDB** operation, including:

DBCC CHECKALLOC

DBCC CHECKCATALOG

DBCC CHECKDB

DBCC CHECKTABLE

Match the following characteristics with the appropriate statement (some may be used more than once):

Can be used to correct allocation and integrity errors on all database objects in a specified database.

Can be used to correct consistency errors in a single specified indexed view.

Can be used to correct consistency errors in a single specified table.

Can be used to correct consistency errors on system tables within the specified database.

Can be used to correct disk space allocation errors.

Question 28

You are the database administrator for two SQL Server 2000 instances. One is used by a Web-enabled Online Transaction Processing (OLTP) application that experiences a large number of transactions each day. The second database is used for generating reports only. You have decided to set up Log Shipping between the source (OLTP) and destination (reporting) databases.

Which of the following DTS configuration options will allow user access to the reporting database?

○ a. Allow ad hoc querying

○ b. Allow database to assume primary role

○ c. No Recovery Mode

○ d. Standby Mode

Question 29

SQL Server monitoring can be accomplished at two levels:

Local Server

Remote Server

Match the following monitoring tools with the appropriate level (some may be used more than once):

sp_monitor

sp_who

sqldiag

SQL Profiler

Question 30

You have a database that has continued to grow in size over the past year. Client access time has continued to slow down. You have decided to add indexes to the primary tables to improve access performance. Will this help to improve access time?

○ a. Yes

○ b. No

Question 31

Will you encounter problems if you enable write-caching on disk controllers used for SQL Server 2000 instances in locations that can experience occasional power failures?

○ a. Yes

○ b. No

Question 32

Clients have complained of poor access to tabular data. You suspect that index fragmentation is the cause. You choose to use DBCC statements to check for fragmentation and defragment a nonclustered index if required. Which two DBCC statements should you use for these actions? [Check all correct answers]

❏ a. **DBCC CHECKALLOC**

❏ b. **DBCC CHECKDB**

❏ c. **DBCC DBREPAIR**

❏ d. **DBCC SHOWCONTIG**

❏ e. **DBCC REINDEX**

Question 33

Several options are available for backing up your data, including:

Differential

File

Filegroup

Full

Transaction Log

Match the following characteristics with the appropriate option:

Allows for point-in-time recovery

Creates a copy of a single data file

Requires a variable amount of file storage for all data files

Takes longer than all other backup types

Question 34

You are the database administrator responsible for the administration of an instance of SQL Server 2000. You have configured a backup schedule as follows:

- A Full backup each Sunday at 4:00 A.M.

- A Differential backup each night at midnight

- A Transaction Log backup every four hours (2:30 A.M., 6:30 A.M., 10:30 A.M., 2:30 P.M., 6:30 P.M., and 10:30 P.M.)

At 10:00 P.M. Saturday evening, a power surge damages two drives on your server that house all of your data and transaction log files. You replace the drives, reinstall SQL Server 2000, and check your backup tapes for available backups from the previous two weeks.

Because you have been awake for over 36 hours, you unthinkingly set three of the tapes on top of the magnetic lock long enough to get your keycard when reentering the machine room. You discover that this has ruined the Differential backups from Tuesday and Thursday, as well as the Transaction Log backups from 2:30 A.M. to 10:30 A.M. on Friday and from 2:30 P.M. to 6:30 P.M. on Saturday.

When performing a restoration of your database, up to what point can you recover the data?

○ a. 10:30 P.M. Monday

○ b. 10:30 P.M. Tuesday

○ c. Thursday night, midnight

○ d. 2:30 P.M. Friday

○ e. 10:30 A.M. Saturday

Question 35

Which of the following actions can help to improve performance during **BULK INSERT** actions? [Check all correct answers]

❏ a. Configure the database to use the Full recovery model.

❏ b. Remove all indexes before the **BULK INSERT**, and rebuild them after completion.

❏ c. Remove the TABLOCK hint.

❏ d. Specify a large **BATCHSIZE**.

❏ e. Specify a small **BATCHSIZE**.

❏ f. Specify the TABLOCK hint.

Question 36

You are the database administrator responsible for the administration of an instance of SQL Server 2000. You have configured a backup schedule as follows:

- A Full backup each Sunday at 4:00 A.M.

- A Differential backup each night at midnight

- A Transaction Log backup every four hours (2:30 A.M., 6:30 A.M., 10:30 A.M., 2:30 P.M., 6:30 P.M., and 10:30 P.M.)

Because of a hardware failure on Thursday evening, you must perform a complete recovery of the **Sales** database. Because this task must be completed before the staff returns for work on Friday, you must accomplish it in the most efficient manner.

Which of the following steps must be taken to perform the most up-to-date recovery possible in the least amount of time? [Check all correct answers]

- ❑ a. Restore all Differential backups since the last Full backup.

- ❑ b. Restore all Transaction Log backups since the last Differential backup.

- ❑ c. Restore all Transaction Log backups since the last Full backup.

- ❑ d. Restore the most recent Differential backup since the last Full backup.

- ❑ e. Restore the most recent Full backup.

- ❑ f. Restore the most recent Transaction Log backup since the last Differential backup.

- ❑ g. Restore the most recent Transaction Log backup since the last Full backup.

Question 37

Is it possible to change recovery models without stopping and restarting the SQL Server or SQL Server Agent services?

- ○ a. Yes

- ○ b. No

Question 38

Which of the following describes a system that is configured identically to a primary server, can be renamed to take the place of the primary server in the event of failure, but is not automatically updated using Log Shipping?

- ○ a. Cold standby server
- ○ b. Linked server
- ○ c. Standby server
- ○ d. Subscriber server
- ○ e. Warm standby server

Question 39

Which of the following are valid database access modes? [Check all correct answers]

- ❑ a. Single-User
- ❑ b. Members of the **db_owner**, **dbcreator**, or **sysadmin** roles
- ❑ c. Mixed-Mode
- ❑ d. Read-only
- ❑ e. Unrestricted

Question 40

You are the database administrator of an instance of SQL Server 2000 that is used in tracking client inventory data during business reorganizations for different clients. The last job has been completed, but you want to keep the old **Inventory** database available in the instance for several more months in case additional reporting is needed. You have imported the new client's inventory data into an identically structured database named **NewClientInv**. To make the new data available through your Web-based application, you must rename the **NewClientInv** database to **Inventory**. Which two commands should you perform to fulfill the stated requirements? [Check all correct answers]

❏ a. In SQL Query analyzer, perform the following command:

```
ALTER DATABASE NewClientInv
    MODIFY NAME = Inventory
```

❏ b. In SQL Query analyzer, perform the following command:

```
ALTER DATABASE Inventory
    MODIFY NAME = NewClientInv
```

❏ c. In SQL Query analyzer, perform the following command:

```
ALTER DATABASE Inventory
    MODIFY NAME = OldClientInv
```

❏ d. In SQL Query analyzer, perform the following command:

```
ALTER DATABASE OldClientInv
    MODIFY NAME = Inventory
```

❏ e. In SQL Query analyzer, perform the following command:

```
DROP DATABASE Inventory
```

❏ f. In SQL Query analyzer, perform the following command:

```
EXEC sp_detach_db 'Inventory'
```

Question 41

Several categories of Database Consistency Console Transact-SQL (T-SQL) command-line statements are available for troubleshooting transactions and integrity checks:

Maintenance

Miscellaneous

Status

Validation

Match the following DBCC statements with the appropriate category:

DBCC CHECKTABLE

DBCC HELP

DBCC INDEXDEFRAG

DBCC OUTPUTBUFFER

DBCC SHRINKDATABASE

DBCC SQLPERF

DBCC TRACEON

DBCC UNPINTABLE

DBCC UPDATEUSAGE

Question 42

Which of the following constraints are used in creating table relationships? [Check all correct answers]

❑ a. Check

❑ b. Foreign keys

❑ c. Linked

❑ d. Primary keys

❑ e. Publisher

❑ f. Subscriber

❑ g. UNIQUE

Question 43

If two processes are mutually locked awaiting the release of the lock held by the other, this condition is called a *deadlock*. You must configure a monitoring job that generates an alert to the operator when deadlocks occur, because system resources remain locked until a member of the **sysadmin** or **dbcreator** role selects which process to terminate.

○ a.   True

○ b.   False

Question 44

Which of the following monitoring tools provide a graphical user interface (GUI) for performing monitoring tasks? [Check all correct answers]

❏ a.   Database Console Commands (DBCC)

❏ b.   Enterprise Manager

❏ c.   SQL Profiler

❏ d.   sqldiag utility

❏ e.   System Monitor

Question 45

Which of the following replication types is often used for disconnected or mobile users?

○ a.   Client-Server

○ b.   Merge

○ c.   Snapshot

○ d.   Read-only

○ e.   Transactional

Answer Key

For asterisked items, please see the textual representaion of the answer on the appropriate page within this chapter.

1. c	16. c	31. a
2. d	17. a, c	32. d, e
3. c, d	18. b	33. *
4. e	19. c	34. e
5. b	20. *	35. b, d, f
6. *	21. b	36. b, d, e
7. b	22. *	37. a
8. *	23. a, b	38. a
9. a	24. e	39. a, b, d, e
10. b	25. c	40. a, c
11. c	26. a	41. *
12. a	27. *	42. b, d
13. *	28. d	43. b
14. c	29. *	44. b, c, e
15. a, e	30. a	45. b

Question 1

The correct answer is c. An Update trigger should be added to the **ON_SALE** column that will send the notification. Answer a is incorrect because the use of a new stored procedure would require a change to the application. Answer b is incorrect because it would not provide notification of updates to the **ON_SALE** column. Answer d is incorrect because the use of a recurring scheduled job checking for any changes since the last test is not the most efficient method of notification. It consumes system resources for the job and change tracking.

Question 2

Answer d is the correct answer. You should create a new domain group, place the New York members into this group, create a login for this group on the appropriate instance, and deny access rights to this login. Answer a is incorrect because removing the Sales group's login rights can prevent necessary access to the instance supporting employee data. Answer b is incorrect because denying login rights to the Sales group prevents access even if granted by membership in another group. Answer c is incorrect because Windows Authentication Mode does not support SQL logins. Answer e is incorrect because removing the New York members of the sales force from the Sales group can affect their ability to access the instance supporting employee data.

Question 3

Answers c and d are correct. You must grant the Guest login access to the **Employees** database, and configure the instance for Mixed-Mode Authentication to make the SQL Guest login available. Answers a and b are incorrect because domain user accounts are not necessary for Anonymous Web access to information contained in the database when using the Guest login under Mixed-Mode Authentication. Answer d is incorrect because changing the **sa** administration login password to blank will not grant Web access but can expose the instance to unauthorized administrative access.

Question 4

Answer e is correct. The **db_denydatawriter** role restricts update capabilities without affecting read permissions. Answers a and d are incorrect because the **db_datareader** and **db_denydatareader** roles affect read access only. Answer b is incorrect because the **db_datawriter** role grants update access. Answers c and f are incorrect because there are no fixed roles **db_dataupdate** or **db_denydataupdate**.

Question 5

Answer b is correct. This will not correct the problem. Arial's membership in the Sales group causes her to inherit the permissions associated with the **db_denydatawriter** role, denying update rights. Arial's domain account must be removed from the Sales group to remove this restriction from her account.

Question 6

The correct answers are:

dbcreator

   Creation and alteration of databases and database objects

serveradmin

   Management of server-wide settings

sysadmin

   Creation and alteration of databases and database objects

   Management of server-wide settings

   Overall administration

Question 7

Answer b is correct. You must also stop and restart the server to start audit logging.

Question 8

The correct answers are:

Server

   bulkadmin

   processadmin

   setupadmin

Database

   User-defined

Question 9

Answer a is correct. Denying Martin's login rights will override the access rights inherited from his membership in the Managers group.

Question 10

Answer b is correct. Windows Authentication Mode does not provide access to the SQL Guest login. You must use Mixed-Mode Authentication Mode for this.

Question 11

Answer c is correct. Data Transformation Service (DTS) packages can be created and scheduled for automated update procedures. Answer a is incorrect because the SQL Query Analyzer is a user interface for manual command-line actions. Answer b is incorrect because the Enterprise Manager is the overall graphical user interface (GUI) for overall database administration and maintenance that provides access to the Data Transformation Service tool. Answer d is incorrect because the SQL Profiler is used to monitor performance traces.

Question 12

The correct answer is a. Distributed transactions across linked servers allow for centralized command actions that access data located on linked servers.

Question 13

The correct answers are:

Desktop Engine

A component that can be distributed with applications

Limited to five concurrent batch processes

Developer

Licensed for development only

Fully featured version

Enterprise

Fully featured version

Evaluation

    Expires after 120 days

    Fully featured version

Personal

    Limited to five concurrent batch processes

    Standalone version for mobile users

Standard

    Designed for small workgroup environments

Windows CE

    Designed for replication of data on Windows CE devices

Question 14

Answer c is correct. Detaching the database, copying its files, and attaching the database to the new server is the easiest and fastest method to move a database from one server to another. Answer a is incorrect because backup and restoration take far longer to complete, especially if verification after creation of the backup is enabled. Answer b is incorrect because it is unnecessarily complicated and takes far more time than is necessary. Answer d is incorrect because it is highly complex, requires significant effort to enact, and can remove access to any other databases on the same server that do not need to be moved.

Question 15

Answers a and e are correct. Because the data will be static, the index does not have to be able to adapt to a large number of updates. Therefore, a high Fill Factor is appropriate, conserving resources by reducing the additional space available for index changes. Answer b is incorrect because a low Fill Factor reserves a large amount of space for index changes. To minimize the impact on backup performance, placing the data into the OldTerm.ndf secondary data file allows for daily file and filegroup backups to exclude this static data. Answer c is incorrect because there is no Mixed recovery model. Answer d is incorrect because the extension .ldf is reserved for transaction log files and is not used for data files.

Question 16

Answer c is correct. Using update triggers on the two columns that update aggregate values in the related **PENDING** column when relevant data is changed is the most efficient method, because they are only called when a relevant change has occurred to the data. Answer a is incorrect because it involves a stored procedure that is executed each time an invoice or receipt is posted and runs even when no backorders are present. Answers b and d are incorrect because they involve aggregate queries against full tables. Additionally, answer b is a recurring job that runs only at set intervals, occurring even when no changes are present and falling out of synchronization if a large number of transactions occur over a shorter period of time than the recurrence scheduling. Answer d is also incorrect because it involves distributed transactions, which are used to access data from remote linked servers. Because this is a single-server solution, distributed transactions are not needed.

Question 17

The correct answers are a and c. A main data file (.mdf) and transaction log files (.ldf) must be present to attach a detached database. Answer b is incorrect because the .mdb extension is used for Microsoft Access databases. Answer d is incorrect because the use of secondary data files (.ndf) is optional and such files may not be present. Answer e is incorrect because Microsoft SQL does not use files with the .rdf extension.

Question 18

The correct answer is b. A table associated with a read-only filegroup cannot be inserted into, updated, or deleted from, but can be viewed if the proper permissions are assigned. On a non-read-only table, the **db_datawriter** role is assigned to allow inserting into, updating, and deleting data, whereas the **db_datareader** role is necessary to view table data.

Question 19

Answer c is correct. You should move the data files (.mdf and .ndf) to one of the new drives to allow for expanded indexing of the data and place the transaction log files on a separate drive to allow transaction updates and data access to occur in parallel. Answers a and b are incorrect because these configurations place data and transaction log files together on a single drive. Answer d is incorrect because it maintains primary data files on a drive that has already been determined to be too small for continued index expansion.

Question 20

The correct answer is:

Publishers

Distributors

Subscribers

Note: Publishers publish the data snapshots. Distributors distribute the published data to subscribers, who receive the published data for use.

Question 21

Answer b is correct. A Data Transformation Service (DTS) package using a script to perform format translation during data import allows for data to be imported in a standard format without risking loss of records that are incompatible. Answer a is incorrect because no translation is involved and any errors result in the loss of imported records or the termination of the import process. Answer c is incorrect because the -i *input_file* argument specifies a file to provide automatic responses to command prompt questions. Answer d is incorrect because the servers are listed as independent servers instead of linked servers, which are required for distributed transactions.

Question 22

The correct answers are:

Client Connectivity Components

Development Tools

Debug Viewer

Management Tools

Enterprise Manager

Query Analyzer

SQL Profiler

Server Components

Replication

SQL Server

Question 23

Answers a and b are correct. Both the Client Tools Only and Connectivity Only installation types install the connectivity components required for connection to SQL Server instances on other machines. Answers c, d, and e are incorrect because Custom, Minimum, and Typical installations are SQL Server installations, not connectivity component installation types.

Question 24

Answer e is correct. Only the net send Windows notification option is available. Answers a, b, and c are incorrect because only POP3 mail service is available and MAPI mail support is required for email notifications. Answer d is incorrect because pager notification by SQL Server 2000 can only be accomplished using email.

Question 25

Answer c is correct. Snapshot replication is useful for creating asynchronous read-only copies of aggregated data. Answers a and d are incorrect because Merge and Transactional replications involve routine synchronization, which create additional network overhead unnecessary for data that only changes weekly. Answer b is incorrect because there is no SQL Server configuration Push replication type.

Question 26

Answer a is correct. The restored database will maintain its original collation after the restoration is completed. Each database can maintain a different collation than the server default collation within an instance of SQL Server 2000.

Question 27

The correct answers are:

DBCC CHECKALLOC

Can be used to correct disk space allocation errors.

DBCC CHECKCATALOG

Can be used to correct consistency errors on system tables within the specified database.

DBCC CHECKDB

Can be used to correct allocation and integrity errors on all database objects in a specified database.

Can be used to correct consistency errors on system tables within the specified database.

Can be used to correct disk space allocation errors.

DBCC CHECKTABLE

Can be used to correct consistency errors in a single specified indexed view.

Can be used to correct consistency errors in a single specified table.

Question 28

The correct answer is d. Standby Mode allows the destination server to remain accessible to users. Answer a is incorrect because there is no Allow User Access option. Answer b is incorrect because the destination database is used for reporting only, not to allow transactional posting. Answer c is incorrect because the No Recovery Mode prevents user access to the standby database.

Question 29

The correct answers are:

Local Server

sp_monitor

sp_who

sqldiag

SQL Profiler

Remote Server

SQL Profiler (requires a separate instance for each monitored server)

Question 30

Answer a is correct. Indexes are used to improve tabular access performance. Clustered indexes must be regularly rebuilt for tables experiencing a large number of additions, deletions, and modifications because clustered indexing physically rearranges tabular data storage.

Question 31

Answer a is correct. Write-caching disk controllers hold (cache) data to be written in RAM pending drive availability. If power is lost during a write operation, all cached data is also lost. This can result in generating a number of errors that will be detected by your regularly scheduled **DBCC CHECKDB** consistency maintenance check.

Question 32

Answers d and e are correct. **DBCC SHOWCONTIG** checks for database fragmentation, and **DBCC REINDEX** performs the same tasks as the **DROP INDEX** and **CREATE INDEX** statements. Answers a and b are incorrect because they check for consistency errors rather than index fragmentation issues that may be affecting performance. Answer c is incorrect because the **DBCC DBREPAIR** statement does not affect an index. It is included solely for backward compatibility and allows a database to be dropped.

Question 33

The correct answers are:

Differential

Requires a variable amount of file storage for all data files

File

Creates a copy of a single data file

Filegroup

Full

Takes longer than all other backup types

Transaction Log

Allows for point-in-time recovery

Question 34

The correct answer is e. You can recover the Full backup from last Sunday at 4:00 A.M., the Differential backup from Friday night at midnight, and the Transaction Log backups from 2:30 A.M. through 10:30 A.M. on Saturday. All data entered after 10:30 A.M. on Saturday will have to be reentered.

Answers a and b are incorrect because a more recent Differential backup is available than the lost Differential backups from Tuesday and Thursday and only the last Differential backup is required to restore all changes since the last Full backup to that point. Answer c is incorrect because the loss of the Transaction Log backups from Friday morning will not prevent the use of a later Differential backup from Friday night. Answer d is incorrect because the loss of the Transaction Logs from early Friday prevent the recovery to any point in time after that, until the next Full or Differential backup available.

Question 35

Answers b, d, and f are correct. **BULK INSERT** performance can be improved by removing indexes before the insertion and rebuilding them afterwards, specifying a large **BATCHSIZE**, and specifying table-level locking using the TABLOCK hint. Answer a is incorrect because the Full recovery model logs each change to the data and can actually slow performance. The Bulk-logged recovery model is a better choice. Answer c is incorrect because without the TABLOCK hint, record-level locking will be used rather than table-level locking. Answer e is incorrect because a small **BATCHSIZE** causes the **BULK INSERT** transaction to occur as a series of small insertion tasks, each of which are applied after successful completion or rolled back if a failure occurs. This creates additional overhead during the **BULK INSERT** action.

Question 36

Answers b, d, and e are correct. To perform the most up-to-date recovery possible in the least amount of time, you must restore the most recent Full backup, the most recent Differential backup since the last Full backup, and all Transaction Log backups since the most recent Differential backup.

Answer a is incorrect because only the most recent Differential backup since the last Full backup is required. It contains the information found in all earlier Differential backups since the last Full backup. Answer c is incorrect because a more recent Differential backup has been performed since the last Full backup. If no Differential backup had been created, all Transaction Logs since the last Full backup would have been required. Answers f and g are incorrect because all Transaction Logs must be applied since the last Differential or Full backup (if no Differential backup was made since the last Full backup). If any Transaction Log backups are omitted or missing since the last Differential backup, no later Transaction Log files can be used in the restoration.

Question 37

The correct answer is a. Yes; it is possible to change the recovery model while the database is in operation. Changing from the Full recovery model to the Bulk-logged model before performing **BULK INSERT** and **bcp** updates can improve performance during the bulk action. Changing back to the Full recovery model after completion of all bulk update actions returns the database to the default recovery model without requiring a server restart.

Question 38

Answer a is correct. A cold standby server is an identically configured server that does not automatically synchronize with the primary server using Log Shipping. Answer b is incorrect because a linked server has been configured for distributed transaction processing. Answer c is incorrect because both cold and warm standby servers are "standby" servers. Answer d is incorrect because a subscriber server is used in replication scenarios and requires both a publisher and distributor for continued updates to its data. Answer e is incorrect because a warm standby server is one that maintains synchronization with the primary server using Log Shipping.

Question 39

Answers a, b, d, and e are correct. When setting access restrictions on the database Properties screen, you can restrict access to members of the **db_owner**, **dbcreator**, or **sysadmin** roles, as well as to Single-User, Unrestricted, and Read-only modes. Answer c is incorrect because Mixed-Mode is an authentication mode, not an access restriction mode.

Question 40

The correct answers are a and c. To keep a copy of the old **Inventory** database available within the instance and rename the new database as **Inventory**, you must first rename the current **Inventory** database as **OldClientInv** and then re-name the **NewClientInv** database as **Inventory**.

Answer b is incorrect because it would attempt to rename the current **Inventory** database to **NewClientInv**, which is already in use. Answer d is incorrect because it would attempt to rename the not-yet-created database **OldClientInv** to **Inventory**, which is already in use. Answer e is incorrect because it would result in the deletion of the current **Inventory** database and you must keep a copy of this database available for reporting. Answer f is incorrect for this same reason, although by detaching the database instead of deleting it, the files remain on the server and so could be recovered. However, they are not available for reporting without first reattaching them.

Question 41

The correct answer is:

Maintenance

   DBCC INDEXDEFRAG

   DBCC SHRINKDATABASE

   DBCC UPDATEUSAGE

Miscellaneous

   DBCC TRACEON

   DBCC UNPINTABLE

Status

   DBCC OUTPUTBUFFER

   DBCC SQLPERF

Validation

   DBCC CHECKTABLE

Question 42

The correct answers are b and d. Primary and Foreign key constraints establish table relationships. Answer a is incorrect because a Check constraint is used to verify input data before record creation occurs. Answer c is incorrect because there is no constraint named Linked. Linked servers are used for processing distributed transactions. Answers e and f are incorrect because Publishers and Subscribers are two server roles during replication. Answer g is incorrect because the UNIQUE constraint prevents the entry of duplicated data in the specified column, guaranteeing uniqueness of each record in a single table.

Question 43

Answer b is correct. When two processes are deadlocked, SQL Server 2000 creates a monitoring process that selects the deadlock victim to be terminated based on which deadlocked process is the least expensive in terms of resource utilization.

Question 44

The correct answers are b, c, and e. The Enterprise Manager, SQL Profiler, and System Monitor provide graphical user interface (GUI) consoles for monitoring various aspects of the SQL Server 2000's operation. Answer a is incorrect because the DBCC commands are command-line statements. Answer d is incorrect because the sqldiag utility is an executable command-line monitoring utility.

Question 45

Answer b is correct. Merge replication is often used for remote or disconnected users, because changes to data resynchronize with the Publisher when the next connection occurs. Answer a is incorrect because client-server is a database topology, not a type of replication. Answer c is incorrect because it produces a read-only snapshot of data from the Publisher. Answer d is incorrect because the Snapshot form of replication is the read-only form. There is no Read-only replication type. Answer e is incorrect because Transactional replication requires network connectivity to perform data updates on the Publisher.

Glossary

· ·

alert

An automated response to an event. Used to signal an operator that the event has occurred or to trigger a job in response to conditions on the server.

Analysis Services

An optional package for online analytical processing (OLAP) of large data structures. Used for data warehousing and data mining projects.

attaching a database

Method for creating a new database that uses existing data and transaction log files. The existing database is first detached and copied or moved before it is attached again. *See also* detaching a database.

attribute

One element of data within a record. Attributes are represented as columns within a table.

auditing

Process using the SQL Profiler utility to trace and record security-related activity, such as failed and successful logins.

authentication

The process of establishing the necessary credentials to connect to networked resources such as an instance of SQL Server 2000.

authorization

The process by which a user's access rights and permissions to perform tasks and modify objects or data are determined. A login may be granted, not granted (revoked), or denied permissions either directly or through roles.

automation

The programmed scheduling, processing, and success or failure notification of tasks performed by the SQL Server Agent without direct interaction by the database administrator. The three main automation components are Jobs, Alerts, and Operators.

baseline
Normal operational levels determined by monitoring performance statistics for a period of time.

bcp utility
Command-line bulk update program used in batch files and scripted process for such actions as extracting database data into an external data file.

Bulk-logged recovery
A complete recovery model with minimal bulk-transaction logging.

C2 security
A complex and comprehensive set of security provisions used in some governmental networks.

cascaded updates
Option that causes all Foreign key related field values to change when the Primary key value is changed. Cascaded deletions cause all related records to be deleted when the Primary record is deleted, thus avoiding the creation of orphaned records in violation of referential integrity.

client/server architecture
A database architecture that separates user access applications (client) from

the DBMS (server). Distributed client computers access shared resources located on centralized servers.

cold standby server
A standby server that requires manual actions to maintain synchronization with the primary server.

collations
Collections of alphabetic character sets and rules for proper use of certain characters in a language. Collations will affect rules such as alphabetization in applications designed for use in an international forum.

constraints
Limitations or conditions that must be satisfied before data is accepted as valid.

data files
The physical files that comprise a database. A primary data file (.mdf) is used for data storage, and a log file (.ldf) is used for transaction logs. Secondary data files (.ndf) are used for additional data storage. They can improve performance by distributing tables to multiple disks, which allows for parallel access; directing specific tables to particular locations, which minimizes fragmentation on available disks; and modeling the logical database design in physical storage.

Data Transformation Services (DTS)
A graphical bulk operations utility within the SQL Server 2000 Enterprise Manager used for

creating packages that can be saved for reuse or scheduled for later or recurring operations. DTS packages are often used to transfer data from heterogeneous data sources (deriving data from non-SQL databases) by configuring the appropriate OLE DB connection type as required for each source. *See also* OLE DB.

Database Console Commands (DBCC)

Transact-SQL (T-SQL) statements that are a subset of command-line maintenance actions. These are very important because they allow verification of the physical and logical consistency of the database. The DBCC commands are grouped into four categories: Maintenance, Status, Validation, and Miscellaneous. DBCC commands are also referred to as the Database Consistency Console commands in some references.

Database Maintenance Planning Wizard

A graphical user interface (GUI) tool used for scheduling routine maintenance tasks, such as Log Shipping and database backups.

Database Management System (DBMS)

The software that provides access to stored data. The DBMS is responsible for enforcing database structure and rules, maintaining relationships between data, and providing access for client applications, presented in a clear and useful manner. SQL Server 2000 is one type of DBMS.

databases

Organized collections of related information stored so that users can easily access the information and add, delete, update, and display subsets of it based on criteria specified by the user.

deadlock victim

The process in a deadlock using the least system resources that is automatically terminated by default.

deadlocking

Deadlocking occurs when two processes are mutually holding necessary locks. SQL Server 2000 automatically resolves deadlocks by creating an eager deadlock search thread. This thread eventually traces the activity to the deadlock and selects one process as the deadlock victim, which is aborted with an error message returned to the calling application. This enables the other process to be completed. *See also* deadlock victim.

default instance

The default installation of SQL Server identified by the name of the server. Prior to SQL Server 2000, this was the only instance possible.

deny login

Prevention of a login. This action prevents access even if other inherited access rights are granted.

detaching a database

The process of disabling a database without deleting the database files.

This is typically used when moving a database to a new location. Detached databases are no longer listed in the Databases node of the Enterprise Manager and are not available to users. System databases may not be detached. A database may not be detached while in use. *See also* attaching a database.

differential backup
A backup of database information that has changed since the last full backup.

distributed transactions
Transactions against heterogeneous data sources located on remote servers that are configured as linked servers.

Distributors
Element used in server replication for distributing data to Subscribers. *See also* Publishers, Subscribers.

DTC Client
Distributed Transaction Coordinator (DTC) management tool used in multiple server transactions. Distributed transactions are processed on multiple servers at once, allowing for much more rapid processing.

eager deadlock search
A lock monitor process used in identifying and resolving deadlocking conflicts.

English Query
An optional package that allows for plain English querying of the database (for example, "How many products contain paper?").

Enterprise Manager
A graphical utility that provides information useful for monitoring and resolving conflicts. The Current Activity and Database Usage windows provide information necessary for database maintenance.

error logs
A listing of Windows 2000 application errors generated by events within SQL Server 2000.

failover clustering
A high-availability configuration using Microsoft Cluster Service (MSCS)-configured server clusters in which multiple servers maintain access to shared Small Computer Systems Interface (SCSI) storage. It provides automatic redirection of the processing for an instance from one node to another in the event of failure.

filegroups
Grouping of data files that allows for detailed allocation and placement of files and tables, making it easier to add new files on new disks and to expand total storage as requirements increase.

Foreign key
A related field in a table that references a Primary key in another table. *See also* cascaded updates.

full backup
A complete backup of all database files.

Full recovery
The most flexible database recovery model in which data can be recovered to a specified point in time.

heartbeat message
The signal transmitted by each node in a Failover cluster. If the MSCS software fails to detect a node's heartbeat, the node is treated as a failed server.

heterogeneous data
Data derived from non-SQL database sources.

implied permissions
Permissions granted through membership in one of the system roles or inherited by ownership of a database object.

index defragmentation
Process to reorganize index information in an efficient manner that resolves unequal distribution and unused space. It involves the regeneration of indexes in a contiguous layout.

instance
A collection of databases.

jobs
A series of operations to be performed by the SQL Server Agent. Jobs are scheduled for execution or triggered by an alert and may generate operator notifications based on the events occurring on each execution.

keys
Shared columnar data relating tables together. *See also* Foreign key, Primary key.

linked server
Allows SQL Server 2000 to process distributed transactions against heterogeneous OLE DB data sources located on different servers throughout an enterprise environment.

log shipping
An automated process by which a standby server is continually synchronized with a primary server by applying the transaction logs from the primary to the identical databases configured on the standby server.

master server
The central server in a multiserver administration scenario. It stores a copy of all job tasks so that target servers may periodically obtain copies of the jobs that they must perform.

Mixed-Mode Authentication
Allows users to connect to SQL Server using Windows user account validation or SQL Server Authentication, providing backward compatibility with earlier versions of SQL Server and access capability from non-Windows platforms.

MSXOperator
The master server operator configured on the master server. It is the only operator able to receive multiserver job notifications.

multiserver administration

Centralized management process for automated tasks that may be required in an enterprise environment. It uses a master server to store a copy of all automation tasks and one or more target servers that periodically connect to the master server to update the list of jobs that they are to perform. The SQL Server Agent is required for multiserver administration functions.

named instance

Any SQL Server 2000 instance on a server other than the default instance. An installation option made available in SQL Server 2000.

network libraries

Provide communication avenues between client/server applications and multiple server distributed databases.

node

A server in a Failover cluster.

nullability

The ability to use a Null value if no user-supplied value is provided for a record element.

object permissions

Involve the manipulation of data and the execution of procedures within a database.

OLE DB

An application program interface (API) used by Microsoft for access to different data sources.

operators

Individuals responsible for the maintenance of some aspect of an SQL Server instance. One or more operators can be notified of events that meet defined criteria using electronic mail (email), pager notification (using email), or the net send utility available in Windows NT and Windows 2000.

orphaned records

Records that reference deleted related records.

permissions

Rights that grant or deny access to certain functions or database objects. Permissions may be granted at the server, database, or database object level. Permissions may be assigned to roles and logins assigned those roles. Permissions are grouped in three categories: Object, Statement, and Implied.

point-in-time restoration

Option for restoring a database to a particular time.

Primary key

The source field for a tabular relationship. *See also* cascaded updates.

Public role

A special database role assigned to all database users. Anonymous logins via the Guest account have only those permissions granted to this role. Newly created logins have only the rights granted to this role and must be assigned any access permissions on databases and database objects directly or through role assignment inheritance.

Publishers
Element used in server replication for providing data to Distributors. A Publisher can also be a Distributor for its own data. *See also* Distributors, Subscribers.

record
A collection of attributes related to a single item that comprises one row in a table.

recovery model
Standard models for database recovery that differ in terms of availability, recoverability, and optimization of file space during operation. New databases have the same recovery model (Full recovery) as the modal database by default.

recovery plan
A detailed, exhaustive listing of all actions taken to protect data, notify responsible parties if disaster recovery is necessary, and perform the appropriate steps necessary to recover lost data.

referential integrity
Rules that prevent deletion of a record without also removing all related records in a table.

relational database
A database structure that organizes data into related tables, each representing a class of information deemed important. Primary and Foreign keys are used to establish relationships between tables.

relationship
A logical connection between tables formed using Primary and Foreign key relationships.

remote installation
The process of deploying SQL Server 2000 from a central location using the Remote Installation option.

replication
Automatic copying of data and database objects from one database to another and the synchronizing of data between servers. Replication relies on Publishers, Distributors, and Subscribers. Three types of replication are available: Snapshot, Merge, and Transactional.

revoke login
Removal of a login. This action does not block access granted by other inherited login access rights. To prevent inherited access, the login must be implicitly denied rather than revoked.

roles
Groupings of permissions assigned to logins. SQL Server 2000 provides several fixed server and database

roles, as well as the ability to define custom database-level roles.

security

Option for determining login rights to a database. Two layers of security are provided within SQL Server 2000: *Login authentication* is a process that determines whether a user attempting to access data is first allowed to connect to the database. *Authorization* is the process that verifies whether the user, after connecting to the database, has permission to access database objects. Users can be granted, not granted (revoked), or denied access at either of these levels. Permissions can be assigned for both users and roles.

server

The computer system hosting an instance of SQL Server. Also the general term for this computer and the DBMS software together.

SQL Profiler

A graphical tool that allows the monitoring and logging of events within an instance of SQL Server 2000. SQL Profiler provides filtering options to extract useful subsets of monitored data, such as traces of events.

SQL Server Authentication

Process used to establish a SQL Server database connection for users who have earlier versions of SQL Server, remote users who do not have a Windows user account, such as

those attempting to access the SQL Server 2000 instance from a non-NT 4.0 or Windows 2000 domain, and those who have instances of SQL Server 2000 loaded on Windows 98 or Windows ME systems, which do not support Windows Authentication even in Mixed-Mode.

standby server

Server used as a backup if the primary server fails. It is created using the backup and restore functions. Unlike the Failover clustering solution, a standby server must be manually activated. Standby servers are often configured as read-only access options during Full recovery on a failed primary server.

statement permissions

Involve the manipulation of databases and database objects.

stored procedures

Stored programmatic segments designed to allow multi-step scripted SQL language actions using runtime-specified parameters.

Subscribers

Element used in server replication for receiving published data from Distributors. *See also* Distributors, Publishers.

system databases

The databases used by the SQL Server engine. Each instance of SQL Server 2000 has four system databases: **master, modal, tempdb,** and

msdb. These databases are used by the DBMS to maintain state information, provide a template for new databases, provide temporary storage, and manage scheduled tasks.

System Monitor
A graphical tool for monitoring and logging system resources and process activities, accessed within the Windows 2000 Performance Console.

table
A collection of records objects. Each table has a series of columns and rows. Each column corresponds to an attribute of the object represented by the table, and each row characterizes a record.

table integrity
Rules that prevent "bad" data, disallowed actions, or inappropriate data to be entered in a table.

target server
Multiserver administration servers that connect to a master server periodically to update the list of jobs that they must perform. Target servers can only be enlisted by one master server at a time. A target server must be defected from its master server before a different master server can enlist it.

Transaction Log backup
File containing all current transaction log entries.

transaction logs
A serial record of all changes to the data. This record allows the server to roll back (undo) incomplete transactions or roll forward (apply) each in sequence. Transaction log files can be used to synchronize separate databases and to reapply sequential changes to the data files after performing disaster recovery operations.

type integrity
Rules that define the allowable data types for each field in a table.

unattended installation
All information necessary to complete an installation without intervention. An unattended installation setup initialization (.iss) file can be created to deploy instances with identical setup configuration choices on multiple servers or to perform a remote setup using distributed media rather than network installations.

Unicode
A data type using the two-byte character set defined by the International Organization for Standardization (ISO—formerly known as the International Standards Organization) and the Unicode Consortium to facilitate multinational data compatibility.

UNIQUE constraint
This restriction prevents the creation of duplicate data in the appropriate field.

user databases
Contain user-defined data and database objects. Two sample user databases are included when SQL Server 2000 is installed: **Northwind** and **pubs**.

views
Data extracted from one or more tables. Views are used to aggregate data, restrict access to confidential or secure columns, and simplify subset extraction of available data.

virtual log files
Transaction logs that are internally segmented into smaller portions. Transaction checkpoints within the virtual log files mark where all transactions to that point have been applied to the database.

virtual server
An instance of SQL Server 2000 installed on a Failover cluster.

warm standby server
A backup server that is maintained automatically through the use of Log Shipping.

Windows Authentication
Process of granting or denying local and domain users and groups login access to an instance of SQL Server 2000. This mode integrates with native Windows security principles within a homogenous Windows NT 4.0 and Windows 2000 enterprise environment.

Index